# The Digital Silk Road
## China's Technological Rise and the Geopolitics of Cyberspace

**Edited by David Gordon and Meia Nouwens**

'This groundbreaking work combines the best available expertise with detailed datasets to illuminate the complex phenomenon that is China's Digital Silk Road. The understanding it offers is critically important at a time of growing East–West geopolitical and technological competition.'

*– Nigel Inkster, IISS Senior Adviser for Cyber Security and China; former Assistant Chief, Secret Intelligence Service (UK)*

# The Digital Silk Road
## China's Technological Rise and the Geopolitics of Cyberspace

**Edited by David Gordon and Meia Nouwens**

IISS The International Institute for Strategic Studies

# The International Institute for Strategic Studies

Arundel House | 6 Temple Place | London | WC2R 2PG | UK

First published November 2022 by **Routledge**
4 Park Square, Milton Park, Abingdon, Oxon, OX14 4RN

for **The International Institute for Strategic Studies**
Arundel House, 6 Temple Place, London, WC2R 2PG, UK
www.iiss.org

Simultaneously published in the USA and Canada by **Routledge**
52 Vanderbilt Avenue, New York, NY 10017

*Routledge is an imprint of Taylor & Francis, an Informa Business*

© 2022 The International Institute for Strategic Studies

DIRECTOR-GENERAL AND CHIEF EXECUTIVE Dr John Chipman
SERIES EDITOR Dr Benjamin Rhode
EDITOR Dr Jeffrey Mazo
ASSISTANT EDITOR Michael Marsden
EDITORIAL Jill Lally, Haoyu Tong
PRODUCTION Loraine Winter
COVER ARTWORK James Parker

**The International Institute for Strategic Studies** is an independent centre for research, information and debate on the problems of conflict, however caused, that have, or potentially have, an important military content. The Council and Staff of the Institute are international and its membership is drawn from almost 100 countries. The Institute is independent and it alone decides what activities to conduct. It owes no allegiance to any government, any group of governments or any political or other organisation. The IISS stresses rigorous research with a forward-looking policy orientation and places particular emphasis on bringing new perspectives to the strategic debate.

The Institute's publications are designed to meet the needs of a wider audience than its own membership and are available on subscription, by mail order and in good book-shops. Further details at www.iiss.org.

British Library Cataloguing in Publication Data
A catalogue record for this book is available from the British Library

Library of Congress Cataloging in Publication Data

ADELPHI series
ISSN 1944-5571

ADELPHI 487–489
ISBN 978-1-032-48687-1

# Contents

CONTRIBUTORS

**Dr David Gordon** is Senior Adviser for Geo-economics and Strategy at the International Institute for Strategic Studies. He is a former US diplomat and intelligence official, and served as director of policy planning at the US State Department under then-secretary of state Condoleezza Rice. His work focuses on the intersection of security, economics and strategy.

**Robert Koepp** is the Principal of Los Angeles-based Geoeconomix, an independent, creative source for insights into the forces moving global societies, markets, technologies, organisations and governments. An internationally active practitioner and analyst who researches and writes in English, Chinese and Japanese, he is the author of several books and numerous reports, monographs and articles on topics covering geo-economics, global finance, innovation, technology, strategy and public policy.

**Damien Ma** is Managing Director of MacroPolo, the think tank at the Paulson Institute, Chicago. He is the author or editor of *In Line Behind a Billion People: How Scarcity Will Define China's Ascent in the Next Decade*; *The Economics of Air Pollution in China*; and *China's Economic Arrival: Decoding a Disruptive Rise*. He is also adjunct faculty at the Kellogg School of Management at Northwestern University. His advisory and analytical work has served institutional investors, multinationals and various governments. He has published and appeared widely in the media, including the *Atlantic* and the *New York Times*, Bloomberg, the Charlie Rose Show, NPR and CNBC.

**Scott Malcomson** is the author of five books, most recently *Splinternet: How Geopolitics and Commerce Are Fragmenting the World Wide Web* (2016). He has written on technology and geopolitics for *Foreign Affairs*, the *New York Times*, the *Washington Post*, the International Institute for Strategic Studies and many others. He has served at the US State Department and the United Nations, was the foreign editor of the *New York Times Magazine* and is a principal at Strategic Insight Group.

**Meia Nouwens** is Senior Fellow for Chinese Defence Policy and Military Modernisation at the International Institute for Strategic Studies (IISS). Her expertise lies in Chinese cross-service defence analysis, China's defence industry and innovation, as well as China's regional strategic affairs and international relations. She leads IISS research on China's Digital Silk Road and the institute's wider China portfolio.

**Adrian Shahbaz** is Vice President for Research and Analysis at Freedom House, a non-profit organisation dedicated to expanding freedom and democracy around the world. He previously worked as a researcher at the United Nations, the European Parliament and the Organization for Security and Co-operation in Europe. He holds a master's degree from the London School of Economics.

**Paul Triolo** is Senior Vice President for China and Technology Policy Lead at Albright Stonebridge Group, Washington DC. A recognised expert in global technology policy, he was most recently founder, practice head and managing director of the Geo-Technology practice at Eurasia Group. Previously, he spent more than 25 years in senior positions in the US government, analysing China's rise as a technology power and advising senior policymakers on a broad set of technology-related issues. He also serves as a Senior Advisor at the Paulson Institute. He received a master's degree in International Relations from the Catholic University of America.

**Marcus Willett CB OBE** was deputy head of the UK's Government Communications Headquarters (GCHQ), responsible for all its intelligence and cyber operations. He led several major UK government cyber initiatives, including the National Offensive Cyber Programme. He also held posts across the wider UK intelligence and security community. Since leaving government service in 2018, Marcus has been Senior Adviser for Cyber at the International Institute for Strategic Studies, as well as advising the International Committee of the Red Cross and a range of companies in the UK, US and elsewhere on strategic cyber matters.

## ACKNOWLEDGEMENTS

The origins of this book lie in the IISS data-collection effort that seeks to better understand Chinese levers of influence and power projection in the twenty-first century. Huawei's worldwide 5G-network infrastructure projects intensified debates about the nature of China's global technological roll-out through public- and private-sector Chinese companies in what the Chinese government termed its 'Digital Silk Road'. But the issues surrounding Huawei, the focus of so much attention in Europe and the US when this book project began, represented only a small part of the emerging technological competition between the United States and China. Intentionally or not, Chinese terminology and initiatives can be nebulous. The editors of this book therefore saw an opportunity to explore multiple aspects of the Digital Silk Road – its origins, its roll-out, its stakeholders and its recipients – with the ultimate aim to better understand its current impact and its potential consequences for the future global order. This *Adelphi* book complements the IISS China Connects dataset, with one chapter drawing on its data concerning Chinese global digital investments. Both the dataset and this book were made possible thanks to generous support from Robert Rosenkranz.

The editors of this *Adelphi* are grateful to the authors of each of the chapters for their contributions, expertise and dedication to the final product. Views on the Digital Silk Road and Chinese technology investments differ widely, but through their individual chapters the authors have strengthened our understanding of a complex and fast-changing initiative. The editors would also like to thank IISS colleagues, in particular John Chipman, Robert Ward, Benjamin Rhode and Jeffrey Mazo, and the editorial, publications and design teams, especially Michael Marsden and Kelly Verity, for their guidance and assistance with this project. Last but not least, the book would not have been possible without the help of our colleagues Haoyu Tong and Tabatha Anderson, who were instrumental to the IISS China Connects dataset project and to managing the book project, respectively.

# GLOSSARY

| | |
|---|---|
| **AI** | artificial intelligence |
| **ASEAN** | Association of Southeast Asian Nations |
| **AWS** | Amazon Web Services |
| **BRF** | Belt and Road Forum |
| **BRI** | Belt and Road Initiative |
| **BSN** | Blockchain-based Service Network |
| **CAC** | Cyberspace Administration of China |
| **CBDC** | central bank digital currency |
| **CCP** | Chinese Communist Party |
| **DSR** | Digital Silk Road |
| **FDI** | foreign direct investment |
| **ICT** | information and communications technology |
| **IPO** | initial public offering |
| **ITU** | International Telecommunication Union |
| **MFA** | Ministry of Foreign Affairs |
| **MIIT** | Ministry of Industry and Information Technology |
| **MOF** | Ministry of Finance |
| **MOFCOM** | Ministry of Commerce |
| **MOST** | Ministry of Science and Technology |
| **NDRC** | National Development and Reform Commission |
| **OTT** | over the top |
| **PBoC** | People's Bank of China |
| **PLA** | People's Liberation Army |
| **PRC** | People's Republic of China |
| **SOE** | state-owned enterprise |
| **WTO** | World Trade Organization |

# INTRODUCTION

## David Gordon and Meia Nouwens

China's rise is no longer a question. The People's Republic (PRC) today is an economic powerhouse, a growing high-technology dynamo and increasingly a critic of the current international system. President Xi Jinping's centralised rule has marked the end of former president Deng Xiaoping's era of China's 'hiding and biding'. If the second half of the twentieth century was defined by competition between the United States and the Soviet Union, competition between the US and China will define at least the first half of the twenty-first.

Deng's '24-character strategy' called for China to '*lěngjìng guānchá, wěnzhù zhènjiǎo, chénzhuó yìngduì, tāoguāng yǎnghuì*', or 'observe and analyse calmly, strengthen your own position, undertake change with confidence, conceal your true potential, contribute your part, never become the leader'.[1] Deng's strategy provided the strategic underpinnings for China's increasingly successful global engagement over the quarter-century following 1989. In the wake of the

**David Gordon** is IISS Senior Adviser for Geo-economics and Strategy. **Meia Nouwens** is IISS Senior Fellow for Chinese Defence Policy and Military Modernisation.

global financial crisis of 2008, Beijing's ambitious domestic economic-stimulus programme enabled it to lead the global recovery from the Great Recession. As the inconclusive outcomes of the wars in Iraq and Afghanistan damaged America's image, China's status rose.

It was in this context that, shortly after coming to power in 2012, Xi chose the Belt and Road Initiative (BRI) as a way to transcend the self-imposed limitations of the 24-character strategy to a much greater extent than his predecessor, Hu Jintao, had done. Launched in 2013, the BRI embodied China's strategy of shaping globalisation through an intensification of its external infrastructure-development efforts. While Beijing has promoted the multibillion-dollar initiative, which focuses on traditional connectivity infrastructure such as roads, railways and ports, as a socio-economic endeavour for the developing and developed world alike, the promise that it would create 'win–win' opportunities has been greeted with scepticism in some quarters.[2]

Sparked in part by concerns about China's growing global investments, political weight and military modernisation, Western liberal societies have begun to question how peaceful China's rise actually is. The 2020 'Strategic Approach to the People's Republic of China' issued by the Trump administration depicted the rise of a strategic competitor.[3] The administration of President Joe Biden has not strayed far from this competition-driven perception of China, although it has worked more closely with allies and like-minded partners in developing a strategy to counter some of the challenges that China's rise poses to the liberal order. The European Union's 'EU–China Strategic Outlook' in 2019, for example, referred to China as a partner, but for the first time also as a 'systemic rival', and transatlantic dialogues between the EU and US on China have been proposed by the EU.[4]

The BRI and other elements of Xi's nationalistic agenda (see Damien Ma's chapter in this volume) have for some observers cemented the view that China's global engagements have little to do with creating a 'community of common destiny' or tackling global problems such as international terrorism or global warming. The 'Chinese Dream', the slogan for the rise in military, economic and cultural power China seeks to achieve to mark the centenary of the People's Republic in 2049, is, after all, the embodiment of what its constitution calls 'the great rejuvenation of the Chinese Nation' and the return of the country to global centre stage as a great power.[5] China intends to have rebounded from its suffering at the hands of colonial powers in the nineteenth and twentieth centuries, and to have built a 'moderately prosperous society' through 'socialism with Chinese characteristics'.[6] Governments in the liberal West, particularly that of the US, believe that Xi's global initiatives have more to do with overturning at least the last phrase in Deng's 24-character strategy – that China should not become a global leader – despite his statements that China will 'never seek global hegemony'.[7]

Recently, concerns about China's ambitions for global leadership have focused on what may be seen as a particular strand of the BRI, or a spin-off from it: the Digital Silk Road (DSR). Formally launched in 2015, the DSR initially referred to the inclusion of advanced technology in the BRI (see Robert Koepp's chapter in this volume). Its name was a reference to the ancient network of trade routes that connected Europe and East Asia across Central Asia until the sixteenth century. While cyber was initially mentioned in BRI discussions only in the context of fighting cyber crime, by 2017 the DSR had emerged as a centrepiece of the government's BRI strategy and in 2019 it was promoted further at the second Belt and Road Forum (BRF), where it was referred to as an initiative in its own right.

By 2020 the DSR had become a focal point of China's foreign policy, and Xi has continued to promote the idea of cooperation on digital connectivity, for example with members of the Association of Southeast Asian Nations (ASEAN).

But the DSR has received little attention compared to the BRI, and it has not been examined as broadly or as deeply as its parent initiative. It remains poorly understood, both as a government initiative and a commercial endeavour. It is difficult even to define the parameters of the DSR; the little official documentation that exists is ambiguous and sometimes contradictory. Some government documents define the DSR as those digital technologies that increase connectivity or help build digital economies, and point mainly to investments in telecommunications-network infrastructure, including 5G, submarine and overland fibre-optic cables, satellite ground tracking stations, data centres, whole-of-system integrated solutions such as 'smart city' and security-sector information systems, and select 'over-the-top' applications such as financial services and processes (fintech) and e-commerce investments. However, other statements emanating from Beijing include any high technology, such as quantum computing or artificial intelligence (AI) applications for big-data analytics, under the DSR rubric.

The DSR concept has thus evolved into an umbrella term for various activities of interest to the Chinese government in the cyber realm. At the same time, there is no comprehensive list of project types that should be considered part of the DSR. An added complication is that unlike BRI projects, which are usually labelled as such, most overseas information and communications technology (ICT) projects that have been undertaken by Chinese companies are not promoted or labelled as part of the DSR. This ambiguity means that the DSR can – and has – been understood differently by different observers or even participants, including Western analysts, Chinese bureaucrats, Chinese companies and Western govern-ments. The debate over the implications of the DSR centres around one question: is it primarily a commercial or a strate-gic political project, or a combination of both? It is difficult, if not impossible, to answer this question without a common understanding of what the DSR entails. Moreover, technologi-cal change is occurring at a rapid pace, and the perception in a year's time of what the DSR comprises might differ from our understanding today. To reflect the fast-changing nature of China's private-sector technology industries, a flexible approach to understanding the evolving scope of the DSR is needed.

We would argue that a limited definition of the DSR (involv-ing specific technologies, degrees of government involvement and types of financial support) and a more expansive, inclusive understanding of it are complementary. As Paul Triolo puts it in his chapter:

> The DSR is best understood as an umbrella brand-ing effort and a narrative for Beijing to promote its global vision across a range of specific core technol-ogy sectors, rather than as a project or initiative that is being directed or implemented centrally by ministries in Beijing, or as the maximalist DSR concept in which all business operations related to the digital economy are lumped together under its rubric.

The DSR originated in a socio-economic narrative promoted by Beijing that focused solely on connectivity and digital economic growth. This suggested a predominance of service-related, infrastructure and platform projects. However, since its inception – and particularly since the beginning of the global coronavirus pandemic in 2020 – Chinese companies have moved on from building digital-infrastructure networks and diversified into collaborating in e-health, AI and other frontier technologies. These projects also receive support – at least vocal, and sometimes financial – from the Chinese government. It is likely that the mix of projects that makes up the DSR will continue to evolve.

Despite its origins as a component of the BRI, the DSR seems to have developed less as a government-driven initiative than organically through the activities of China's domestic tech giants and ICT industry. It operates according to its own rules: BRI member countries benefit from DSR projects, but the DSR seems to extend beyond the BRI's geographical boundaries. How, then, is the DSR to be understood as a larger initiative? What role does the government play in such a loosely formulated but strategically imperative initiative? Has Beijing simply piggy-backed on the success of China's private tech sector, or is there a larger strategic ambition at the core of the DSR? Or is the DSR a reflection of both commercial trends and government aims?

Beyond these questions about parameters and goals, the same concerns about consequences for global security and critical infrastructure previously voiced with regard to the BRI are now being raised about the DSR. At the heart of such international concerns is not the fact that Chinese companies are becoming globally competitive, but rather the implications of the potential for the Chinese Communist Party (CCP) to use such companies to 'rewire' the global digital architecture, from physical cables to code. Dominance of the international digital ecosystem by Chinese technology could ultimately shift global norms from a free global cyber commons to competing systems of cyber sovereignty or cyber freedom, creating the potential for a further splintering of the internet. The ultimate question is what the lasting implications of such a project are for global connectivity, security and the geopolitical landscape in the future. What will the world look like in 2049 if China has seized the commanding heights of the world's digital ecosystem?

In exploring these questions, this *Adelphi* book is divided into three parts. The first three chapters contextualise the Digital Silk Road, both internationally and domestically. The next two explore the role of the key institutions in the Chinese state and their interaction with Chinese private-sector tech companies that are the key actors in DSR-related activities on the ground. Chapters Six and Seven address the economic, security and governance impact of the DSR in recipient countries. In the Conclusion, we assess the broader impact of the DSR on patterns of economic and technological dependence, on the emerging rules and norms of tech globalisation, and on global geopolitics and great-power relations.

In Chapter One, 'China's investment in digital technologies and the Digital Great Game', Marcus Willett, IISS Senior Adviser for Cyber, does not directly address the DSR but provides the technological and geopolitical context for the contributions that follow. He draws on his deep experience of over three decades in the United Kingdom's signals-intelligence agency GCHQ to explore how and why China has risen so rapidly in the past two decades to become one of the world's leading tech powers. He then addresses the external implications through a case study of how the UK government responded to the US government's campaign against Chinese tech giant Huawei's 5G mobile-technology business in 2019–20. Finally, Willett turns to the deepening tech cold war between Washington and Beijing, and addresses the question of whether the world is heading towards a bifurcation of the digital domain into two competing systems.

In Chapter Two, 'Locating the Digital Silk Road in the Belt and Road Initiative', Robert Koepp, for many years the director of The Economist Group's Corporate Network in Hong Kong, describes how the DSR emerged as a substantially autonomous component of the BRI. He examines the policy entrepreneurship of Lu Wei, the minister who founded the Cyberspace Administration of China (CAC) and the administrator of China's vast online censorship apparatus, who was purged in 2017. Koepp's analysis highlights the increasing attention the Chinese authorities paid to the DSR in the run-up to the second BRF in April 2019. More importantly, he reveals the intricacies of policy formation in China's political system. The origins of the DSR were by no means the result of a neatly organised top-down process.

To complement Koepp's detailed description of the origins and evolution of the DSR as formally and minimally construed, one of us (Meia Nouwens) then explores the wider context in Chapter Three, 'Identifying the Digital Silk Road'. This draws on the IISS China Connects dataset of Chinese overseas ICT projects (which includes all projects involving technologies or supporting goals mentioned in formal DSR policy documents and statements) to examine how the maximalist DSR concept has evolved, who the stakeholders are, how it is financed and how it compares to the BRI. In Chapter Four, 'The Digital Silk Road and the evolving role of Chinese technology companies', Paul Triolo then examines the chicken-and-egg questions regarding the commercial and political motivations behind the DSR from the perspective of China's private tech companies. Triolo, Senior Vice President for China and Technology Policy Lead at Albright Stonebridge Group, focuses on the development of Chinese technology and, on the basis of his extensive connections with leading Chinese scholars, makes the case that China's private-sector tech firms seeking commercial rewards are the principal drivers of DSR activities on the ground, competing with one another for state support. At the same time, he argues that their activities promote the broader geopolitical goals of the state, and that Chinese private firms in the DSR are likely to become more dependent on government support.

In Chapter Five, 'The Digital Silk Road and China's grand strategic ambition', Damien Ma, Managing Director of the MacroPolo think tank at the University of Chicago's Paulson Institute, addresses the question of how the DSR relates to China's broader strategic aims, both domestically and internationally. Ma highlights Xi's role in articulating specific metrics for China's 'national rejuvenation', a theme that has been central to the CCP since well before it came to power in 1949. Ma describes the DSR as a logical deepening of China's efforts, from the early 2000s onwards, to promote Chinese companies 'going out' into the world. Given both the limited size of the domestic market and the push by Washington against Chinese tech firms, the DSR is gaining in strategic importance to Beijing. Ma then addresses whether China has the capability to achieve its strategic aims. The interdependence between the Chinese government and Chinese tech companies is growing in the face of US pressure, but he also highlights potential tensions between CCP ambitions and private-sector interests.

In Chapter Six, 'The Digital Silk Road and normative values', Adrian Shahbaz addresses the question of whether DSR projects aimed at enhancing the public-security capacity of participating countries will enable more authoritarian methods of government. Shahbaz, Vice President for Research and Analysis at Freedom House, argues that the effect on civil liberties and norms will depend upon the type of technology China exports, the political culture of recipient states, and whether those states can or want to implement independent and robust oversight of new surveillance and algorithmic technologies. Through a series of case studies, he shows that where freedom of assembly and association already receive little protection, the DSR appears to have reinforced authoritarian governance, while in fragile democracies, greater political pluralism has been conducive to a degree of public oversight of new surveillance technologies while also leading to resistance by civil society against their use. In established liberal democracies, on the other hand, the effects of the DSR have been relatively neutral. He concludes that the export of the same technologies that China uses to suppress its own population – without the safeguards or transparency claimed for similar Western products – is likely to further erode civil liberties in authoritarian states, to prove threatening in states where institutions or regulations remain fragile, and to challenge existing norms even in liberal democracies. The DSR also enhances China's influence, prestige and economic leverage, contributing to a broader Chinese campaign for an internet under the control of often repressive governments rather than an open one imbued with liberal values.

In Chapter Seven, 'Balancing prosperity and security along the Digital Silk Road', Scott Malcomson shifts the focus from Chinese actors to recipient states. The author of *Splinternet: How Geopolitics and Commerce Are Fragmenting the World Wide Web* (2016) starts by examining how individual countries balance the economic benefits of engaging Chinese tech companies against the risk that those companies and their tech will serve Chinese security at the expense of their own. Not surprisingly, the balance struck between security and prosperity has depended on how much a given country thought it already had of each. As global wariness of Chinese technology increases, Malcomson describes how China's remarkable successes through the DSR have left it more exposed, in terms of the future prospects of its multinationals and its own tech sector, than it expected to be. He raises the prospect that Chinese companies may not reap the rewards of Beijing's enormous investment in building a global telecommunications infrastructure. Even if they do, their dependence on external sources of revenue may lead them to become more vulnerable to the preferences of foreign governments. He concludes that a trend towards local control and data sovereignty reduces the leverage of current and emerging technology superpowers such as China and the US, but though Beijing and Washington appear to be choosing the security of exclusive markets, it is to their ultimate advantage not to force other states to choose which camp to join, which would dampen prosperity for all concerned.

In the Conclusion, we examine the broader and longer-term implications of the DSR. We first explore the interplay between the DSR and global geopolitics, and focus on the question of why China's shift towards greater technological assertiveness has failed to enhance its global standing and influence in the global geopolitical hierarchy. We then examine the changing domestic context facing China's large tech firms, whose support from the state has enabled them to exert outsized influence against more established actors in overseas markets. What Beijing deems acceptable behaviour by Chinese tech firms, however, is now changing. Finally, we look at the question of tech bifurcation, and the related issue of whether there will be Western or local competitors for China's tech champions in the various DSR geographies. Rather than a straightforward decoupling of the Western and Chinese digital domains, the more likely outcome is a patchwork of overlapping legal and normative frameworks.

## CHAPTER ONE

# China's investment in digital technologies and the Digital Great Game

## Marcus Willett

Life in the twenty-first century increasingly depends on a man-made, virtual world. It is where people communicate, learn, play, shop, bank, develop friendships and perhaps meet their future spouses. It is fundamental to the global economy, to international security and influence, and to the global spread of ideas. It is also used by criminals to defraud, terrorists to radicalise, and states to spy and to seek strategic advantage over their adversaries. It is the domain in which, some argue, future wars will be won or lost. While each of these activities has a parallel real-world dimension, the virtual world adds a revolutionary degree of speed, scale and geographical reach.

This virtual world has many shorthand descriptors, often used loosely: 'cyberspace', 'the internet', 'the web', or the 'online' or 'digital' environment. Essentially, it is a realm of computer networks in which information is created, stored, shared and communicated. Although virtual, this world rests upon physical foundations or 'hardware' – computers, microchips, phones,

**Marcus Willett** is Senior Adviser for Cyber at the IISS.

## Artificial intelligence

Software systems that can improvise and adapt to new environments or generalise and apply knowledge to different scenarios. Examples include systems that can understand human speech and act as virtual assistants, compete with humans in complex games such as chess or Go, operate machinery autonomously, translate between human languages, or handle financial investments.

## Blockchain

A database shared or distributed between networked computers, which enables the linking of digital records using cryptography to record transactions between two parties efficiently and in a verifiable and permanent way without the involvement of a trusted third party. The earliest widespread use of blockchain technology was to implement the cryptocurrency bitcoin and its imitators.

servers, switches, data centres, fibre-optic cables, cellular radio towers and antennae, and communications satellites. Across this hardware run coded 'software' applications (such as Facebook or TikTok). Both hardware and software can be categorised as ICT or simply as 'digital technology'.

The evolution of digital technology has been and remains rapid. Blockchain and AI are merely the latest iterations, as is the 'Internet of Things', where household appliances, roads, cars and cities are enabled by digital technology to become 'smart'. If, as some argue, the advent of digital technology is the 'third industrial revolution', its use to enable the growing automation of human activity has been called the 'fourth'.[1]

The contemporary structure and governance of the global internet reflects a balance between the interests of multiple stakeholders, including companies and governments, the visionary coders who created it, and its everyday users. Since the internet's inception, however, the development of the digital technology that underpins it has been dominated by American technical innovators and companies, and by the United States' perception of its national interest. The US remains the world's only digital superpower.

Sixteen of the world's top 50 digital-technology companies in 2021 were American, while most of the others were based in states closely allied to the US: Japan had ten, Western Europe seven, Taiwan six, South Korea two, Mexico one; the remaining eight were Chinese.[2] The US was the first state to develop national strategies and military doctrine around the use of 'cyber power'. It has developed the world's largest commercial sector devoted to cyber security. Purported intelligence leaks since 2013 have alleged the strength of its cyber-intelligence capabilities, including how they might exploit US commercial dominance in digital technology.

Most other states have recognised their dependency on digital technology for future prosperity and security. This is especially true of China, whose regional and wider aspirations have brought it increasingly into competition with the US. Beijing believes it cannot meet those aspirations in today's digital-dependent world if it is not itself a digital power. The ruling CCP also recognises the ideological threat posed to it by the Chinese people's use of digital technology, given the internet's crucial role in the spread of ideas. China has therefore taken measures over the past two decades both to insulate itself from perceived threats stemming from US technological dominance and to increase its own digital influence worldwide. Washington has made increasingly robust efforts to counter this in what has been described as a 'Digital Great Game'.[3] This is the wider context for China's DSR initiative.

## China's digital beginnings

China's investment in digital technology can be traced back to the early 1980s, with the telecommunications companies ZTE and Huawei founded in 1985 and 1987 respectively. President

Jiang Zemin became one of the first world leaders to advocate strongly for investment in electronics and information technology as a means of industrial transformation.[4] In 1995, China launched its first commercial internet service, with a few hundred thousand of its population moving online by the following year. In 1996 the Chinese government issued an edict barring unfiltered access to the global internet, the origin of the so-called 'Great Firewall'. The Chinese internet-services conglomerate Tencent Holdings Ltd was founded in 1998. By 2000, 1.8% of the Chinese population were online, rising to 34% by 2010 and around 60% by 2019.[5] Following revelations of the role that the internet played in the succession of 'colour' revolutions and movements beginning with Georgia's 2003 'Rose Revolution', China has argued at the United Nations in favour of the principle that states should have greater control over their 'sovereign' cyberspace, a concept now generally labelled 'cyber sovereignty'.[6] Beijing also implemented a series of internal initiatives to enforce this principle within China itself. One example, launched in 2003, was China's 'Golden Shield Project' (*Jīndùn Gōngchéng*), involving the use of digital technologies to transform the way the Chinese authorities collect, analyse and transmit information, enabling them to track individuals in real time as they move across offline and online spaces. Another initiative was the 2009 decision to ban Facebook, YouTube and Twitter from Chinese networks (along with Google in 2010) for failing to comply with the country's censorship laws.

A 1993 Chinese military strategy labelled 'Winning Local Wars under High Technology Conditions' provides an early indication of China's perception of the military use of digital technologies.[7] Subsequently, the public revelation of aspects of emerging US cyber doctrine and the US campaigns in Kosovo (1999) and Iraq (2003) all reinforced for China the importance of digital technology in modern conflict. An authoritative Chinese analysis of the Kosovo campaign, produced in 2000, attributed NATO's victory to 'total information dominance' resulting from disruption of the Federal Republic of Yugoslavia's tele-communications system.[8] Jiang subsequently updated the 1993 strategy, describing the US 'Revolution in Military Affairs' as really being a revolution 'in military informatisation' and concluding that 'informatised' warfare would become the main type of warfare in the twenty-first century.[9]

Subsequent years saw a well-publicised global prolifera-tion of both cyber criminality and state-run cyber operations, involving many actors. As well as 'passive' spying operations involving the observing or copying of data passing across networks, there has been a growing catalogue of 'active' cyber operations that have interfered with code or data, denied access to data or leaked data publicly to achieve both cognitive and physical effects. Taking only state-led activity, the cata-logue includes many operations by Russia, including those against Estonia, Georgia, Ukraine, the World Anti-Doping Agency and Western democratic processes; US retaliation against one of the Russian organisations responsible; opera-tions by the US and Israel against Iran, and subsequent Iranian retaliations; Iranian operations against Saudi Arabia; North Korean operations against the global banking system; joint US, British and Australian operations against the Islamic State (ISIS); and many more. Some states have used cyber capabilities in unrestrained ways, damaging unintended victims, with the Russian use of the NotPetya virus and the North Korean use of the WannaCry virus two notable examples. Some of these state cyber operations have been aimed at critical national infra-structure – financial institutions, oil and gas companies, power grids and plants, transport sectors and core communications infrastructure. Operations to reconnoitre and gain a presence on these sorts of networks, occurring every second, are now a permanent feature of cyberspace, carrying a significant risk of miscalculation. Other risks include the proliferation of state capabilities to criminals or terrorists and the ease with which states can find effective offensive cyber tools on the open market. All of this will have contributed to China's sense of the advantages it could gain, and the risks it could better manage, if it became able to exert greater influence over the future development of cyberspace.

But the major shock for China occurred in 2013 with the allegations in the purported leaks by US National Security Agency contractor Edward Snowden of the likely extent of US and allied cyber capabilities and operations, and the role that US commercial dominance of the world's digital industry might have played in securing a twenty-first-century strategic advantage for America. As just one example, the Snowden cache includes supposed details about a US operation (BULLRUN) described as a 'Sigint enabling' project that 'actively engages the US and foreign IT industries to covertly influence and/or overtly leverage their commercial products' designs' to make them susceptible to US (and allied) signals-intelligence collection.[10] That same year, the well-publicised exposure of a People's Liberation Army (PLA) cyber unit by Mandiant, a US cyber-security firm, would have added to the Chinese sense of unease. The result has been an ongoing Chinese perception of the superiority of the US in the cyber domain and a determination to catch up.

**The Xi reforms**

In 2014, Xi announced China's intent to transition from a 'cyber power' (*wǎngluò dàguó*) to a 'cyber superpower' (*wǎngluò qiángguó*).[11] He introduced a wave of Chinese internet-related organisational reforms, regulations and legislation, culminating in his 2018 creation of the Central

Cyberspace Affairs Commission (CCAC) under his own chairmanship to manage internet-related issues, including the expansion of Chinese online services, cyber security and internet censorship. The Cyberspace Administration of China (CAC), established in 2014, was to be the CCAC's executive arm, with responsibilities including the cataloguing and certifying of 'key network equipment'; the regulation of virtual private networks, internet portals, and data stored outside China by Chinese companies; and the review of devices made by foreign countries. All of this was paralleled by a surge in cyber operations conducted by the Chinese state, mostly aimed at stealing the intellectual property of other states on an industrial scale, judging by the large number of such operations caught in the act.

In a 2016 speech, Xi identified the gap between China and foreign countries in the development of 'core internet technologies' as particularly severe, with China's reliance on foreign vendors as 'our biggest threat'.[12] This followed the 2015 publication of Xi's 'Made in China 2025' strategy, intended to create an indigenous and competitive high-tech digital industry within ten years. The aim was to have 40% of core internet technologies made in China by 2020 and 70% by 2025. Underpinning all this, there are three technologies that will probably have the greatest bearing on China's ability to shape the future of cyberspace – semiconductors (or microchips), quantum computing and AI. Microchips are the engine at the heart of

### Quantum computing

Use of the properties of quantum physics to store data and perform computations. Rather than using binary bits, quantum computers employ quantum bits (qubits) using physical systems such as the spin of an electron or the orientation of a photon. In theory, qubits can represent different things at the same time through a phenomenon called quantum entanglement, allowing much faster computation than traditional computers.

most digital technology, while quantum computing and AI will provide an ability to process data at such unprecedented volumes and speeds that they will be transformational for any nation that can master them.

Today there is clear evidence of the strides China has made in the last 20 years towards developing an indigenous industrial base for digital technology. Of the eight Chinese firms in the top 50 digital-technology companies in 2021 – China Mobile, Huawei Investment, China Telecom, Lenovo, Tencent Holdings, China United, China Electronics and Xiaomi – the first two were in the top ten. That put China in third place globally, behind the US and Japan. At the same time, Chinese investment in digital research and development is now on a par with that of the US, while Chinese companies have been securing more international patents than US companies.[13] China also has the advantage of a huge domestic market for digital technologies, with one billion of the world's estimated 4.5bn internet users.[14]

China has made considerable headway on quantum computing and AI, for example by developing a world-leading quantum processor (66 superconducting qubits) in 2021 and by advances made in AI-assisted 'smart city' image-recognition and computer-vision software, which have been deployed to hundreds of cities in China and elsewhere.[15] That said, China has continued to depend heavily on Western scientific research and development, often through investment in or collaboration with Western firms and universities.[16] China has become competitive globally on a range of other digital technologies. Its flagship telecommunications company Huawei is an acknowledged world leader in 5G mobile communications, and in 2020 it was for a brief time the world's largest manufacturer of smartphones.[17] Since 2018, Lenovo has been the world's leading personal-computing company.[18] The use of Chinese

## The cloud

A network of internet servers dedicated to the storage, management and processing of data as a single digital ecosystem, rather than by local servers or personal computers. Cloud-based applications allow connected users to access computing power, and data and storage, on demand.

software applications (QQ, WeChat, TikTok) is growing worldwide, with TikTok overtaking Facebook to become the most downloaded application globally and in the US in 2020 and 2021.[19] Tencent has invested heavily in US video-game companies. Alibaba has become a major provider of cloud systems in Asia. In July 2020, China launched the final satellite of its new *Beidou* satellite network, created as a rival to the US Global Positioning System (GPS).

As for semiconductors (or computer microchips), in 2016 China imported 90% of its microchip consumption. As part of Made in China 2025, Xi committed US$150bn to ensuring that 70% of the microchips used by Chinese industry in 2025 would be made domestically. China has also set aside US$1 trillion in government funding for advanced chip development and manufacturing, part of which will be used to invest in third-generation chip projects.[20] In 2020, however, only about 16% of the microchips used in China were made there, and according to industry forecasts the figure will not even exceed 20% by 2025. Not only is that far short of the announced goal, but a significant proportion of those chips will still be produced by foreign companies operating in China.[21] Meanwhile, China's own leading producer of chips, Semiconductor Manufacturing International Corporation, is still unable to produce the most cutting-edge chips and is unlikely to be able to catch up within a decade. The microchip story is therefore symptomatic of a wider issue: the complex, entangled and globalised nature of digital technologies, each with often opaque, multinational supply chains. China itself continues to rely significantly on eight US companies for the provision of digital technology. Chinese observers have called these firms – Apple, Cisco, Google, IBM, Intel, Microsoft, Oracle and Qualcomm – 'the eight guardian warriors'.[22]

While competition between China and the US on digital technology, complete with its cyber dimension, had been ongoing since the early 2000s, it took a significant new turn in 2019–20 with the robust measures taken by the US against Huawei's 5G mobile-technology business. 5G brings major enhancements to existing 3G and 4G mobile digital technology – greater bandwidth, faster speeds, better quality and instant connections. It is this faster, smarter layer that will enable innovative applications described as the Internet of Things, including smart vehicles, smart roads, smart household appliances and smart cities. 5G is the key technology enabling the so-called fourth industrial revolution.

Many countries were already turning to Huawei to build their 5G networks when in mid-2019 the Trump administration effectively banned the use of Huawei equipment in the US by adding the company to its list of 'entities' subject to government licensing control. The administration gave as its reason its belief that 'Huawei has been involved in activities contrary to the national security or foreign policy interests of the United States'.[23] This followed the 2018 designation of Huawei by the US intelligence community as 'untrusted', on the grounds of the company's perceived connections to the Chinese state and military. The US also cited the Chinese National Security Law of 2015 and Intelligence Law of 2017 requiring Chinese companies to act on behalf of the state when required to do so, and pointed to a litany of intellectual-property theft, 'racketeering' and sanctions-busting. Finally, in June 2020, the US Federal Communications Commission (FCC) formally designated Huawei and ZTE as national-security threats, stating that 'Huawei is highly susceptible to influence and coercion by the Chinese government, military and intelligence community'.[24] In March 2021, the FCC reaffirmed this designation and extended it to three other Chinese tech firms – Hytera Communications, Hangzhou Hikvision Digital Technology and Dahua Technology – calling them an 'unacceptable risk' to national security, and the US Department of Commerce placed further restrictions on Huawei's suppliers, preventing them from supplying items that can be used with or in 5G devices.[25] In June 2021, the FCC unanimously gave initial approval to provisions allowing the formal banning of approvals for equipment used in US telecommunications networks from companies designated national-security threats, and revoking previous approvals.[26] Throughout, the US specifically highlighted the risk that the Chinese state could use Huawei's technology to conduct cyber espionage and enable the sabotage of critical national telecommunications networks. The US also actively encouraged other countries to ban the use of Huawei equipment in their networks.

By the end of 2021, some countries had followed suit with a complete ban (these included Australia, Japan, New Zealand, Taiwan and the UK), and many Western European countries made it almost impossible for Huawei to win relevant contracts. Other countries declared that they intended still to allow Huawei equipment in their 5G networks (these included Argentina, Brazil, Italy, Russia, Saudi Arabia, South Africa and Turkey), or were so far down the path of using Huawei equipment and software in their 5G networks that they appeared unlikely to be able to change track even if they wanted to (this was true particularly of countries in Southeast Asia).

## Playing the Digital Great Game
US actions against Huawei, as well as those attempted by the Trump administration against Chinese software applications

such as TikTok and WeChat, appear to reflect a significant inten-sification of the 20-year contest between the US and China over the future of cyberspace, each believing that digital dominance will bring it long-term strategic and economic advantages. It has been argued that the intense competition between the US and China will produce a 'bifurcation' of the internet, forcing coun-tries to choose between two digital-superpower blocs, each with its own cyberspace ecosystem. It is already the case that there are two competing models of internet governance. The one that is currently dominant is described as 'multi-stakeholder' and advo-cated as 'internet freedom'. It is a model largely unchanged since the internet's inception in the late 1960s and early 1970s, through the advent of email, domain names and the Internet Protocol (IP), and the rise of the United States' digital mega-companies. It emphasises trust, open-mindedness, consensus and the applica-tion of existing international law to cyberspace, while contending that the nature of cyberspace defies the traditional structural models of national and international governance.

By contrast, the principle of 'cyber sovereignty' as espoused by China (among others) argues for greater state control and governance of the internet, using traditional-looking gover-nance structures and protectionist domestic legislation and seeking a body of new, cyber-specific international law. With its Great Firewall, including the banning of foreign applications that will not abide by its censorship laws, China has already set about creating its own 'sovereign' piece of cyberspace.

Yet sitting beneath these different governance models today are digital technologies and supply chains of an entangled, multi-national nature. For example, the US Semiconductor Industry Association objected to the Trump administration's closing of the final loophole in its ban on the provision of US microchip technology to Huawei on the grounds that such restrictions would 'bring significant disruption to the US semiconductor industry', and that 'sales of non-sensitive, commercial products to China drive semiconductor research and innovation here in the US, which is critical to America's economic strength and national security'.[27] One might say that there is one internet, with its supporting digital-technology market, but two governing systems. The whole is held together by global technical standards that ensure the underpinning technology works, regardless of the governance model under which it is required to operate. Such technical standards for each new type of digital technology are agreed and set internationally by well-established bodies, such as the International Telecommunication Union (ITU), the European Telecommunications Standards Institute and the mobile-technology workhorse, the 3rd Generation Partnership Project. This complex standards process means that, whichever smartphone you use, whichever mobile network you connect to, and whether you are in Beijing or Washington, your phone will still work, even if the software applications available to you may be different according to the respective 'governing system'. The bifurcation theory argues that all this could be unstitched by attempts to exclude Chinese companies and equipment from key global markets, exacerbating the existing internet-governance divide by adding competing national hardware and software, competing supply chains, and even competing national technical standards. In this view, such techno-nationalism would result in two separate digital ecosystems and, at its extreme, two separate internets divided along superpower lines, evoking echoes of the Cold War. China, with a monopoly on its own massive internal digital market, would be able to concentrate its entire overseas effort on the developing world through the DSR.

But US and Chinese technology and the global economy it supports are entangled in ways the US and Soviet Union never were, and which are extremely hard to disentangle. It may be worth looking further back in history for an alternative analogy:

the competition between the British and Russian empires for influence in Central Asia in the nineteenth century, the so-called 'Great Game'. The twenty-first-century Digital Great Game also involves two economically connected major powers contesting a new, unexplored and continually shifting space, marked by fluid commercial and security alliances. Just as the British and Russians aimed to spread their respective influence throughout Central Asia through exploration and trade, so the US and China hope to spread their influence globally through advances in, and export of, digital hardware and software.

Both Washington and Beijing seem to consider each other's companies as latter-day equivalents of Britain's East India Company: commercial fronts for the strategic ambitions of their parent state (with China's National Security Law an attempt to control its own companies the way the British government tried to control the East India Company with Pitt's India Act of 1784). That is how Beijing, not unreasonably, views the eight guardian warriors, and how the US, again not unreasonably, views Huawei.[28] Countries other than the US and China face the hard reality that, at present, they are perhaps the latter-day equivalents of Bokhara, Khiva and Merv: left to choose to which power they will be digitally beholden.

All states should recognise that a Digital Great Game has been under way for 20 years; that it has intensified markedly in the last couple of years, with increasingly robust tactics; and that it will continue for the foreseeable future. While both US and Chinese tactics may vary over time, the DSR has all the hallmarks of being one of the game's enduring battlegrounds.

## CHAPTER TWO

# Locating the Digital Silk Road in the Belt and Road Initiative

Robert Koepp

China is not a monolith. Despite the DSR's origins within the BRI, its formation involved multiple agencies within China's political system and its evolution within the party and state bureaucracy reflects complex decision-making processes and positional jockeying between top-level officials. The DSR's geographical scope also extends beyond that of the BRI. Ultimately, while the DSR was conceived as part of the BRI and has benefited from the opportunities that this broader initiative provided, the idea of a DSR has become akin to a global initiative in its own right.

## The DSR's origins

The first inkling of official Chinese government interest in developing a Digital Silk Road (*shùzì sīlù*) came with proclamations about ICT components of the BRI, the most prominent of which was the March 2015 document 'Visions and Actions to Promote Joint Construction of the Silk Road Economic

**Robert Koepp** is the Principal of Geoeconomix, a Los Angeles-based consultancy.

Belt and 21st Century Maritime Silk Road' (*Tuīdòng Gòngjiàn Sīchóu Zhīlù Jīngjì Dài hé 21 Shìjì Hǎishàng Sīchóu Zhīlù de Yuànjǐng yǔ Xíngdòng*).[1] Also referred to in government shorthand as the BRI action plan, this document was jointly issued by three powerful, long-standing central-government bodies, the National Development and Reform Commission (NDRC), the Ministry of Foreign Affairs (MFA) and the Ministry of Commerce (MOFCOM), under authorisation from the State Council (a large, cabinet-like executive body headed by China's premier). The plan references advanced ICT infrastructure for the BRI in an unnumbered subsection of Section 4, concerning 'Important Points of Cooperation'. Typical of documents of this type, its phrasing is declarative:

> Jointly advance the construction of transnational fibre-optic cables and other trunk-line communications networks, improve the quality of international communications interconnectivity, and open up an Information Silk Road. Hasten development of interlinked fibre-optic cables and related equipment, plan construction of transcontinental submarine fibre-optic cable projects, and complete aerial (satellite) information passageways, and expand information exchange and cooperation.[2]

The concept of an Information Silk Road (ISR, *Xìnxī Sīchóu Zhīlù*), as described in the 2015 BRI action plan, reflects the themes of the BRI undertaking following its public unveiling by Xi in the autumn of 2013. The DSR's initial defining attributes emphasised hard-wired aspects of communications technology, aligning with the BRI's prevailing orientation as a massive programme for construction-based infrastructure projects. The focus on hardware is also not surprising considering that the announcement came from three old-guard bureaucracies.

It did not take long for a newer organ of state, the CAC, to join the fray. From its founding on 27 February 2014, the CAC was given an unusually high degree of prominence and positioning in the central government and CCP, with Xi serving as the CAC's chair and Premier Li Keqiang as its vice-chair. The body's name in English sounds more modern and powerful – and better reflects its true mission – than its name in Chinese, *Guójiā Hùliánwǎng Xìnxī Bàngōngshì*, which simply means 'National Internet Information Office'. Like other Chinese government institutions, the CAC is paired with a political organisation; in this case it was originally paired with the CCP's Central Leading Team of Internet Security and Informatisation (*Zhōngyāng Wǎngluò Ānquán hé Xìnxīhuà Lǐngdǎo Xiǎozǔ*). At the conclusion of the annual National People's Congress in March 2018, this leading-team status was upgraded to that of a fully fledged party commission, the CCP Office of the Central Cyberspace Affairs Commission (OCCAC, *Zhōnggòng Zhōngyāng Wǎngluò Ānquán hé Xìnxīhuà Wěiyuánhuì Bàngōngshì*), further intensifying the politicisation, political duties and political power of the CAC. Although every government organ in China is ultimately overseen by and beholden to the CCP, the CAC/OCCAC is explicitly conjoined in ways that other key, functionally specific central-government bodies such as the MFA and MOFCOM are not.

The CAC took the lead in championing, expanding and rebranding the ISR according to its own ideas for digitalising the BRI. Its founding minister and China's first 'internet tsar', Lu Wei (previously head of the CCP's propaganda department for the city of Beijing), first publicly referred to a DSR when touting the benefits of 'the digital and cyber Silk Road' on 6 July 2015 at the China–EU Digital Cooperation Roundtable in Brussels.[3]

The timing of Lu's visit was itself significant, representing the first visit by a high-level Chinese official to Brussels following the summit between the EU and China at the end of June 2015. The summit had commemorated the 40th anniversary of the establishment of EU–China diplomatic relations and marked a milestone towards implementing the EU–China 2020 Strategic Agenda for Cooperation. The joint statement issued at the summit's conclusion declared that 'both sides confirmed their strong interest in each other's flagship initiatives, namely the Investment Plan for Europe, and the Belt and Road Initiative' and 'acknowledged the key role of the digital economy in their societies and the importance of close cooperation in that field'.[4] The conference where Lu promoted the DSR was hosted by ChinaEU (then known as the ChinaEU Association for Digital), a Brussels-based lobbying group focused on advocacy for Chinese government and commercial ICT interests. Lu explained at the roundtable that in order to 'connect this digital and cyber Silk Road across the two continents', the CAC hoped 'to see more Chinese Internet companies "going out" to [investing in] Europe, and more European enterprises entering the Chinese market'.[5] Around six months before the July roundtable, Lu had described an encompassing vision for Chinese and European collaboration on internet development in a speech entitled 'Shaping an Interconnected World, Sharing a China–EU Common Dream'.[6] So, right from the DSR's inception, a role for Europe in facilitating its implementation was clearly being envisaged.

**Formalising the DSR**

Back in China, CAC officials moved quickly to broadcast a broadened, policy-endorsed positioning of the DSR within the scope of the BRI and other central-government programmes. At the 15th Forum on Internet Media of China (a government-orchestrated gathering of digital providers, used to reinforce official policies) held in Guangdong in mid-July 2015, a CAC vice-minister exhorted Chinese internet businesses and media platforms to contribute to the BRI by constructing a 'digital Silk Road' to 'upgrade traditional industries within and beyond China's borders'.[7] The forum was described as having been 'organised' by chinadaily.com.cn, the web platform for the CCP's English-language mouthpiece, *China Daily*; 'co-hosted' by the Central Propaganda Department-controlled All-China Journalists' Association and major national news websites; and 'led' by the CAC.[8] The forum's theme for the year was 'E-path to One Belt, One Road'. Pronouncements on the DSR by the CAC were further linked to central-government designs for 'Internet Plus' (*Hùliánwǎng Jiā*). Essentially a Chinese version of the Internet of Things, Internet Plus represents a national objective (one often associated with Made in China 2025, another major strategy unveiled in the key year of 2015) that Premier Li first announced in his annual Government Work Report at the March 2015 National People's Congress. Connecting the DSR to Internet Plus provided the initiative with an additional bureaucratic endorsement at the highest level, demonstrated by a State Council website post (republishing a *China Daily* article) entitled 'Digital Silk Road Linked to "Net Plus"'.[9]

As officials refined and elevated concepts around the DSR, Beijing adjusted its descriptions to outsiders of the BRI's parameters. Within six months of issuing the BRI action plan, the initiative's triumvirate of ministerial overseers – the NDRC, MFA and MOFCOM – showed signs of recognising that China's centrepiece foreign economic programme did not translate well, literally or figuratively. The BRI's full title, the Silk Road Economic Belt and the 21st-Century Maritime Silk Road, is as clumsily worded in the original (*Sīchóu Zhīlù Jīngjì Dài hé 21 Shìjì Hǎishàng Sīchóu Zhīlù*) as it is in English. 'One Belt, One Road' is a direct translation of the popularised shorthand Chinese styling, *Yídài Yílù*. This phrasing remains the BRI's constantly employed and unproblematically articulated buzzword in Chinese. However, even though technically accurate, the English translation (with its acronym 'OBOR') sounds somewhat ominous. 'One Belt, One Road' connotes a sense of Chinese singularity and unilateralism, an association that Beijing assiduously seeks to avoid. In September 2015, the three government bodies announced that, when explaining matters to the outside world, 'Belt and Road' would replace 'One Belt, One Road' officially in English, and that rather than refer to the BRI undertaking as a 'programme', 'agenda', 'strategy' or 'project', it should be described simply as an 'initiative'.[10] These authorised restylings of the BRI made no mention of the DSR. Rather, the only official statement regarding the DSR's positioning was the State Council's posting, issued around the same time, that connected a 'digital Silk Road' with Internet Plus.[11]

The idea of a DSR as a fully fledged and formalised component of Beijing's grand strategy for the BRI is nevertheless very real. The effective launch event for the DSR as a concerted, formally blessed concept within the BRI was the CAC's second annual World Internet Conference (WIC, Shìjiè Hùliánwǎng Dàhuì), which ran from 16–18 December 2015. Also known as the Wuzhen Summit, the annual WIC gathering constitutes an ongoing effort by Beijing to promote its version of the internet's purpose and principles. This mainly entails recasting the ideal of global interconnectivity based on a borderless, unencumbered network flow into Beijing's vision of 'internet sovereignty'. At the opening day of the 2015 WIC, two full sessions focused on the DSR. They were both entitled 'Digital Silk Road – Win–Win Cooperation' (Shùzì Sīlù – Hézuò Gòngyíng), reflecting China's standard assertion of the BRI's reciprocal benefits. Among the key achievements listed after the conclusion of the conference was a declaration of '"Digital Silk Road" construction'.[12]

The manner in which the ISR was officially announced by three central-government bodies and then quickly redefined and globally promoted by Lu and the CAC is suggestive of the power that he and the CAC could wield. Lu made the WIC the CAC's signature contribution to strategic messaging for the digital components of the BRI, and for advancing the CCP's overriding objective of making internet sovereignty an accepted norm of global internet governance. The 2015 WIC, in which the DSR held centre stage for the first time, was notable for its expanded size (attracting over 2,000 attendees, representing more than 120 countries and regions) and for being graced with the presence of Xi himself, who delivered the conference's opening speech. During his tenure at the CAC, in addition to acting as China's internet czar, Lu was considered a leading national figure and an integral member of Xi's inner circle.

**Idealising the DSR**

Reflecting Lu's appreciation for and use of digital communication channels, the DSR's domestic unveiling at the Forum on Internet Media in July 2015 served to introduce China's news media to the significance of the DSR and the role of the CAC (and the Chinese online-media apparatus that it rules over) in promoting the concept. Leading up to the December 2015 WIC, articles appearing in the Chinese press aimed to drum up public enthusiasm. In a jargon-laden opinion piece appearing online on platforms operated by the popular Nanfang Daily media group, and further amplified through widely accessed and influential sites like those operated by the CCP mouthpiece *Global Times*, one author rhapsodised that 'Digital Silk Road – Win–Win Cooperation' brought together the 'already tremendously successful' BRI and 'China's internet wave' with the power to draw in 'every household in the global village'.[13] The significance of such postings lies in their demonstration of the effort authorities would exert to promote the BRI's digital powers to a domestic audience. They are just one illustration of the degree to which the BRI and DSR serve the CCP's interests as a domestic as well as an international political instrument.

The leaders of China's major technology companies were also enlisted to the cause of championing the DSR. Accompanying Lu on his inaugural DSR roadshow to Brussels were senior executives from Alibaba, Baidu, China Mobile, China Telecom, China Unicom, Huawei, Tencent, Xiaomi and ZTE.[14] At the first DSR-themed session at the 2015 WIC, ZTE's chief executive, Shi Lirong, delivered a speech titled 'M-ICT: Time to Build an Information Silk Road' (M-ICT: *Xìnxī Sīchóu Zhīlù Chàngtōng Zhèngdāngshí*).[15] According to a *China Daily* article recapping the highlights of Shi's speech, ZTE's interpretation of the DSR embraced an 'idea of creating a smart city ... to collect and share all the information in transportation, education and government affairs ... The decisions on city operation will be made scientifically by using big data rather than just depending on city governors' wisdom.'[16] Joining ZTE's Shi on stage to deliver presentations discussing the DSR's 'information infrastructure partnership' were Jin Liqun, president of the Asian Infrastructure Investment Bank; Stephen Ho, CEO of CITIC Telecom International; Xu Luode, executive vice president of the Bank of China; and Sun Pishu, chairman and CEO of Inspur Group. 'Welcome the 5G era', the straightforward title of the address by Houlin Zhao, secretary-general of the UN's ITU, suggested the scale of the ambition harboured by the DSR's backers.

After the initial series of official statements about the DSR in 2015, and the accompanying media hype and corporate endorsements, the BRI, including its technological aspects, received gradually increasing, though uneven, levels of government support. The following year provided an opportunity to reassess some of the loftier expectations for the Chinese economy, the BRI as a whole, and China's technology sector. That year GDP growth dropped to 6.7%, the slowest pace in more than 25 years, while the National Bureau of Statistics recorded a growth rate of 18.1% for the tech sector, significantly lower than its initial estimate of 22.2%.[17] In its review of BRI projects in 2016, the NDRC warned of dangers from 'irrational' overseas investments and suggested that traditional infrastructure projects – rail and oil-pipeline projects, for example – might be 'more deserving than others'.[18] By 2017, however, the BRI had become enshrined in CCP orthodoxy. That year, the central government launched an internal purge of the CAC, beginning with an anti-corruption investigation of Lu Wei that led to his removal from office in early 2018. Coinciding with the administrative house-cleaning, the DSR was transformed into a centrepiece of BRI strategy.

Among the changes made to the CCP's constitution that were adopted at the 19th Communist Party of China National Congress in October 2017, a codification of the objective to 'push forward construction of the Belt and Road Initiative' received special attention.[19] The insertion of the BRI into the heart of party doctrine took most observers by surprise. This was the first time a non-domestic economic programme had been permanently politicised to such an extent. Along with including 'Xi Jinping Thought' in the CCP constitution, the upgrade of the BRI underscored that, in addition to the demand for greater obeisance to the man himself, people and organisations in China would need to further commit to the realisation of Xi's BRI agenda to be considered fully compliant with party dictates.

Less than a month after the party congress, the anti-corruption agency announced the detention of Lu. The initial nondescript standard charge, 'serious violations of political discipline' (*yánzhòng wěifǎn zhèngzhì jìlü*), was followed up by an unusually detailed list of alleged offences, from the banal ('accepting bribes') to the salacious ('trading power for sex') to the hubristic ('behaving tyrannically') to the ironic, given Lu's prominent role in online censorship as operator of the Great Firewall ('preposterously criticising the CCP Central Committee').[20] Considering the extent of the charges and the vitriol accompanying them, and that other top-ranking officials who had fallen from grace were usually sentenced to life imprisonment, Lu's sentence of 14 years was light. This perhaps owed to his unique contributions to propelling China's propaganda machine into the internet era.

Despite the fall from grace of its founding director, the CAC continued to operate and champion the DSR, although with far less flair than under Lu. It was just weeks after Lu's sentencing that the CAC's counterpart organisation in the CCP was elevated from the status of a leading team to that of a commission, demonstrating the institutional resilience of the projects under the CAC's dominion. Restructured and re-empowered, the CAC focused on consolidating its political base. This was no easy task. Despite its name, the CAC is not alone in exercising functional bureaucratic authority over the Chinese cybersphere and related digital realms. It must contend with other powerful administrative bodies such as the Ministry of Industry and Information Technology (MIIT) and the Ministry of Science and Technology (MOST). Yet in addition to its raised status, the CAC's continuing influence is indicated, for example, by its uninterrupted annual hosting of China's WIC, now a major international showcase event.

## The DSR's evolution

There is an inherent physical connection between the BRI and the DSR, as ICT products and services have become integral parts of modern infrastructure. Analysis by Carnegie Mellon University shows that even when the primary Chinese motivation is to channel excess capacity through the BRI's mainstay of basic infrastructure projects, digital technology still gets bundled in. Beijing's efforts to absorb parts of its excess industrial capacity through large-scale infrastructure building cannot be realised without the support of digital equipment and services. For example, even in a low-technology environment such as Laos, a BRI project to connect the country's railway system with China includes US$3.67 million for ICT services.[21] As a regional director of Huawei points out, the company benefits greatly from the BRI not only because the ICT sector is one of the targeted areas but also because many non-digital infrastructure projects, such as high-speed railways, airports and oil pipelines, all rely on ICT products to achieve system integration.[22]

Accordingly, the DSR should not be considered simply an adjunct element of the BRI, but an inseparable and under-pinning component. The digital dimensions of the BRI have evolved into formidable forces of China's foreign policy – conceptually, in practice and in strategic intent. Xi's ongoing interest in furthering the DSR was clearly on display at the April 2019 BRF. In the opening address, he referred to the DSR by name for the first time, securing its place within the BRI's wider endeavours and deepening DSR ties with foreign states within the context of China's international relations. Xi argued that

> we need to keep up with the trend of the Fourth Industrial Revolution, jointly seize opportunities created by digital, networked, and smart develop-ment, explore new technologies and new forms and models of business, foster new growth drivers and explore new development pathways, and build the digital Silk Road and the Silk Road of innovation.[23]

## Smart city

An intelligent network of connected sensors and machines, embedded across all city functions and services, that transmit data to a central authority. By analysing such data, governments are able to improve the quality of life and efficiency of urban environments.

Just as the 2019 BRF highlighted the role of the Ministry of Finance (MOF), in addition to the NDRC, in overseeing the BRI, it also drew attention to the institutions beyond the CAC that now have responsibility for and provide support to the DSR. In this regard, the government stakeholders in the DSR include the NDRC, the MOST, the MIIT and the Export–Import Bank of China (Eximbank). The variety of stakeholders in the DSR was reflected in the large number of DSR and DSR-affiliated agreements and projects that were signed at the forum. DSR-associated announcements appear in a lengthy tally of accomplishments, the 'List of Deliverables' (*Chéngguǒ Qīngdān*), attributed to the 2019 BRF.[24] Under the subtitle 'Strengthening Practical Cooperation', global leaders attending the BRF pledged to 'encourage digital infrastructure including transnational fibre-optic highways, promoting e-commerce and smart cities, and helping narrow the digital divide while drawing on international good practices'. A bulleted section of the communiqué under the heading 'Sectoral multilateral cooperation initiatives and platforms' referred to the DSR as an initiative in its own right, the 'Digital Silk Road Initiative' (*Shùzì Sīchóu Zhīlù Chàngyì*).

Looking ahead, beyond its political and economic positioning, the DSR is continuing to expand geospatially through cross-border infrastructure installations and virtually throughout cyberspace. Given the borderless nature of the digital domain and its embodiment of the future of economic evolution, the DSR concept operates far beyond designated BRI geographies. From this perspective, the DSR is not merely embedded in Beijing's strategy for global economic expansion: it is the ultimate, potentially unbounded extension of One Belt, One Road.

## CHAPTER THREE

# Identifying the Digital Silk Road

**Meia Nouwens**

Although the BRI is well defined, the few official documents published by the Chinese government specifically on the DSR give little indication of what it actually entails. As described in the 2015 BRI action plan, the Information Silk Road, as part of the BRI, focused narrowly on physical-infrastructure projects related to ICT, as well as on information-sharing systems in the areas of shipping, trade and finance (see Chapter One). In his address to the 2017 BRF, however, Xi referred to 'a' digital silk road focusing on emerging technologies such as 'digital economy, artificial intelligence, nanotechnology and quantum computing … big data, cloud computing and smart cities'.[1] This broader conception was expanded upon in his speech at the 2019 BRF (where he spoke of 'the' DSR), and in an address at the China–ASEAN business summit in 2020, to include 5G, e-commerce, blockchain and telemedicine.[2]

Without a clear understanding of what types of projects are included or should be excluded from the DSR, different

**Meia Nouwens** is Senior Fellow for Chinese Defence Policy and Military Modernisation at the IISS.

observers will base their conclusions on widely varying inter-
pretations. Since 2020 the IISS has been developing a dataset,
China Connects, of Chinese ICT projects around the world,
including those explicitly part of the BRI, those involving
technologies specifically mentioned in DSR policy documents
and statements, and those assessed to support the Chinese
government's publicly stated purpose for the DSR. It thus
defines the DSR dynamically, allowing fact-based analysis of
the narrowly defined DSR initiative and of how the maximalist DSR concept has evolved, who the stakeholders are, how
it is financed and how it compares to the BRI. (Unless otherwise specified, data and conclusions in this chapter are drawn
from the China Connects dataset, updated in autumn 2022.)

## The China Connects methodology

The China Connects dataset compiled by the IISS comprises Chinese infrastructure and digital-connectivity projects and investments that have taken place outside China and involved at least one Chinese stakeholder. It covers 173 countries and four territories.

The dataset includes projects that China's central government, ministerial agencies or state media have officially recognised as forming part of the BRI enterprise launched in 2013, as well as projects that Chinese stakeholders have undertaken since 2010 in response to Beijing's overseas infrastructure campaign but for various reasons have not received explicit endorsement from the Chinese state. Projects undertaken since 2000 involving 5G technology, academic programmes related to digital technology, data centres, e-commerce, e-governance, fibre-optic network technology, fintech, people-to-people connection programmes, satellite technology, surveillance and security, smart cities, submarine and overland fibre-optic cables, telecoms, and transfer of digital knowledge/technology are included under the DSR rubric to encompass China's global digital-infrastructure investments preceding and after the launch of the DSR initiative.

A team of IISS researchers fluent in Mandarin, English, French, Italian, Arabic, Spanish, German and Japanese compiled the dataset based on open-source primary and secondary sources, including government and industry documents and media reporting. Information for each project is triangulated. A minority of cases have fewer than three sources listed, due to insufficient publicly available information.

## Within and beyond the BRI

Just as Chinese companies were involved in the construction of roads, railways and ports in other countries long before the 2013 launch of the BRI, Chinese ICT activity abroad had been ongoing for years before the DSR was officially named in 2015. For example, Chinese telecoms giants such as Huawei and ZTE were active in Southeast Asia, sub-Saharan Africa and Europe as early as 2000 through the roll-out of previous generations of national telecommunications networks. In 2003 and 2004 ZTE signed contracts with companies in Russia, India and Ethiopia; in 2004 Huawei signed its first 3G contract in Europe with Dutch mobile-telecoms company Telfort; and ZTE and Greece's OTE contracted to build an ADSL (asymmetric digital subscriber line) network for the 2004 Olympic Games in Athens.[3]

When the DSR has featured in official documents and speeches it has usually been presented as part of the BRI, but the two initiatives differ in their geographical scope, stakeholders and financing structures. Although 127 countries had officially signed up to the BRI through memorandums of understanding (MoUs) by 2020, only 16 had signed an MoU for the DSR.[4] However, 165 countries could be considered recipients of projects and technologies that fall under the broadest definition of the DSR. Many of these are liberal democracies in Europe and Latin America, which have largely rejected offers to sign up to BRI membership. While the UK, for example, is not a member of the BRI, it can be considered part of the DSR under the maximalist definition. No European country, however, has to date formally confirmed its participation in the DSR, and many – for example France, Poland and the UK – are resisting (or considering resisting) the integration of Chinese technology into their national digital ecosystems.

Whereas the BRI mostly provides significant infrastructure to developing and emerging economies, with some inroads into developed economies, the DSR has extended to countries across the spectrum, with Chinese companies rolling out different generations of technology depending on recipients' development and connectivity. In 2015, for example, while ZTE signed an agreement with SoftBank Group to deploy its 5G trial technology in Japan, it was working with Smartfren in Indonesia to deploy 4G, and Huawei won a contract to deploy fibre-optic connectivity to 500 administrative centres in Lomé, Togo.[5]

The BRI is centrally directed by the NDRC as well as a small leading group within the CCP, and implemented by state-owned industries, with participation from Chinese regional and provincial governments. The DSR, in contrast, is carried out by a mixture of state-owned enterprises such as ZTE and Chinese private-sector tech companies and internet giants such as Alibaba. State-owned enterprises have primarily rolled out physical-infrastructure projects, reflecting the state's virtual monopolisation of this sector in China, while private-sector companies dominate services and platforms (that is, software working on top of physical telecommunications infrastructure).

While China has witnessed a domestic technology-industry boom, DSR-related projects tend to be monopolised by China's champion tech companies. The majority of projects are dominated by Alibaba and Tencent. Huawei, Hikvision, Uniview and Dahua dominate security-related sector; Alibaba, JD.com and Tencent dominate e-commerce; and Alibaba and Tencent are the biggest players in fintech. Companies that traditionally operated in the provision of physical network infrastructure, such as Huawei, are increasingly moving into the cloud-computing space and competing with newer private-sector companies such as Alibaba and Tencent. This reflects their attempts to find new areas of business growth following US restrictions that limit their access to supply chains of critical components and consequently their ability to offer physical-infrastructure projects.[6]

These differences between the BRI and DSR have implications for how the two initiatives are financed and for the degree of control the Chinese government potentially exerts over them. In 2018, for example, Beijing's cumulative commitment to the BRI was around US$575bn.[7] While the majority of funding for BRI projects is provided by a consortium of four state-owned commercial banks, two state-owned 'policy banks' and the Silk Road Fund, less than 10% of DSR-related projects report receiving Chinese state support.[8]

Most of the financial support for DSR projects from Chinese policy banks has been directed towards developing economies. Of these loans, 55% have been provided to countries in Africa, while another 30% of DSR projects reporting state financial support have taken place in Central Asia, South Asia or the Pacific Islands. Five countries in Latin America (Mexico), Southeast Asia (Malaysia) and Central and Eastern Europe (Romania, Russia and Ukraine) have also received this form of support.

Projects that receive funding from Chinese policy banks such as Eximbank have generally involved the provision and roll-out of physical technologies: brick-and-mortar data centres, e-governance projects, surveillance-technology projects such as Huawei's 'Safe City'-branded products, and national telecommunications networks. In some of these projects, banks have provided financial assistance for setting up entirely new network infrastructure, while in others the funding went towards upgrading an existing network. In 2016, for example, Huawei signed a three-year project with Ukraine's fixed-line operator Ukrtelecom to modernise and expand the country's national telecommunications network.[9] Huawei had previously acted as one of Ukrtelecom's major technology partners in other roll-outs. China Development Bank (CDB) supported the 2016 strategic-partnership agreement financially, with a first tranche of credit amounting to US$50m, with repayment due in 2022.[10]

Loan packages for DSR-related projects tend to be smaller than those in connection with the BRI. For example, the 2015 loan from CDB to Russia's MegaFon for a DSR-related project was worth US$600m through two credit facilities, compared to US$1.3bn in Chinese loans to Sri Lanka for Hambantota Port.[11] The difference could to some extent reflect a lack of transparency in reporting DSR-related funding of infrastructure projects, but could also reflect the fact that such projects tend to be smaller and less expensive, and therefore more affordable for a recipient country or company.

The state-owned and state-linked companies that have dominated physical-infrastructure projects abroad often leverage the support of Chinese policy banks for lines of credit and cheap financing to undercut their Western competitors. In 2004, for example, Nigeria received US$200m in loans from CDB to buy Huawei equipment. Lending rates were reportedly well below the benchmark one-year lending rate in China, by as much as five percentage points.[12] Chinese state funding thus subsidises commercial risk investment in the area of physical ICT technology.

There is little evidence of public financing from Chinese policy banks for projects involving the provision of services or platforms. Chinese commercial internet companies have invested large sums abroad in competitor companies or start-ups, without the involvement of policy banks. This might suggest that Chinese private-sector companies are commercially able to absorb any risk investment on their own without the guarantee of support from policy banks. As the demand for services and platforms increases, the dominance of private-sector companies in the DSR may grow along with it, ultimately diminishing the need for state policy-bank support for the DSR overall.

**Safe Cities**

Huawei's proprietary brand of smart-city public-security projects, incorporating the physical and technical infrastructure required to support biometric-identification databases, video-surveillance networks, and the use of AI and big-data analytics by public-security operators.

Finally, despite the government's promotion of the DSR as a socio-economic endeavour aimed at increasing connectivity and improving rural life, the vast majority of projects are located in urban areas and serve urban needs. Moreover, projects such as Safe Cities that include surveillance technology or are linked to security services, intended to increase a government's ability to monitor and control citizens, are three times more common than smart-city projects.

## Technological, economic and geographical trends

The evolution of the DSR reflects the evolution of technology and the growth of Chinese companies at home. In addition to investing in new markets, Chinese companies have also built on existing projects in foreign countries by offering upgrades as new generations of technology become available. The type and geographical focus of DSR-related projects will thus naturally shift over time, with consequences for the relationship between the Chinese government and the companies active in the DSR.

Many categories of physical-infrastructure project, for example, have declined in relative importance in recent years. This trend began in 2016, only a year after the DSR's launch, and could be due to the saturation of international markets. Projects in 5G technology have been a notable exception, however, with numerous Huawei and ZTE 5G projects launched with increasing frequency beginning in 2015. The downward trend in pre-5G projects and gradual increase in 5G projects are connected: as a new generation of national telecommunications infrastructure is adopted, pre-5G infrastructure will naturally decrease.

The number and diversity of projects begun each year has also steadily increased since 2015, when Chinese companies started 105 DSR-related projects abroad. By 2019 that figure was 355, although it fell to 245 in 2020 during the coronavirus pandemic. The DSR initiative is not necessarily the cause, however, since for Chinese tech companies facing a saturated domestic market, going global has been a necessity for commercial survival. Only a few days after becoming CEO of Alibaba in 2015, for example, Daniel Zhang told his employees that the company 'must absolutely globalize' and that the company would 'organize a global team and adopt global thinking to manage the business … If not, we won't be able to last.'[13] Other Chinese tech companies followed suit, though their motivations may not necessarily have been the same.

In 2015 the largest single category of new DSR-related projects involved pre-5G telecommunications infrastructure; the second and third largest involved surveillance technology and transfer-of-knowledge projects respectively. By 2020 the principal categories were data centres, surveillance-technology-related projects, 5G, terrestrial- and submarine-cable projects, transfer-of-knowledge projects, fintech and academic programmes (see Table 1).

The relative growth of services and platform projects has been particularly significant since the start of the DSR. Between 2015 and 2019, for example, the number of new fintech projects per year grew almost fourfold; smart-city projects doubled; surveillance- and security-related projects, already significant before 2015, also doubled; and data centres grew more than twentyfold. Although there were reports as early as 2013 of BRI projects not yet under way years after they were supposed to begin, this does not appear to be the case for DSR-related

Table 1: **New DSR-related projects by technology type, 2015 and 2020**

|  | 2015 | 2020 |
|---|---|---|
| 5G | 4 | 22 |
| Data centres | 5 | 116 |
| E-commerce | 5 | 2 |
| E-governance | 1 | 1 |
| Fintech | 3 | 12 |
| Transfer-of-knowledge projects | 14 | 15 |
| Academic programmes | 10 | 11 |
| People-to-people connection programmes | 0 | 1 |
| Satellite technology | 1 | 2 |
| Surveillance and security | 15 | 30 |
| Smart city | 3 | 6 |
| Terrestrial or submarine cables | 2 | 16 |
| Telecoms (pre-5G) | 42 | 9 |

Source: IISS China Connects

projects (see Figure 1).[14] Of the DSR-related projects agreed in 2014, 84.8% had been completed as of 2021, while 8.6% were ongoing, 3.8% were still in the planning stage, and 2.8% had been halted or cancelled. For projects begun since then, the figures were 65.7%, 24.9%, 5.9% and 3.5% respectively.

The geographical focus of the DSR will increasingly be the Middle East and Southeast Asia. Roughly 16% of Chinese overseas tech projects have taken place in sub-Saharan and North Africa, due to the high demand for and relative lack of infrastructure there. But around 40% of the projects in this region and in Latin America, and 33% of those in Europe, pre-date the 2015 launch of the DSR, whereas some 76% of those in the Middle East and Southeast Asia have begun since then. These regions have not only benefited from greater Chinese investment in services and platforms, but also continue to be important recipients of Chinese physical telecommunications infrastructure. They offer growth markets for the future trajectory of the DSR and significant opportunities for Chinese tech companies. Indonesia, for example, is ASEAN's largest ICT

Figure 1: **Status in 2022 of DSR-related projects begun since 2001, by year of commencement**

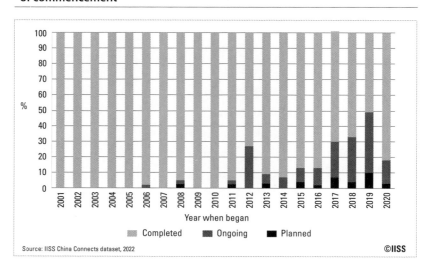

Source: IISS China Connects dataset, 2022                                                   ©IISS

market, and its digital economy is forecast to grow to US$133bn by 2025. Although around 40% of the population still does not have access to the internet, the population is largely young, tends to be tech savvy, and is already a major consumer of technology apps and products. Chinese companies are increasingly targeting the country's market for cloud and Internet of Things applications and the hardware that enables them.[15]

The relationship between the state, the CCP and the private sector in China is currently in flux. Due to the size and influence of companies such as Alibaba and Tencent, the government increasingly sees them as threats to state and party control. As the DSR moves away from the provision of physical-infrastructure projects towards a focus on cloud-based services and platforms, it threatens to become less dependent on state-backed financing and less vulnerable to centralised government control over its trajectory and development. The start of a government crackdown on private tech companies (see Chapter Four) was signalled in 2020 by the three-month disappearance from public view of Jack Ma, a founder and former executive chairman of Alibaba Group and one of the wealthiest individuals in China, following his criticism of Chinese banks and regulators for stifling innovation. Part of this effort includes passing new laws and regulations regarding the sharing of digital records and data collected from social media, e-commerce and other businesses.[16]

Whether Chinese tech firms can maintain their current international dynamism while facing greater restrictions at home is a vital question for the future of the DSR. The power struggle between the CCP, the state and the private tech sector could potentially derail the initiative by stymieing the growth and success of some of the main stakeholders. As Fred Hu, founder of investment firm Primavera Capital in Hong Kong (as well as an investor in Ant Group and member of its board), put it in 2020, a month after the Chinese government had scuttled Ant Group's US$34.5bn initial public offering (IPO), 'you can either have absolute control or you can have a dynamic, innovative economy. But it's doubtful you can have both.'[17] Other players rationalise the party's moves against large tech companies as beneficial to innovation. Andy Tian, CEO of Beijing social-media start-up Asia Innovations Group, has said that the moves mean 'competition in China will be fiercer than in the US' as smaller companies will be able to compete against their larger counterparts.[18]

Foreign pushback against Chinese technology projects and infrastructure is also increasing. In August 2020 the US launched the Clean Network initiative to persuade allies and partners to exclude Chinese vendors from their national 5G telecommunications networks. By November 2020, 50 countries (including 31 of the 37 members of the Organisation for Economic Co-operation and Development, 27 of the 30 NATO members and 26 of the 27 members of the EU) had signed up to the initiative or (as in the case of the EU's 5G Toolbox) had agreed that their own initiatives had synergies with it.[19] But by early 2021, several European countries, including NATO members Italy and Turkey, had still not decided whether to allow the use of Huawei equipment in their national 5G networks. By the end of 2020, only 15% of Chinese 5G projects had been officially halted or cancelled, most of them in US-allied or like-minded states. India and Canada are the latest countries to restrict the integration of Huawei's technology into their national 5G networks, announcing the decisions in May 2021 and May 2022 respectively.[20] In Europe, only the UK and Sweden have officially banned the use of Huawei equipment in their national networks.[21] Most other European countries have agreed to allow only 'trusted vendors' into national networks, without banning Huawei outright. In developing and emerging economies, however, the vast majority of Chinese 5G contracts have survived this pushback. Indeed, there is a disconnect between the rhetoric of 'global pushback' against Chinese tech projects and what can be observed in practice, perhaps reflecting a tendency on the part of the majority of developing and emerging economies to put prosperity ahead of politics, prioritising connectivity needs and digital economic growth over issues of allegiance.

There is also a disconnect between national technology policies and the reality on the ground. For example, although Poland has signed up to the Clean Network initiative, restricted the use of Chinese technology in its national networks and generally backtracked from its earlier enthusiasm for Chinese digital technology, some local projects involving Chinese technology – such as contracts between local governments and Hikvision to use Chinese-made surveillance cameras to control traffic – have apparently not been halted or cancelled.[22] Dahua's Polish subsidiary, meanwhile, remains active throughout the country.[23] What is decided at the national level does not always result in coordinated action at the regional or local level.

The US-led normative effort to create global pushback against Chinese technology (particularly in 5G networks) has had limited effect. Restrictions on Chinese companies' access to core components will probably have a greater impact on their ability to roll out future generations of networks than arguments based on norms and ideological considerations. Furthermore, most of the DSR's broad range of technologies appears so far to be largely unaffected by restrictions in recipient states. While national policies have largely focused on 5G and network roll-outs, Chinese technology projects in fintech and e-commerce, for example, have faced significantly less pushback. As the future trajectory of the DSR probably lies in the provision of such services and platforms, national government policies in recipient states have yet to significantly alter its short-term trajectory.

## CHAPTER FOUR

# The Digital Silk Road and the evolving role of Chinese technology companies

## Paul Triolo

Understanding the relationship between Chinese tech firms and the Chinese government is challenging. Official statements and documents may give the impression that there are rooms full of cadres deciding on how Chinese tech conglomerates should expand internationally. The sweeping statement by official media during the government-sponsored BRF in April 2019 that the DSR 'not only promotes the development of the digital service sector, such as cross-border e-commerce, smart cities, telemedicine, and internet finance, but also accelerates technological progress including computing, big data, Internet of Things, artificial intelligence, blockchain, and quantum computing' implied that all things technology related were being coordinated through a state-sponsored initiative.[1] But in reality, the role played by the Chinese state in these technology sectors is much less important than such statements imply. The DSR is best understood as an umbrella branding effort and a narrative for Beijing to promote its global vision across a range

**Paul Triolo** is Senior Vice President for China and Technology Policy Lead at Albright Stonebridge Group, Washington DC.

of specific core technology sectors, rather than as a project or initiative that is being directed or implemented centrally by ministries in Beijing, or as the maximalist DSR concept in which all business operations related to the digital economy are lumped together under its rubric.

The main drivers of the core DSR are Chinese private companies, which often use the label to gain policy support for their pursuit of overseas commercial expansion. The DSR today is in many respects like a set of franchise businesses, evolving in parallel with the degree of involvement and broader priorities of Chinese ministries. Chinese private-sector companies sometimes brand projects they have developed themselves as part of the DSR, in order to receive political – and perhaps financial – support from Beijing, while the state generally has no involvement in day-to-day operations. There is no compelling evidence, for example, that CCP committees within the headquarters of large multinational firms such as Huawei, Alibaba or ByteDance have any say over the companies' operational decision-making. Nor, moreover, would such committees be equipped to intervene in any substantial way in the running of such large and complex businesses. In fact, informal discussions with officials at large Chinese companies and other observers suggest that the subject of the DSR per se is rarely addressed at the executive level or discussed to any significant extent within the firms, which are driven by commercial considerations. As one senior Huawei executive put it, 'I've never heard anyone at Huawei use the phrase "Digital Silk Road". In fact, I'm not sure I've ever actually heard anyone anywhere use it.'[2]

Nevertheless, it is likely that government officials can and will increasingly seek to leverage Chinese companies' participation in digital projects abroad to advance Beijing's broader strategic objectives. China's leaders are eager to exploit the advantages that the country's leading technology firms, mostly private, have in relation to their international competitors, particularly in areas such as next-generation infrastructure, including 5G mobile and cloud services. This will not happen via party committees attached to the companies, but rather via the key ministries that support BRI projects, including the NDRC, the MIIT and the MOF.

Over the past five years, leading Chinese internet, e-commerce, payments and AI-platform conglomerates such as Alibaba, Tencent and JD.com, and to a lesser extent Baidu (as well as Huawei and state-owned telecoms carriers such as China Mobile, China Telecom and China Unicom) have all expanded their global footprints, particularly in countries and regions that are part of the BRI. But for these companies the primary driver of expansion has been the potential for larger user bases and stronger market share, much more than adherence to the concepts of the BRI or the DSR. They are all eager to compete in emerging markets with leading US companies in 'over the top' (OTT) services, for example. These include smart cities, cloud services, mobile payments and social-media applications. They will eventually also encompass AI, autonomous vehicles, and Internet of Things technologies and services.

A small number of digital projects do originate via high levels of state influence. They are likely to be linked to state-backed BRI projects where digital infrastructure is required or desired to support the operation of the project. Such state-driven digital projects could expand in number in the years ahead in the wake of BRI expansion. But for the most part, the global expansion of Chinese private tech companies will be driven by business requirements and the desire to develop global brands, not by bureaucrats in Beijing with limited knowledge of company operations or the highly competitive business sectors in which they operate.

State support for Chinese companies operating in foreign markets usually does not involve the degree of coordination that Beijing has implied and foreign observers have assumed. The growth of Chinese tech companies in many emerging markets preceded the development of the BRI and DSR, and long-standing business relationships, both with foreign governments and with private-sector partners, have only recently been branded by Western observers as identifiable with the DSR. While these ostensible DSR policy incentives supported projects orchestrated by Beijing after 2015 as well as ordinary business growth, many self-branded DSR projects did not enjoy any political or financial state backing at all.

Officials in Beijing are coalescing around a more expansive vision of the DSR. Across emerging markets as well as developed economies in Asia and Europe, Beijing will seek to invest resources to help the country's tech giants pursue commercial opportunities and be involved at all levels of the digital-infrastructure build-out, from fibre-optic and wireless infrastructure to telecommunications carrier services and the provision of OTT applications services. Chinese tech companies will be cheered by this more ambitious approach because it is in keeping with what they have already been doing to expand into overseas markets.

Beijing may be gearing up to both dramatically increase financial support and attempt to assert a more activist role with respect to some DSR-branded projects, particularly as part of the post-pandemic recovery, where the critical role of digital infrastructure and the need to boost investment are now widely recognised, and regulators are playing a more active role in constraining the business models of large technology platforms. This is already creating a more complex operating environment for Chinese DSR-related companies, especially in Europe, where US efforts to pressure governments into limiting the role of Chinese tech companies have had the most impact. Despite these developments, the DSR will remain at its core a franchise effort, with individual businesses continuing as the main drivers of the initiative, using the DSR label to gain policy support – via loans, subsidies and political support – in their pursuit of overseas commercial expansion.

## Core DSR technologies

The set of technologies that form the core of the DSR includes telecommunications infrastructure and associated sectors such as data centres, cloud services and select OTT applications, including financial services. Chinese researchers identified 1,324 overseas investment and cooperation projects involving 201 companies in 2018–19, of which only 57% were related to these core technologies (see Table 2).[3]

Table 2: **Chinese companies' overseas digital-transformation projects, 2018–19**

| Sector | All projects | DSR core technologies | Representative companies |
|---|---|---|---|
| E-commerce | 85 | 0 | Alibaba, JD.com, Suning, NetEase |
| Communications infrastructure | 211 | 211 | Huawei, ZTE |
| Digital finance/fintech | 136 | 0 | Alipay, China UnionPay |
| Smart cities | 264 | 264 | PingAn, China TransInfo, Inspur, China Mobile, UBTech |
| Industrial internet | 189 | 189 | State Grid Corporation of China, PCITC, China Satellite Communications |
| Intelligent terminals | 115 | 0 | Transsion, APUS, Xiaomi, Oppo |
| IT services (incl. cloud) | 88 | 88 | AliCloud, Tencent Cloud, Baidu Cloud, Kysun |
| Media/ entertainment | 236 | 0 | TikTok, Boomplay |
| | 1,324 | 752 (57% of total) | |

Source: author's research; Fudan Institute of Belt and Road & Global Governance

The Chinese tech companies involved in these projects fall into six categories:

- *Infrastructure and enterprise-equipment vendors.* This group – which includes telecoms vendors Huawei and ZTE, along with server giant Inspur – consists of a mixture of mainly private-sector and some state-linked companies that have benefited from a large domestic market. Inspur has recently stepped up its marketing and made major inroads in some emerging markets in Africa.[4] In this category, Chinese firms face stiff competition from European vendors Nokia and Ericsson, and from South Korean giant Samsung. Some have benefited from official BRI-related lending, but many had established a presence in foreign countries which later participated in the BRI long before the BRI or DSR were thought of. Huawei CEO Ren Zhengfei, for example, claims that because his company's contracts are usually for short-term projects and involve much smaller amounts of money than the large infrastructure projects that are part of the BRI, 'we have no connection with the initiative'.[5]
- *Consumer-electronics vendors.* These are all private-sector firms. Companies such as mobile-phone maker Transsion and smartphone vendors Oppo, Vivo and Xiaomi are all becoming major players in emerging markets, including some that are part of the BRI and some that are not, such as India. Transsion, for example, is one of the dominant lower-end handset providers in Africa. Drone makers DJI and XAG are also making inroads in emerging markets, both within and outside the BRI.
- *State-backed telecommunications providers and private IT-services providers.* In this category, China's leading mobile and fixed-line carriers China Telecom, China

Unicom and China Mobile have differing levels of involvement in countries participating in the BRI. These companies are particularly active in Africa and Central Asia. In Southeast Asia, China Telecom and China Mobile are most active in Cambodia, Indonesia, Malaysia, Myanmar and Papua New Guinea. Such companies are likely to become a more important part of the DSR. They face competition from a host of global carriers including Vodafone, Telenor, Verizon and AT&T. Also in this category, Alibaba and Tencent are the leading Chinese companies in cloud services, along with Huawei, and are playing growing roles in this sector in some BRI countries, competing directly with big Western players such as Amazon, Microsoft and Google.

- *Industrial internet companies.* Although this category receives much less attention in Western analyses of the BRI and DSR, the companies in it are set to become important players in what is a very competitive space, including in smart energy. For example, the State Grid Corporation of China has invested in, constructed and is now operating energy networks in countries participating in the BRI. It focuses on projects such as precision active repairs, photovoltaic cloud networks, smart-vehicle networking and virtual power plants.[6] Chinese smart-energy companies are competing against capable Western firms including ABB, Siemens, eSmart Systems, Schneider Electric and EDF, along with US companies such as General Electric, Itron, Cisco, OSI, Honeywell, Tantalus, Grid4C and C3 Energy.

- *Providers of smart-city services.* The leading Chinese players in this category are Alibaba, Huawei and ZTE. This is a complex sector that also includes companies offering key components of a smart-city suite of hardware and software, such as Hikvision and other security-camera firms that provide security systems, and AI companies offering smart cameras for traffic monitoring. Huawei and Alibaba function more as systems integrators and have a diverse set of offerings, such as Alibaba's 'City Brain'. Major competitors include ABB and Siemens.

- *Over-the top players.* These are all private companies that are already playing a major role in the DSR, especially in Southeast Asia and Africa, and whose importance under the DSR umbrella is set to increase because they bring the added value – in payments, cloud services, AI and smart-city applications – that governments and other companies and users are looking for in many BRI countries. Chinese players in this arena are going up against major US payments companies such as Visa and Mastercard, and technology companies such as Apple.

None of these companies has a dominant role in its sector, with the partial exception of Huawei in emerging regions such as Africa and Central Asia. From the perspective of individual Chinese companies, therefore, the DSR is by no means a sure bet in terms of competitiveness. Many Chinese investments take the form of joint ventures with local partners, which the Chinese government often encourages. But on the whole, Chinese companies have established a stronger presence in the digital-technology sector in foreign markets than those from any other single country. US pressure on Huawei's supply chains, and its campaign to get allies and other like-minded countries to ban the firm from 5G-network roll-outs, has dramatically changed Huawei's trajectory globally, and particularly in Europe, but in general those efforts have not slowed the expansion of Chinese tech firms in BRI countries.[7]

Alibaba Cloud, or Aliyun, is a typical example of a Chinese company involved in the DSR. Driven by strategic business priorities and the desire to compete with US leaders Amazon, Microsoft and Google, it is clearly targeting emerging markets. Within these markets, particularly in Southeast Asia, Aliyun is targeting lower-value market segments such as mass (as opposed to high-end) e-commerce, small and medium enterprises, and start-ups, where requirements are less sophisticated and full enterprise-cloud solutions of the type offered by leading Western competitors may not be required. As part of the Alibaba conglomerate, Aliyun is also leveraging the gains of parent company Alibaba in e-commerce and logistics, and those of Ant Financial and its Alipay infrastructure in payments and digital transactions. This package of services on offer from the broader conglomerate is not driven by bureaucrats in Beijing but by corporate strategists in Alibaba's Hangzhou headquarters. But the firm is also leveraging the goodwill, open doors and expansive development programmes that BRI investments are creating in some countries, especially in Southeast Asia. Another, more significant marketing point for the Alibaba companies is that they are far more nimble and flexible than their large Western competitors in terms of compliance and market-entry positions in these markets.

Aliyun exemplifies how a company's efforts to expand can complement Beijing's strategic priorities along with those of the local authorities and the regulatory complexities of the local market. In Southeast Asia, Alibaba and Aliyun have accommodated local regulatory concerns on issues such as law enforcement, cross-border transfers of personal data, and compliance with local requirements. The regulatory environment around these issues is not well developed in many emerging markets, allowing Alibaba some leeway in interpreting how to comply. In Indonesia, for example, Alibaba has opened two data centres, and pitches them as supporting Jakarta's Digital Economy Vision.[8] Alibaba/Aliyun are similarly leveraging BRI goodwill in Brunei, Cambodia, Myanmar, the Philippines and Thailand, which are all countries where Huawei has had close relationships with telecoms carriers.[9]

Recent developments concerning the BRI and DSR in Malaysia offer another way of looking at Beijing's implicit and explicit priorities. On returning to office in May 2018, prime minister Mahathir Mohamad put Chinese BRI projects under review. He threatened to cancel the East Coast Rail Link project, the largest BRI project in the country, then approved a significantly downsized and less costly version. He signed an agreement to develop a new US$500m AI park with Chinese start-up SenseTime, and was also supportive of Alibaba/Ant's electronic World Trade Platform (eWTP) project in Kuala Lumpur, aimed at helping small and medium enterprises find new markets outside Malaysia.[10] With regard to 5G and mobile networks, Mahathir initially appeared supportive of Huawei.[11] In 2020, however, after delaying 5G-spectrum auctions, Malaysian officials decided they should expand their options.[12] In May 2021 the MOF called for bids from eight vendors – Cisco, Ericsson, Fiberhome, Huawei, NEC, Nokia, Samsung and ZTE – of which only two were Chinese.

Chinese tech-company activity in Malaysia suggests that leading Chinese players are drawn to more developed markets where the authorities are eager to deploy advanced technologies to improve government functions, reduce traffic congestion and plug small and medium enterprises into global markets. Although Beijing supports these efforts by private tech firms in Malaysia, government ministries are more focused on the large BRI projects that are under way there. While some Chinese firms have probably benefited from Malaysian government support, Mahathir's return to office shows that a change of regime can mean a shift in attitude towards the presence of Chinese companies in critical national infrastructure.

**Looking forward: the technical DSR**

Over the next few years, Chinese companies are likely to take their operations within the DSR's core technological sectors in a variety of directions.

*Digital infrastructure*

Before 2019, Huawei and ZTE were closely involved in developing 5G-technology networks in third-country markets. Both companies were also involved in bids around the world for undersea and terrestrial telecommunications cables, among other ICT infrastructure. However, under pressure from US diplomatic efforts as part of the Clean Network initiative, and from restrictions on the firm's access to semiconductors, Huawei appears unlikely, as of mid-2022, to compete successfully for 5G contracts in more advanced markets, especially in Europe. So far, it has not faced similar difficulties in its developing-country markets, including in Southeast Asia, the Middle East, Africa and Latin America. But it is too early to predict the long-term status of Huawei's 5G-infrastructure capabilities.[13] Just before the US tightened restrictions on Huawei's supply chains in August 2020, the firm was among the bidders for a major 5G project in Thailand operated by Advanced Info Service (AIS), the country's largest mobile carrier.[14] ZTE appears likely to be a major beneficiary of Huawei's troubles in Thailand, and is also poised to expand its role in developing telecommunications infrastructure elsewhere in Southeast Asia and in other BRI regions.

*Telecoms services*

Chinese carriers have ramped up the installation of non-standalone 5G infrastructure domestically, and at the end of 2021

China led the world in terms of numbers of 5G base stations installed, with plans to reach two million by the end of 2022.[15] Chinese carriers are beginning to issue tenders for full stand-alone networks to support industrial internet applications. Success in these early efforts to support advanced applications such as autonomous vehicles, smart factories and smart cities would help Chinese vendors of 5G equipment and providers of 5G carrier services to market such products in BRI countries.

### Data centres and cloud services

Chinese companies are likely to attempt to expand DSR-related infrastructure such as the data centres and cloud services critical to smart cities, which in turn integrate such services with elements such as 5G networks and OTT applications. There is some confusion, however, around the use of particular data centres built or operated by competing Chinese tech companies. Alibaba, for example, has at least 23 data centres outside China. In 2021 it opened two operations in the UK along with its second data centres in both Indonesia and Japan, and in March 2022 it unveiled its first data centre in South Korea after announcing a South Korean cloud region in October 2021.[16] As of April 2022, Aliyun (or Alibaba Cloud) was operating 26 cloud regions and 82 availability zones globally. But its data centres in developed-country markets such as the UK and Japan principally support Chinese tourists, who prefer to use Alipay and other services, and hence should not be considered part of the DSR. In other cases, Alibaba is building data centres to compete directly with major Western players in advanced-country markets. In 2019, for example, Alibaba discussed partnering with BT Cloud in the UK to offer its cloud services, which would allow it to compete with Amazon Web Services (AWS). Alibaba Cloud is already competing with AWS in South Korea.

Alibaba/Aliyun are intent on marketing smart-city capabilities already deployed in many cities in China. In May 2020
Aliyun announced a partnership with local smart-traffic-system
controller Sena Traffic Systems to build a traffic-management
system in Malaysia.[17] Alibaba views the deployment of smart-
city applications, often coupled with Aliyun cloud services, as
a growth area, particularly in Southeast Asia.

In contrast, Huawei is focused on cloud services, viewing
them as a critical part of its smart-city and AI offerings. In fact,
with growing US pressure on its other business lines, the firm
appears to regard the expansion of its cloud-services footprint
as one way to survive the onslaught.[18] In November 2019, for
example, Huawei announced its Cloud and AI Innovation Lab
in Singapore, which opened in February 2021 and is intended
to align with the city-state's Smart Nation strategy.[19] In some
markets Huawei is also expanding its data-centre presence, for
example in Thailand's Eastern Economic Corridor (EEC), where
Alibaba, JD.com and Tencent have also expressed interest in
investing.[20] Thailand's AIS is also set to invest up to US$1.4bn
in 5G infrastructure in the EEC, which will be a major test of
Huawei's ability to win 5G-infrastructure projects and data-
centre business as it seeks to shore up supply chains under US
pressure.[21] The company will also face stiff competition from
European 5G vendors and other Chinese players as it tries to
maintain a foothold in Thailand. It is unclear what Beijing's
preferences are in this regard, or whether Chinese government
ministries will play any role in this competitive environment.

Huawei is also in talks with countries in Central Asia,
Southeast Asia, Africa and elsewhere to promote smart-city
projects. In Africa, for example, it has built a series of data
centres to support its various business lines, including several smart-city offerings, most of which are focused on 'Safe
City' public-security solutions involving AI applications and

security-related technology such as networked surveillance cameras. In 2019 it won a US$172.5m contract to support the Konza Technopolis Data Centre and Smart Cities project in Kenya.[22]

In many cases smart-city projects are announced with much fanfare before the required investment has been secured, and while the priority applications and timelines are still unclear. In addition, most smart-city projects involve multiple vendors and Chinese companies may play only limited roles, typically providing one or several key pieces of technology. Huawei and other Chinese companies do not appear to be using a consistent model: each smart-city project will probably see different degrees of Chinese involvement (both by companies and government) and of Chinese government support.

*Over-the-top services*
Chinese companies are attempting to promote their wholly owned payments platforms or blockchain solutions as part of the DSR. For example, Alibaba is prioritising the global expansion of its payment platform AliPay. Such platforms are alternatives to Western payments systems and are aimed at Chinese tourists travelling abroad, with a focus on those in Europe, Asia and Australia. But the assumption by some observers that these efforts had strong political support from Beijing has been challenged by the political attacks on Alibaba founder Jack Ma and the restrictions subsequently imposed on the firm by Chinese regulators. This is significant considering Alibaba's planned investments in banks and insurance firms, and its major investments in payments companies in Asia and Europe. Alibaba's Ant is a 'super app' that combines Apple Pay for offline payments, PayPal for online payments, Venmo for transfers, Mastercard for credit cards, JPMorgan Chase for consumer financing, iShares for investing, and an insurance-brokerage function. The cancellation of Ant's scheduled IPO in late 2020 and the imposition of tighter regulatory

controls over the company will slow the emerging Chinese dominance of fintech in BRI countries and especially in Southeast Asia, the most dynamic fintech region in emerging markets.

Blockchain developments by Chinese entities could turn out to be one of the next major elements of the DSR. Although China bans cryptocurrency exchanges and initial coin offerings, Beijing is set to leverage the underpinning technology. At the Hainan Free Trade Zone & Global Digital Economic Forum in December 2019, Chinese officials discussed blockchain applications with officials from Bahrain, Indonesia, Kazakhstan and Russia, and some countries signed an agreement on blockchain and the digital economy.[23] The following April, an alliance of Chinese tech companies, banks and government agencies launched the so-called Blockchain-based Service Network (BSN), designed to supply a low-cost global infrastructure for developing blockchain-based applications.[24] A six-month pilot for the project took place in Singapore. The founding members of the BSN included the State Information Centre (SIC), China UnionPay, China Mobile and payroll-services company Red Date.

The BSN's underlying infrastructure consists of more than 100 so-called Public City Nodes (PCNs) – collections of servers providing computing power and storage located inside data centres at the regional level. Nearly all the network's PCNs are provided by one company, the cloud-services arm of China Mobile. But while the SIC envisions hundreds of PCNs launching abroad, only seven PCNs exist overseas as of May 2022, of which six are operated by non-Chinese cloud-computing companies.[25] Indeed, the negligible to non-existent role that China's largest public cloud-services incumbents in the private sector, such as Alibaba and Tencent, play in the BSN is striking, suggesting that the BSN might have as much to do with competition between China Mobile and the big cloud-services companies, with the government moving in to support the former.

In September 2021 the BSN launched support for developers in Hong Kong and Macau, via what Red Date officials have called BSN International (one of the project's two arms launched in July 2020; the other is BSN China).[26] A Red Date official claimed in late 2021 that there were already more than 30 projects in development via Hong Kong and Macau, and that the site had attracted a lot of attention from developers.[27] The development of the BSN and its extension beyond China's borders have a number of important ramifications. One is the potential use of BSN structures and services, including a non-public version called Private BSN, as a platform for bank-to-bank or business-to-business cross-border transactions. Another is the potential use of the BSN as a platform for deploying a central bank digital currency (CBDC) as part of regional or global payments systems.

In what could be a major development for the DSR, moreover, Red Date is planning to build a payments layer on top of the BSN and claims already to have significant support from banks and technology companies. The company says this is a global project, called the Universal Digital Payment Network (UDPN), with five banking firms in Europe, the US and China discussing how such a system could be deployed. According to a draft UDPN White Paper, the project addresses the issue of inter-operability between CBDCs and other digital currencies by creating a global payment messaging network, designed to support regulated, fiat-backed blockchain-based currencies (stablecoins) and CBDCs across both decentralised and centralised currency systems. The goal of the UDPN is to create a common decentralised network and associated standards: the messaging backbone for efficient and seamless cross-border payments across protocols and systems.[28] According to a Red Date official, it can be seen as a SWIFT-like system for digital currencies.[29]

Should the Chinese government become a more active proponent of accelerating the BSN's use overseas, for example via the

People's Bank of China (PBoC), it would mark a shift to a more active and direct role by the state in influencing which private-sector activities are supported through the DSR. Such an effort is most likely in countries where Chinese companies are already involved in DSR-related activities and where the government either shares or is neutral towards Beijing's vision of cyber sovereignty. In such countries, governments and companies will not be concerned about China's leadership of an effort that drastically lowers the cost of blockchain-based government services such as supply-chain monitoring and property tracking. If the BSN's apparent domestic issues are resolved and it receives Beijing's full support, the effort could accelerate the global deployment of Chinese-led blockchain protocols,[30] Chinese technological and support infrastructure for these protocols, and state-authorised encryption standards.[31]

In April 2020 the PBoC began testing a CBDC that Beijing views as an eventual alternative non-dollar payments system, potentially for some BRI partner countries.[32] A more significant consequence of this digital RMB (eRMB) is its potential to shift the balance of power between China's banks and its big tech firms. Chinese regulators have concluded that the big tech firms are abusing their advantages over traditional banks, which have been losing market share to the digital giants, and need to be reined in. The digital RMB is part of the broader toughening of the regulatory regime around big fintech. Though Beijing aspires to lead the development of alternative, non-US-controlled payments systems, there are many significant political, economic and technological hurdles facing this effort, starting with the issue of RMB convertibility.[33]

### Security and surveillance products

Chinese private-sector companies are seeking to market their security and surveillance products, either directly or as part of broader deals involving projects such as smart cities, as part of the DSR, but they face major challenges. China's domestic laws and regulations such as the 2016 Cybersecurity Law continue to be misaligned with international best practices, particularly in key areas such as data governance and data privacy. Despite claiming that their cloud-services and payments offerings are in alignment with Europe's data-governance regime, the General Data Protection Regulation (GDPR), big technology firms such as Alibaba, Tencent and Huawei will come under increasing scrutiny in developed-country markets around their data-handling practices.

Chinese companies that export facial-recognition technology and potentially privacy-invasive cyber infrastructure are, however, finding government partners in emerging-market countries that are eager to deploy such instruments. This is a demand-driven market. While there is little evidence that Beijing has a master plan to market a 'techno-authoritarian' model led by Chinese technology companies, China does support efforts to align some global technology standards developed by organisations such as the ITU with proprietary technologies used by Chinese suppliers, to potentially give Chinese firms an advantage over competitors, though there are no clear examples of that support proving decisive in standards development or adoption.[34]

### Looking forward: the political DSR

Since 2015, Chinese technology firms including Huawei and ZTE have played a significant role in setting global technology standards for 5G. Other Chinese tech firms are eager to become major players in their sectors, which would grant their own intellectual property a greater role in global standards-setting processes. Though motivated by commercial gain, Chinese companies' pursuit of this path will also help advance Beijing's desire for greater influence over internet infrastructure and the internet-governance regime. A growing alliance of Western governments, however, holds that greater involvement by Chinese companies in multilateral technology standards-setting could be detrimental to their national interests. The issue of Chinese firms' participation in global standards-setting bodies is set to become increasingly fraught.[35]

In the short term, as BRI countries seek a post-pandemic boost to their digital-infrastructure capacity, China's tech conglomerates, including both private-sector and state-linked firms, are likely to receive new state backing to help them respond to this increased demand. Chinese ministries will also push to boost domestic players and extend geopolitical influence in reaction to campaigns such as Clean Network and the targeting of Chinese tech champions such as Huawei. To the extent that US–China relations continue to worsen, Chinese tech industrial policy could scale back or even abandon cooperation with US, European, Japanese and South Korean players, instead pursuing a separate digital ecosystem and standards-setting process that would include a subset of BRI countries (see Chapter One).

If this dynamic took hold, the DSR could evolve into a state-driven project, with ministries in Beijing playing a greater coordinating role. Under this bifurcation scenario, Chinese officials would increasingly view the DSR (and other initiatives such as the BSN and eRMB) as providing the building blocks of a technology and fintech ecosystem that adheres to Beijing's concept of data and digital sovereignty. DSR projects, whether aligned with Beijing's geopolitical ambitions or largely independent of them, would focus on emerging markets, with Chinese tech companies largely abandoning markets in countries unwilling to comply with Beijing's preferences. Already, major tech players including Alibaba, Huawei, Tencent and ZTE, along with leading Chinese AI companies, have basically exited the US market. Finally, in this global-digital-realignment scenario, the fight for spheres of digital influence within key emerging markets would accelerate, and two competing models of cyberspace would emerge as faith in global supply chains, inter-operability and standards-setting ebbed away.

With fewer DSR countries capable of financially support-ing large digital investments, Beijing's coordinating role in facilitating the DSR appears poised to grow.[36] However, any increase in state sponsorship of private-sector engagement in the DSR would probably be seized upon by Washington to reinforce its narrative that Chinese technology companies are 'untrusted' vendors. In the final 18 months of the Trump administration, intensifying US–China strategic competition lent new momentum to a US 'whole of government' effort to curb the use of Chinese technology. Initiatives such as the Clean Network programme drew further lines between competing Western and Chinese technological ecosystems or spheres of influence.[37] The Biden administration has begun to put its own stamp on these strategies but looks likely to continue the effort to restrict the ability of key Chinese tech firms to expand globally. Biden has generally favoured a more multilateral approach to China, however. For example, in April 2022, the White House issued a Declaration for the Future of the Internet signed by the US and 60 partners, in which language clearly aimed at Chinese technology firms included a call to foster societies where 'individuals and businesses can trust the safety and the confidentiality of the digital technologies they use and that their privacy is protected', and where 'technology is used to promote pluralism and freedom of expression'.[38]

Similar language is being used in discussions around ICT supply chains in the EU–US Trade and Technology Council (TTC), the Quad Critical and Emerging Technology Working

Group and the Indo-Pacific Economic Framework. However, as the list of signatories to the Declaration for the Future of the Internet included almost no countries in Africa or the Middle East (the solitary exception was Niger), the signs are that it will be challenging to get buy-in for US policies among countries that have signed up to the BRI or are heavily dependent on Chinese technology companies.[39]

Biden-administration officials have also continued to push programmes in developing countries designed to challenge Beijing's initiatives such as the BRI and the backing of Chinese firms as part of the DSR. In May 2022, for example, US Deputy Secretary of State Wendy Sherman highlighted the work of UK-based mobile-network company Africell, which is competing with Huawei in Angola, saying the US believes that

> when countries choose Huawei, they are potentially giving up their sovereignty. They are turning over their data to another country. They may find themselves bringing in a surveillance capability they didn't even know was there … So we've been very public about our concerns about Huawei, and so we are glad that Africell can provide to the people of Angola a safe, capable tool in their hands to reach out to the world.[40]

Sherman's remarks were the latest in what is likely to be a prolonged US government effort in Africa to use the Build Back Better World (B3W) concept to counter the BRI and DSR.[41] This effort dovetails with G7 and US efforts under B3W to finance alternatives to China-backed infrastructure projects in emerging markets, with special emphasis on regions such as Africa where Chinese firms have carved out dominant positions. Huawei's position in the African market is long-standing, with Angola offering a good example: the company has partnered with Unitel, one of the four carriers in the country (the others are Movicel, state-backed Angola Telecom, and now UK-based Africell), and in 2021 it invested around US$60m in two technology-training centres as part of a project to boost development of the Angolan digital economy.[42]

Africell has raised over US$200m in the past three years, almost half from the US International Development Finance Corporation (DFC), and has acquired equipment from Western suppliers such as Ericsson and Nokia. US government financing via the DFC has been deployed in a limited manner in Africa to counter the types of deals Huawei is able to offer to carriers, although Huawei is not a carrier like Africell, which holds operating licences in other African countries. An explicit condition of DFC financing is that a carrier cannot use any Chinese technology for its networks. The battle between companies backed by initiatives such as the BRI/DSR and B3W is likely to intensify in Africa as the Biden administration prioritises the provision of alternative financing structures for African carriers, including novel arrangements like those involving DFC-backed Africell.

Restrictions on Huawei's access to US technology seem unlikely to be removed, but the Biden administration appears to eschew some Trump-era tactics that they view as heavy-handed, such as pressuring other countries to adopt Huawei bans by threatening to cut off intelligence-sharing with them. This could improve Huawei's prospects in markets such as India and Southeast Asia, and in Brazil and other parts of Latin America. Via the TTC, the administration is seeking to closely coordinate with European allies on investment reviews involving Chinese firms and critical-infrastructure-related deals, and it is working with the TTC and other like-minded allies, including Japan, to coordinate industrial policies around 5G and other technology issues. Wider China-related data-governance issues could be included in a broad tech-alliance push that would potentially put pressure on large Chinese DSR-related platforms. Although increased state sponsorship of Chinese private-sector engagement in the DSR will make Beijing's goal of expanding its influence over global cyberspace and internet governance more challenging, Beijing will almost certainly redouble its efforts to push the DSR and digital-economy issues to the forefront of its foreign policy, creating the conditions for a much more visible struggle with democratic countries over how telecommunications, data, financial, social and other networks are built, operated and governed, the critical issue of how technical standards for these networks are developed and patents are enforced, and who is allowed to participate in those processes.

## CHAPTER FIVE

# The Digital Silk Road and China's grand strategic ambition

Damien Ma

The DSR fits into Xi's broader strategic ambitions for China. Although much has changed since he took power as CCP general secretary in 2012, these grand ambitions have not. Although he declared a 'new era', and his more overtly assertive foreign policy demonstrated a distinct break from the more cautious approach of earlier leaders, he cast his approach as fully within the CCP's long-standing *raison d'être* for rule: the party is the rightful leader that will shepherd China towards 'national rejuvenation' (*mínzú fùxīng*).[1] The DSR and the broader BRI are the latest phase in Beijing's 'Going Out' strategy in pursuit of this goal and China's aim of becoming the leader of the developing world.[2] Private-sector technology companies play a key role in the DSR, but the increasingly overt efforts by party and state authorities to influence their behaviour, including recent major interventions against some of China's most important companies, create a dilemma. Without a dynamic and prosperous private sector, China

**Damien Ma** is Managing Director of the MacroPolo think tank at the Paulson Institute, Chicago.

simply will not be able to obtain the economic power and influence it hopes to project via the DSR.

### Two centenary goals

Modern China, according to the CCP creation myth, was born out of the party-led struggle against prolonged weakness. That myth hinges on the historical binding force of the 'century of humiliation', defined as the period from the beginning of the First Opium War in 1839 to the founding of the People's Republic in 1949, and marked by the domination of imperialist foreign powers.[3] Every Chinese leader since Mao Zedong has reiterated that it would take another hundred years for China to climb back to its former glory. The year 2049 will not just mark a century of CCP rule; it is the target date for achieving full national rejuvenation, including China's re-emergence as a great power globally.

The national-rejuvenation policy has been compared to a '100-year marathon', a stealthy strategy to supplant the US.[4] But it has long been out in the open. Paramount leader Deng Xiaoping believed that, to develop the Chinese economy, a stable external environment was an absolute necessity, and that this should be the overriding theme of China's external policy for an extended period. His 1992 injunction to 'hide your capabilities and bide your time' meant that China must keep its head down to develop its own economy and capabilities while avoiding foreign adventurism and the premature projection of its power.[5] Accordingly, Deng set out to settle China's border disputes, patched up relations with Japan and formalised relations with the US, in part by deciding to postpone any definitive resolution of the Taiwan issue.

Under Deng's hand-picked successors, presidents Jiang Zemin and Hu Jintao, there were two decades of continuity with his 'China first' precept and its focus on developing China's economy. Jiang's keystone achievement was taking China into the World Trade Organization (WTO). But it was Hu who presided over the consequences: a decade of explosive growth that allowed China to leap to the position of the world's second-largest economy. China could no longer 'hide' its formidable economy and growing capabilities, and sought to reassure the world that the intent behind its national-rejuvenation was benign. On the eve of Xi's ascension to power in 2012, it was already evident that China might well even surpass the US in aggregate purchasing power over the next 15 years. This landmark was achieved in 2017, although measured by the dollar exchange rate, China's GDP in 2020 was only 66% of that of the US, despite the country having nearly four times as many people.[6] Eager to put his own stamp on national rejuvenation after becoming general secretary, Xi's first order of business was to offer up the 'Chinese Dream' (*Zhōngguó Mèng*) as a unifying national concept.[7] The Chinese Dream is about prosperity and national g lory, defined as a collective hope for restoring China's lost national greatness. Accompanying Xi's platform was a more assertive global approach to moving towards rejuvenation, a shift from a 'passive' to an 'active' rise. Impatience underpins Xi's version of national rejuvenation, particularly in the rhetoric, the tactics and the scope of the projects his administration has pursued.

Xi has held steadfast to the goals that Deng first outlined but has gone further in formalising the party's commitment to achieving them. At the 19th Party Congress in 2017 they were included in the CCP constitution:

> The Congress holds that national rejuvenation has been the greatest dream of the Chinese people since modern times began, and that it is a solemn commitment our Party has made to our people and to history. The Congress endorses the inclusion of the two centenary goals and the Chinese Dream of national rejuvenation into the Party Constitution.[8]

The first centenary goal was set for the hundred-year anniversary of the founding of the CCP in 1921. By 2021, China aimed to become a 'moderately prosperous society' that had eradicated extreme poverty and escaped the middle-income trap. In short, it would be well on its way to converging with high-income economies.[9] Xi's triumphalism during the party's 2021 centennial celebrations reflected his confidence that these goals had been achieved. The second centenary goal was set for the hundred-year anniversary of the PRC. By 2049, the aim is for China to have achieved national rejuvenation, generally interpreted as matching or even surpassing the US in comprehensive national power (a concept embodying economic, military, political and cultural metrics).[10]

Xi took the opportunity to make a personal modification to the centenary goals by adding a mid-point goal: by 2035 the Chinese economy should be twice the size that it was in 2020, China should be at the level of a 'moderately advanced' country, basic 'socialist modernisation' should have been achieved, and China's role and status in the world should be much greater. This new time frame reflected Xi's likely intention to stay in power or at least exert significant influence until 2035, and the fact that the period 2020–35 would span three five-year plans (FYPs), starting with the 14th FYP, which has been imbued with added significance because it is being touted as the pivotal transition from the completion of the first centenary goal to the pursuit of the second.[11]

## National rejuvenation and the DSR

Xi has thus essentially hung his legacy on the next 15 years. The ambitious projects he has rolled out, particularly the massive US$1trn BRI, under which the DSR falls, will therefore probably need to see significant progress before the national-rejuvenation status update in 2035.[12] Indeed, the BRI and DSR are the central elements of Xi's effort to raise China's global profile and status. From Beijing's perspective, aligning the BRI/DSR with national rejuvenation makes both political and economic sense.

Politically, the BRI was in part a response to the US 'pivot' to Asia, which Beijing warily viewed as a doubling down on Washington's alliances in the Pacific to contain and constrain China. Xi's response was to pivot west and pave a path among states not aligned with the US, a 'geostrategic rebalancing' strategy first proposed in 2012 under the rubric 'Marching Westwards' by Wang Jisi, at the time dean of the School of International Studies at Peking University.[13] More importantly, however, the BRI and DSR seek the actualisation of the long-standing CCP aim for China to become a leader of the developing world and a potential model for economic development. Since the Mao era, Beijing has aligned itself with the 'Third World' and supported various African countries against colonialism.[14] But, under the self-imposed constraints of 'hide and bide', these efforts were less than robust. Now more than ever, Beijing sees an opportunity to assume leadership of the developing world, including the G77, with which it increasingly wants to increase coordination.

Since the early 2000s, Beijing has pursued its Going Out strategy to facilitate Chinese companies' global expansion.[15] China has long sought to build its own multinational companies, like those of the US that have become synonymous with American economic might and influence. That strategy certainly fits under the rubric of national rejuvenation, since it is difficult to achieve global-power status without companies that serve as extensions of a country's economic vitality and dynamism. Such a strategic aim may appear grandiose, but it also has narrower goals. Beijing hoped that Chinese companies, particularly state-owned firms, would become more efficient if exposed to competition in different markets. Moreover, given the excess corporate savings that Chinese companies had accumulated, China could become a deployer of capital rather than merely receiving it from foreign investors.

The BRI and DSR are the most ambitious manifestation of Going Out so far. In an external environment where China's traditional Western export markets have become less receptive to it, the salience of the BRI has grown in recent years. For instance, the US and some of its staunchest allies are unlikely to embrace Chinese exports and investments to anywhere near the extent that they did during the 2000s. Having arrived at that assessment, Beijing has recently called for 'dual circulation', a hedging approach that is meant to rely more on its domestic market ('internal circulation') to drive growth.[16]

But this domestic market, while expanding rapidly, has limits. With 600m people still living on just US$150 per month, according to Li Keqiang, Chinese consumers simply cannot yet replace Americans and Europeans as the principal drivers of the global economy.[17] This compels Chinese companies to seek additional markets for their products and services, which will increasingly flow towards developing countries in Southeast Asia, Africa and Latin America, all of which are within the scope of the BRI and DSR. This trend has been most pronounced in Southeast Asia, where Chinese companies have dramatically expanded their footprint (see Chapter Four).

This push for markets is aligned with the focus on new digital infrastructure in the 14th FYP.[18] Ostensibly a stimulus for the domestic economy, the digital-infrastructure build-out will also have spillover effects in foreign markets. For instance, in a virtual conference call with Latin American counterparts in 2020, China's Foreign Minister Wang Yi specifically touted new infrastructure and the digital economy as areas of cooperation.[19] Whether by necessity or as a matter of grand strategy, Beijing appears to increasingly believe that DSR markets can offset some of, if not all, the volatility in Western markets. Over the next few years, this seems set to become an increasingly urgent strategy in the face of US–China competition over global markets and technology.

The DSR initiative can in some respects be considered 'Going Out 2.0'. The original Going Out strategy in the 2000s focused on investing in extractive industries and commodities to support energy-intensive economic growth and urbanisation. Going Out 2.0, on the other hand, is focused on using Chinese technology to build industries of the future in emerging markets. It is mainly led by private firms, rather than the state-owned enterprises (SOEs) that dominated the previous phase. Unlike SOEs, which tend to build the infrastructure and then leave, Chinese private firms either are already present in DSR markets or want to sell into them over the long term. Private firms have a stronger vested interest in DSR markets than state firms do in BRI markets.

The original Going Out policy had only vaguely defined goals, while Going Out 2.0 appears to be more strategic, with more considered objectives. These state objectives are geo-economic and commercial rather than political: expanding the market share of Chinese firms, deepening the role of Chinese supply chains, and distributing content and cultural products via Chinese platforms. If these objectives are achieved, the DSR will create a market ecosystem in which Chinese technologies and content platforms are dominant. While private firms are the main actors in the DSR, the Chinese state is using diplomatic and political means to facilitate their success. In turn, the success of Chinese companies in DSR markets directly supports the legitimation of China as a global power by normalising its presence in the everyday lives of consumers in developing countries.

Intent is one thing, capability is another. Unlike the original Going Out policy, the success and sustainability of the DSR hinges on China's private sector. Chinese firms are now capable of offering to markets along the DSR the full range of technologies on which the digital economy depends. To be sure, there will continue to be some SOE involvement in the DSR (for example in mobile networks, 5G base stations, smart grids, and charging stations for electric vehicles). But the most important state player in the DSR will be the PBoC, as the first central bank to roll out a digital currency.[20]

The creation of China's eRMB (still undergoing testing) is not about to dethrone the US dollar.[21] The digital currency is simply the renminbi in different form. It could help to internationalise the Chinese currency, especially if Beijing aggressively promotes it for trade and e-commerce transactions along the DSR. But China's ambition for the eRMB appears, at least for now, to be more prosaic – it is mainly a way for the central government to have greater control over financial data and to encourage the replacement of cash by digital transactions. The creation of the eRMB is also a defensive move to prevent the spread of non-official digital currencies and cryptocurrencies, which the PBoC believes would limit its ability to monitor financial transactions and would facilitate capital flight. But the creation of the eRMB does not change the reality that private companies are essential to the DSR. The Chinese state needs to manage its intentions for the DSR in the context of private-sector interests, particularly those of the tech giants that are already operating or are engaged in projects in DSR markets.

One of the biggest sources of growth for Chinese tech companies is that the quality of their products has increasingly converged with that of products from advanced economies, in some cases even surpassing it.[22] This gives China an unprecedented advantage: in virtually all DSR markets it is a technology leader by some distance and may be the only viable choice when it comes to building digital infrastructure or offering certain products. A parallel advantage that China wields is the cost of deployment, especially with regard to digital infrastructure. For instance, Huawei is known for providing high-quality 5G-network equipment that is less costly than its competitors' products, and the company claims that its latest 5G base stations are also cheaper to operate.[23] And when it comes to the deployment of 5G, Chinese state-owned telecoms companies can certainly get subsidies from the government and partner up with local telecoms operators.

At the same time, Chinese private tech firms will be expected to continue investing in digital infrastructure on their own as part of the emphasis on new infrastructure in the 14th FYP.[24] Tencent has already announced that it plans to spend US$40bn on digital infrastructure such as cloud computing. The 14th FYP also contains more details on funding for new infrastructure, which will take the form of public–private partnerships (PPPs). The extent to which the PPP financing model is already part of the DSR is hard to determine. In contrast to the BRI more generally, a substantial proportion of DSR investments are self-financed. This is why DSR activities did not suffer the sharp slowdown witnessed by most BRI programmes during 2019–20.[25] It is also why the lack of a defined financing model should not significantly affect private tech firms' ability to participate in the DSR. For one thing, they are generally well capitalised and are capable of investing on their own rather than relying on state financing. Secondly, since these companies already have a foothold in various markets along the DSR, they will probably continue to invest in those markets as long as the commercial rationale makes sense. Thirdly, China also has a burgeoning venture-capital ecosystem, and big tech companies such as Baidu, Alibaba and Tencent have their own venture arms. This additional source of funding could target investments in promising companies and start-ups in DSR markets.[26] For these reasons, over the medium term, momentum could well shift from the BRI to the DSR.

**The party, the state and the private sector**

The assumption that relations between the government and China's tech giants were in balance was dramatically called into question by the moves in late 2020 against Alibaba-affiliated Ant Financial and Alibaba executive chairman Jack Ma. After Huawei, Alibaba has been the second-most important Chinese tech giant for the DSR. In 2021 its cloud service had revenues of roughly US$9bn, and since 2018 has had the largest share of the Asia-Pacific market (rising from 20% in 2018 to 25% in 2021), beating its competitors Amazon and Microsoft.[27] But Alibaba's overseas success may have enhanced its ability to expand its role in China's domestic financial structure in a way that increased both systemic risk and the risks to traditional Chinese banks. Combined with Ma's independent political views, this led Beijing to impose anti-monopolistic restraints on the company. In the months that followed it became clear that Alibaba was not an isolated case, and that Beijing was intent upon reining in tech giants more generally.

Such moves raise questions about the future of the DSR. To what extent can private firms escape the gravity of state influence? If DSR projects become driven more by political motives than by commercial objectives, would conflicts of interest between a tech company and the state be resolved in favour of the latter? If the state reins in China's tech giants, will they continue to be able to innovate and retain the competitive advantages that have been critical to DSR success?

The power of the private sector has risen dramatically since the 1990s and has become the main engine of economic growth and job creation in China. Its importance was formalised in the early 2000s in Jiang's 'Three Represents' theory, in which private entrepreneurs were considered productive forces of the socialist market economy.[28] It was, in essence, his attempt at making capitalism safe for the CCP.

But even before Xi's moves to increase party control, the CCP was wary of a private sector that could pose an independent challenge, and has always attempted to exert some level of control over the private sector to ensure that its objectives aligned broadly with national goals. Inserting party committees into private firms has been one tactic. According to the CCP's own data, 1.6m private businesses (a small fraction of the total) have party committees.[29] This effort was stepped up in 2015, when businesses were seen by the authorities as the leading source of rapid capital flight.[30] Focusing on state or private ownership, however, obscures a more subtle rule of thumb in China's political economy: firms of a certain size and influence, regardless of ownership, will invariably attract the party's attention.[31] The 'BAT' (Baidu, Alibaba and Tencent) tech firms, for example, all have party committees.

The existence of a party committee does not necessarily mean it has power within a private firm. Party committees do not appear to have voting power on corporate boards, nor do they seem to have any notable influence on company strategy or major decisions. Despite fears about private firms ceding operational autonomy to party mandates, there is evidence that the party committees in private firms have aligned themselves more as facilitators of the businesses. In contrast with the track record of party organisations in SOEs, those in private companies work to support the management and provide services to the employees. This business-oriented party building has made the party more relevant to private businesses and strengthened its organisational presence in the sector.[32]

For the many major private firms that are publicly listed in Hong Kong or New York, there is a substantial operational transparency. Although an increasing number of companies are including paeans to 'Xi Jinping Thought' in their annual reports, it is hard to tell whether that verbiage reflects concrete actions by their party committees.[33] But if party committees were heavily influencing performance and outcomes, it would probably deter investors and affect stock prices.

The existence or absence of such committees does not, therefore, appear to have influenced the recent actions of the Chinese leadership or key regulators towards Chinese tech companies. This does not mean the CCP exerts no influence on private firms, but such influence is not just in one direction. In many cases there appears to be a symbiotic relationship in which each side sees some benefits. One Chinese study of private firms concluded that 'the integration of private entrepreneurs by the ruling party is not one-sided, nor is it a simple exchange based on information, resources, power inequalities and patron–client power relations … it is manifested more as collusive and mutualistic relations based on mutual political trust'.[34]

In general, private firms view a good relationship with the party as necessary to protect them from unexpected policy changes. In this sense, accepting the presence of party committees is a form of 'government relations with Chinese characteristics'. It is fundamental for a company to broadly align with the national strategy of a country in which it operates. But in 2021, as Beijing reiterated its commitment to the DSR and Western pressures on Chinese technology issues increased, the government sought greater influence over Chinese tech companies. In July, the CAC publicly announced a cyber-security investigation of ride-sharing giant Didi Chuxing just days after it completed a US$4bn IPO in New York. As with the failed Ant IPO, this signalled that, at the very least, Beijing will not let tech companies' financing plans stand in the way of regulation.

The growing pressure on China's big tech companies gives them even more reason to publicly align with the BRI and DSR. First and foremost, these initiatives are consistent with the companies' growth strategies. But there is another reason: the companies can also shape policies associated with the DSR to their advantage. Just as US administrations regularly tap the expertise of the private sector on specific policies and initiatives, the CEOs of Chinese private companies are often members of the Chinese People's Political Consultative Conference (CPPCC), the main vehicle by which private businesses provide suggestions and proposals to the national government.

Tencent founder Ma Huateng (also known as Pony Ma), for example, is a CPPCC member and offered seven suggestions to the leadership at the 2020 National People's Congress.[35] Those included accelerating policy decisions on new infrastructure and industrial digitalisation, the renewal of rural China through the digital economy, improving healthcare services, and pushing for breakthroughs in the Shenzhen pilot demonstration area. Ma's proposals ostensibly supported national policies already in the works but also subtly pushed for initiatives where Tencent stood to benefit – such as the idea of pouring more resources into Shenzhen, where the firm is based. Alibaba, for its part, produced a presentation for the second BRF in April 2019, touting how the company has contributed to the DSR and will continue to do so, and detailing the tremendous market opportunities available to the company.[36] The presentation also proclaimed that Alibaba had helped more than 100,000 Chinese firms sell their products and operate in global markets. The core message seems to be that Alibaba enthusiastically supports the DSR through its business strategy.

These examples illustrate how private tech firms are attempting to play in a political environment where they need to balance managing the party with promoting their own corporate interests. There is nonetheless a very broad alignment of interests in supporting an initiative such as the DSR that the party promotes as generating benefits for the Chinese economy. Rather than passively accepting the party's influence, however, these companies adroitly advocate and shape policies within the confines of the broad national strategy, aiming to realise their own growth potential. It is perhaps no surprise, therefore, that the new digital-infrastructure initiative echoes Tencent's and Alibaba's suggestions and plays to their strengths. The party has no interest in killing the geese that laid the golden eggs. But, as the Alibaba case demonstrates, even if the party exhibits a lighter touch on the operations of private tech firms, they are still subject to a wide range of state mandates. There is no such thing as a Chinese company that is too big to be taken on by the state.

Chinese tech companies must also walk a fine line with regard to data disclosure and censorship. They cannot flout Chinese domestic policies, even when operating beyond China's borders and even when compliance could negatively affect their prospects in some DSR markets. This has raised hackles in Western markets, where there is increasing concern that accepting Chinese products is tantamount to accepting CCP norms of censorship, mass surveillance and data insecurity.[37] In addition, there is wariness about anti-competitive behaviour among Chinese firms, even if they are private, because of concerns over perceived CCP influence. Bans on Chinese products have already been imposed in India (covering dozens of apps), the UK (on Huawei's 5G equipment) and the US (against Huawei more generally). These companies have now tempered their expectations when it comes to markets like the UK and US, where their access will be limited. But the potential loss of India is a more important bellwether, as it is a non-aligned country and a major DSR market (although not an official BRI partner) in which Alibaba, Tencent and ByteDance have already invested substantially.[38] ByteDance, the company that created the extremely popular TikTok app, claimed in 2019 that India's ban was costing it up to US$500,000 a day.[39]

Framed as a response to border clashes with China, the Indian government's app ban highlights the vulnerability of Chinese tech firms to asymmetric responses to China's military strength. Chinese technology firms have been leaders in the Indian market, and such a ban could open the door for US rivals (for example Facebook and Amazon) that are increasingly competing with their Chinese counterparts in third countries. However, many Indian firms also have partnerships with Chinese firms and depend on their capital, which will make any such decoupling much harder to achieve in reality.

Beijing's recent assertive 'wolf warrior' diplomacy could undermine its efforts to harness its diplomatic tools and influence to smooth the way for Chinese companies to do business in DSR markets. This could well open rifts between the private sector and the Chinese state. The globalisation of Chinese companies – a clear goal of Going Out 2.0 – may end up stalling as a result of the CCP's mishandling of the external environment. If the linking of commerce and domestic policies makes life more difficult for China's tech companies, they could find themselves facing a more problematic and costly relationship with the government, as is the case for much of China's broader private sector.

## Grand ambition: realised or deferred?

Since taking office, Xi has doggedly pushed the notion of civilisational continuity as the crux of Chinese nationalism. Its modern incarnation, the PRC, is merely the latest evolution of a proud and uninterrupted civilisation that has already brought great contributions to humanity – in the words of twentieth-century American Sinologist Lucian Pye, it is 'a civilization pretending to be a nation-state'.[40] Reviving the Silk Road in the twenty-first century as a distinctly Chinese idea of connectivity is in keeping with this perspective and fits under Xi's rubric of national rejuvenation. With digital highways as a foundation and data flows as currency, the DSR's immediate objectives are commercial in nature: to be a state-supported medium for the globalisation of Chinese companies, technology and standards. Without a dynamic and prosperous private sector, China simply will not be able to obtain the economic power and influence it hopes to project via the DSR.

The DSR initiative is taking on added urgency in the face of the Western volte-face on Chinese companies and products, and the rapid deterioration in comity between Beijing and Washington. Chinese big tech companies can no longer count on significant growth markets in the West, particularly in the US. Their prospects in Northeast Asia are also constrained by direct competition from Japanese and South Korean firms across similar industries and technologies.[41] Doubling down on the DSR seems to be the only viable route in the medium term. The next two billion consumers to be enfranchised into the digital economy are not in the US or in China; third markets from Southeast Asia to Africa and Latin America are the new arenas of tech competition. China's Tencent and Alibaba are, for example, competing with Facebook's ecosystem in Southeast Asia, while American firms are relishing potential opportunities in India after the ban on Chinese apps. Further afield, Chinese companies have first-mover advantage over their American or European counterparts.

As well as a foothold in markets where Western firms have only a minimal presence, China's other advantage is that its companies supply a diverse range of products that can be sold in both developing and developed countries. Hardware companies such as Transsion and Oppo make affordable smartphones for African markets. At the same time, companies such as Huawei, Tencent and Alibaba can compete with their Western counterparts by offering top-of-the-range products and services. Or to put it another way, China's manufacturing ecosystem is so broad that it can simultaneously supply the countries of the G77 and the G20.

The success of the DSR cannot be untethered from the success of Chinese tech firms in those markets; achieving Beijing's strategy and its national-rejuvenation agenda requires the alignment of state interests with those of private firms. But the continuation of this alignment cannot be assumed. A misalignment of state and commercial interests could derail the DSR initiative because private companies might be less inclined to enter markets based solely on political mandates, where the commercial rationale is vague.

The crucial role of private companies in the DSR, combined with their importance in the Chinese domestic economy, suggests that the CCP will need to exercise restraint in influencing their activities. It will want to serve as a facilitator of Chinese companies in DSR countries, rather than obstructing them. As such, Beijing will probably need to reassess its management of the external environment and consider whether continued backlash against its policies will end up constraining those companies' ability to compete in DSR markets. But will it be willing or able to do so? Having shifted from a 'peaceful' to an 'active' rise under Xi, the Chinese leadership may need to consider whether at least some relearning of the lessons of Deng is in order. China may no longer be able to hide, but biding its time may in fact make ambitious projects within the BRI and DSR more palatable and smooth the way for their execution. Xi's speech at the second BRF in 2019 hinted at a more multilateral BRI – but that was before COVID-19 and the advent of wolf-warrior diplomacy.

The DSR timetable probably runs until at least 2035, the midway point between the two centenary goals that Xi has particularly stressed. If it succeeds, Chinese companies will have become a normal presence across emerging markets and will increasingly become the face of China's economic might and soft power. China will be a technology superpower and an exporter of innovation with a roster of world-class tech companies operating in diverse markets and producing high-value products globally. It will, in other words, be well on its way to achieving its grand strategic ambition of national rejuvenation.

CHAPTER SIX

# The Digital Silk Road and normative values

Adrian Shahbaz

The DSR will have significant implications for human rights and democratic governance in states that use Chinese surveillance or public-security technology to suppress their populations. Many of the projects offered through the DSR are modelled on initiatives within China to digitise public databases, collect residents' biometric information, install vast video-surveillance networks, and provide the police with centralised command centres equipped with AI and data analytics. These technologies have helped China become the world's most intrusive digital authoritarian state.

The CCP uses informatisation, surveillance and algorithmic decision-making in service of its broader 'social management' policies that seek to prevent and control even the most innocuous perceived threats to 'social harmony', public order and regime stability.[1] Would-be protesters face the world's largest network of surveillance cameras, with AI systems that recognise individuals' identities and in some cases their ethnicities

**Adrian Shahbaz** is Vice President for Research and Analysis at Freedom House.

and emotional states.[2] Automated systems censor keywords on social media, track public sentiment online and flag individuals for suspicious behaviour. Biometric-data collection and real-name registration renders anonymity virtually impossible.[3] In the hands of dictators and would-be authoritarians, these tools allow for mass co-option and the targeted repression of opposition movements.

The DSR's effect on civil liberties and norms in participating countries will be determined by the type of technology China is exporting, the ability or desire of recipient states to sustain mechanisms for independent and robust oversight of new surveillance and algorithmic technologies, and the administrative capacity of authoritarian (or would-be authoritarian) states. DSR projects consisting solely of 5G telecommunications infrastructure and fibre-optic cables may have limited direct implications for a recipient state's normative values. Just as China embraced Western computing hardware without adopting liberal democracy, so may purchasers of certain Chinese technologies experience few challenges to their governance models. The norms and societal assumptions embedded in public-security and -surveillance systems (such as Huawei's 'Safe City' projects), however, prime them to serve as tools for authoritarian governance and social control.

While the import of surveillance technologies by liberal democracies carries the possibility that states or local authorities might use them to erode civil liberties, such erosions are more likely to be severe in existing autocracies or states lacking robust safeguards. Chinese digital authoritarianism is a product both of advanced technologies and a sophisticated state apparatus of repression that has developed over many decades. States may be able to import the former fairly swiftly but may not be able to replicate the latter so easily. When attempting to evaluate the effect of the DSR on normative values worldwide, moreover, it is essential to recall that Western firms have for many years also exported technologies that can be and have been used to surveil and suppress local populations. While the DSR may magnify and accelerate digital authoritarianism, it is not the only factor contributing to this global trend.

The DSR may also have indirect effects on internet freedom worldwide. Since the advent of the internet in the 1990s, the CCP has considered the enabling of transnational and free information exchange a serious threat to party rule and has promoted the principle of cyber sovereignty as a key element of its security policy. Efforts to export Chinese technology are motivated by a combination of geopolitical and commercial factors, contribute to broader Chinese influence campaigns, and should be understood within the wider context of growing Chinese investments in foreign media, diplomatic manoeu-vrings, and overseas training on technology, digital media and political-party management. While the adoption of Chinese technology does not in itself make a closed, sovereign inter-net more likely within a given country, the DSR may still have meaningful implications for the future of a global open internet, if only through its role in China's broader diplomatic activities.

## The CCP and cyber sovereignty

The internet's pioneers promoted a set of normative values governing the early deployment of digital technologies, best articulated by John Perry Barlow's 1996 'Declaration of the Independence of Cyberspace'.[4] Techno-libertarianism was co-opted by Silicon Valley and Washington, which supported the early internet's development and delegated key oversight functions to multi-stakeholder agencies. The administration of US president Bill Clinton outlined five 'Principles for Global Electronic Commerce' in 1997, one of which stated that 'govern-ments must adopt a non-regulatory, market-oriented approach to electronic commerce'.[5] These norms generally aligned with US democratic values of decentralisation, institutional checks and balances, the independence of civil society and free enterprise.

Political leaders have long viewed digital technology with ambivalence. Governments have sought the economic and educational benefits of expanded internet access but, like all historical technological advancements, many have feared its destabilising impact on society, cultural norms and regime stability. In 1985, US secretary of state George Shultz postulated that totalitarianism was incompatible with advances in information and communications technology.[6] President Clinton made a similar prediction in 2000 during a speech calling for the US to ease China's entry into the WTO, in which he likened the CCP's attempt to control the internet to 'nailing Jell-O to the wall'.[7]

These assertions proved to be wishful thinking. The CCP has embraced technological innovation while rejecting the normative values promoted by the US and other Western nations. Chinese people today enjoy widespread (if filtered) internet access, a bustling digital economy and greater geopolitical clout. But their political system is no more open than it was upon the country's accession to the global internet and free-trade system – in fact, it is less so. Digitalisation has increased Beijing's capacity for social governance and public surveillance.

The notion of 'cyber sovereignty' has provided rhetorical cover for Chinese authorities to co-opt technology for political, social and religious repression. One of the earliest uses of the term was in a 2010 White Paper from the State Council's Information Office, calling for China's internet sovereignty to be protected and respected.[8] Already concerned by the 'colour revolutions' of the 2000s, officials in Beijing had viewed with alarm recent events in Iran, when local and diaspora Iranians

mobilised on US social-media platforms to share information about protests and police violence in the aftermath of the
disputed 2009 presidential election.[9] The state-run *People's
Daily* published an editorial on the Iranian demonstrations
arguing that they were the result of 'online warfare launched
by America, via YouTube video and Twitter microblogging,
spread rumours, created splits, and sowed discord between
the followers of conservative and reformist factions [*sic*]'.[10]
Chinese suspicions further hardened after the internet-fuelled
'Arab Spring' protests of 2010–12 and Edward Snowden's
revelations in 2013 about the US National Security Agency's
global surveillance activities.

On the international stage, Chinese diplomats have called for
the application of national sovereignty to the internet. Beijing
has used the annual World Internet Conference in Wuzhen to
promote not only China's narrative of win–win cyber cooperation and the successes of its domestic technology industry, but
also its concept of cyber sovereignty. Xi opened the 2016 WIC,
before an audience consisting of the heads of major US and
Chinese technology firms, with an explicit call for greater cyber
sovereignty.[11] Chinese efforts have included media initiatives, such as a 2014 op-ed by Lu Wei, director of the CAC, in
the *Huffington Post*, calling for respect for 'each other's cyber
sovereignty, internet governance, major concerns and cultural
differences'.[12] The importance of internet or cyber sovereignty
was underlined in a 2015 article published by a member of the
PLA's Strategic Advisory Committee: 'if a country loses its
cyber sovereignty … It will result in the loss of control over the
guidance of online public opinion, sparking serious unrest and
upheaval in society, directly challenging state power.'[13]

Other authoritarian regimes also consider the internet an
instrument for Western intervention but, unlike China, only
began to institute strict information controls after large-scale

domestic protests made them fear for the survival of their regimes. Iran was one of the first countries to experience mass protests in the social-media age, and is the furthest along in developing its own national information network modelled on China's. After the Islamic Republic's brutal suppression of the Green Movement in 2009, most Western ICT firms left the country – but Chinese firms took their place, and have helped Tehran to suppress the populace. Similarly, after years of relative internet freedom in Russia, mass protests against President Vladimir Putin from 2011 produced a complete re-evaluation of cyber norms, including closer contacts between Russian officials and the architects of China's Great Firewall.[14] In May 2019, Putin signed legislative amendments to expand the country's cyber sovereignty. Described as the 'sovereign internet law', these provisions instructed the telecommunications regulator to develop a mechanism to cut off Russia from the global internet during extraordinary situations.[15]

The global trend towards embracing cyber sovereignty is not driven solely or even mainly by China and the DSR. The concept has gained broader prominence as governments across the democratic spectrum seek good- and bad-faith solutions for many of the social harms wrought by social media. A growing number of governments have adopted policies in accordance with the notion of cyber sovereignty.[16] More democratic (though still illiberal) leaders in Brazil, India and Turkey have considered legislation to mandate that all companies store data on local servers, driven by security or economic factors.[17] And even Washington has taken measures to ban Chinese apps from doing business in the US, threatening a digital decoupling with China.[18]

Yet Chinese technology exports, often driven by local demand for cheap and effective software and hardware, do indeed boost China's influence in foreign states, and contribute to Beijing's broader efforts to recruit such states as supporters in its diplomatic endeavours. Chinese officials lead three of the 15 major UN agencies (down from four in 2020); no other country has more than one.[19] Chinese diplomats build alliances with like-minded states to promote norms of sovereignty and non-interference, as well as to curb criticism of their own country's poor human-rights record.[20] For example, in June 2021, a group of 65 countries organised to resist a Canadian resolution citing human-rights abuses in Xinjiang.[21] Reflecting on China's rise, an Indian government official said that 'if you control important levers of these institutions, you influence norms ... you inject your way of thinking'.[22] By cementing closer connections with policymakers throughout the developing world, the DSR will continue to enhance China's standing in international forums and provide diplomatic support against criticism of its policies towards Hong Kong, Xinjiang and Taiwan – as well as its attempts to promote cyber sovereignty in international forums.[23]

## Digitalising authoritarianism

Recent digital innovations carry strong connotations of state control, ubiquitous surveillance and novel forms of techno-governance. Although the DSR is likely to address genuine governance challenges related to urban development, public safety and sustainability, policymakers should remain clear-eyed when considering the likely implications of, for example, AI-enabled surveillance for democracy and human rights in those recipient states vulnerable to autocratic governance. Developments within China itself illustrate how these tools can be applied to administer a new form of digital authoritarianism.

For decades, Chinese officials have pursued informatisation or digitalisation policies as part of the party's long-standing

efforts to apply a 'systems engineering' approach to governing society.[24] The launch of the internet in China coincided
with a series of 'Golden Projects', beginning in 1993, to build
digital, inter-operable and connected databases to strengthen
governance and improve information-sharing among state
agencies.[25] From 2003, the 'Golden Shield Project', also known
as the National Public Security Work Informatisation Project,
developed security agencies' operational capacity through a
vast system of population databases, ID tracking and internet
surveillance, offering immediate access to the records of every
Chinese citizen.[26] In addition to tracking individuals' movements and transactions, the platform is used by local officials
to identify and report signs of social instability to law enforcement, and there is a separate database of residents who might
threaten social and regime stability.[27] Another project, 'Golden
Gate', involves an electronic data interchange to link customs
posts for international trade.

The Chinese party-state quickly built an advanced, multi-
level censorship regime through investments in filtering
technologies, strict media controls and harsh rules for operators
and users. Party cadres conduct overt and covert programmes
to shape public opinion online, while officials block access to
information sources and digital platforms that fail to comply
with requests to remove an ever-growing list of banned terms,
or to hand over their users' data to law enforcement. Activists,
journalists and ordinary citizens face arbitrary detention and
severe prison terms for voicing their opinions online. Research
from the Central Party School speaks of mining the 'opinions,
behaviours, emotions, footprints, and other characteristics'
of individuals to 'unearth hidden negative opinions, predict
their development, intervene in advance, and effectively
resolve public opinion problems to reduce the risk of societal
safety incidents'.[28] In 2022, Freedom House ranked China as

the world's worst abuser of internet freedom for the eighth consecutive year.[29] Chinese social media and messaging apps automatically censor certain keywords deemed offensive to state sensibilities for users located both within and outside the country.

China has built the world's largest and most intrusive surveillance apparatus. Officials have embraced surveillance technologies as part of the government's 'prevent and control' strategy and embarked on a number of public-security projects to pre-empt large-scale displays of dissatisfaction through a mix of co-option and targeted repression.[30] Video surveillance has been a key component of China's state-led social-management policies, beginning in 2005 with the 'Skynet' project to deploy cameras throughout urban centres. In 2015, nine government agencies launched the 'Sharp Eyes' project to expand China's national public-security surveillance network, particularly in rural regions, in order to compensate for limited police resources.[31] The plan called for universal coverage by high-definition cameras of 'key public areas', 'public areas of residential communities' and 'important parts of key industries'. The NDRC also requires local authorities to use 'modern technologies such as data mining, face recognition, license plate recognition, [and] intelligent warning systems'. To encourage local officials to implement Sharp Eyes, in 2017 the CCP enacted an anti-terrorism law that included provisions for fining officials who failed to establish 'public safety video and image information systems'.[32] In 2020, 18 of the world's 20 cities with the most surveillance cameras per capita were in China.[33]

Grid management is another component of the state's embrace of technology for social governance. Under this system, urban areas are divided into units overseen by a local administrator. The grid manager monitors a range of issues in their neighbourhood, takes measures to anticipate or deal with problems, and records residents' unusual or problematic activities in a unified and digitalised public-security platform.[34] In February 2020, the CCP-run *Global Times* described the grid system as using 'high-tech digital platforms, social volunteers and local police … [to] actively find and handle social issues for … residents'.[35] That same year, grid management was hailed by the *South China Morning Post* as a reason for China's alleged low COVID-19 case count in Wuhan. Grid workers supposedly enforced lockdown orders, collected health information through temperature checks, and delivered food and medicine to residents.[36] Reportedly, a member of each household was required to report their family members' body temperatures to the grid's WeChat group every day, with the data then fed into the police's 'big data platform'.[37]

The latest technological tool in the state's apparatus for social management is the 'smart city'. Chinese firms estimated the domestic market for smart-city products at US$1.1trn in 2018. The State Council's Ministry of Housing and Urban–Rural Development has encouraged various bureaucracies and local authorities to develop smart-city pilot projects across the country, approving almost 300 (out of a total of around 800) by early 2019.[38] China's trend towards the centralisation of smart-city projects has led to greater inter-operability between local smart-city systems and national government databases, although much work remains to unify the systems and databases of various bureaucracies.[39]

By blanketing China's urban and online spaces with internet-enabled cameras, sensors and monitoring systems, the authorities hope not only to distribute law-enforcement resources more efficiently but also to expand their strategy of prevent and control. The growth of smart cities has generated a large market for Internet of Things technology, big data, cloud services and AI. The government has supported the growth of emerging AI technology companies as part of attaining Beijing's target of becoming a global leader in the field by 2030.[40] The image-recognition companies SenseTime, Yitu, Megvii and Cloudwalk are all valued at several billions of dollars.[41]

Under the guise of counter-extremism, Beijing has brutally repressed the Uighurs and other minority groups in the province of Xinjiang. US journalists have referred to Xinjiang as an 'incubator' for new AI surveillance tactics, noting how security officials from other provinces often go there to learn about the latest policing tactics ahead of broader implementation.[42] Grid policing is combined with CCTV cameras, big data and permanent 'convenience police stations' to monitor the local population.[43] Investigations by the *New York Times* and the non-governmental organisation Human Rights Watch revealed that the China Electronics Technology Group Corporation (CETC) has built a mobile app allowing police officers at checkpoints and on patrol in Xinjiang to rapidly access a database of over 60m people and record information. Residents – mainly Uighurs and others from Muslim backgrounds – have to swipe biometric identity cards in order to pass through checkpoints in the provincial capital of Urumqi. A security researcher observed that the city has a huge number of checkpoints – approximately 10,000. Some individuals are also obliged to install a spyware app, 'Clean Net Guard', that monitors their online activities.[44]

The US Department of Commerce has accused dozens of Chinese companies, public-security bureaus and police officials of human-rights violations in Xinjiang and prohibited US exports to them through its Entity List, which includes Dahua, Hikvision, iFlytek, Megvii, Meiya Pico, SenseTime, Yitu and Yixin.[45] Hikvision, the world's largest maker of video-surveillance cameras (and partly owned by the CETC), explicitly noted the ability of its facial-recognition projects to profile Uighurs and other ethnic minorities in marketing materials. An analysis of Yitu source code and Cloudwalk marketing materials found similar capabilities.[46] By 2019, police units in at least 16 regions and provinces had submitted procurement calls for such ethnic-minority-recognition technologies.[47]

### Exporting tools for digital repression

In 2018, Freedom House noted Chinese AI surveillance products in 18 of the 65 countries covered by its annual 'Freedom on the Net' report.[48] A more expansive global study in 2019 by the Carnegie Endowment for International Peace documented these same tools in a total of 63 countries, while in early 2020, Brookings reported 'Chinese surveillance and public security technology platforms … in at least 80 countries'.[49]

Smart cities have become a crucial component of the DSR. The CAC has referred to them as a 'strategic opportunity' for the overseas expansion of Chinese businesses through the BRI, while Xi has referenced them in speeches on the BRI.[50] A 2020 search of the websites of 65 Chinese companies involved in smart-city technology found 34 to be exporting such technology through their involvement in development projects in 106 countries.[51] Smart-city projects often have a substantial public-security component, which has significant implications for normative values in participating countries. Huawei is a leading provider of such projects under its Safe City brand of smart public-security systems. In autumn 2019 there were Huawei Safe City initiatives in at least 52 countries (of which 37 were classified as 'partly free' or 'not free' by Freedom House), while Huawei's own 2018 annual report noted projects in 'over 700 cities across more than 100 countries and regions'.[52]

China is a leader in the biometric-identification systems that underpin smart cities and public-security projects. The Chinese state-run company China National Electronics Import and Export Corporation (CEIEC) markets its biometric-ID service not only as a system for biometric-data collection, secure storage, card manufacturing and data-processing terminals, but also as a 'big data analysis platform' for 'government decision-making' on issues such as 'population behaviour'.[53] The company has offices in Algeria, Angola, Argentina, Bolivia, Cuba, Dubai, Ecuador, Egypt, Kazakhstan, Kenya, Laos, Mexico, Myanmar, Pakistan, Peru, Russia, Saudi Arabia, Sri Lanka, Tanzania and Venezuela. A list of 'strategic partners and customers' includes emergency services in Angola, Bolivia, Ecuador and Venezuela.

China does not, to be sure, have a monopoly on selling surveillance technology to authoritarian regimes.[54] For example, before Uganda and Zambia used Huawei engineers to help them spy on dissidents, they were purchasing tools from private firms such as Israel's NSO Group, Italy's Hacking Team or the Anglo-German Gamma Group. Nor are Chinese companies the only players in the public-security-platform industry. AI surveillance technology from US companies including IBM, Palantir and Cisco has been documented in 32 countries.[55] Indeed, US and Canadian companies were among the early primary suppliers for the Golden Shield Project.[56] US firms have long had a presence in China's own domestic smart-city industry. Similarly, US chipmakers, storage manufacturers and other companies had long been in the supply chains of companies such as Huawei, Hikvision and others implicated in human-rights abuses in Xinjiang, before the US bans with regard to Huawei were imposed in 2019 and 2020.[57]

Western firms have, however, emphasised the comparative openness, security and flexibility of their systems, granted municipalities and the public open access to city data, and insisted on open-source rather than proprietary software.[58] Closed systems present economic and cyber-security risks because they lock in one company as the sole perpetual service provider and do not easily allow for independent security audits of systems. US companies also face some degree of domestic oversight from a free press and advocacy groups, who have been successful in shaming large US and European firms for their complicity in human-rights abuses.[59] In China, companies do not face the same type of oversight from an independent civil society.

The experience of importing Chinese technology has varied, depending largely on the domestic political context and geopolitical interests of individual countries. Autocratic governments view China's cyber-sovereignty model as essential for fostering social and economic development while maintaining state control over civil society. Where freedom of assembly and association already receive little protection – in Iran, Kazakhstan and Uganda, for example – the DSR appears to have reinforced authoritarian governance. In contrast, greater political pluralism and a more open civic space – in Ecuador and Zambia, for example – have provided for greater public oversight of new surveillance technologies, as well as for resistance by civil society against the use of Chinese technology to help reverse democratic norms. Similar dynamics are present in Malaysia and Serbia, where elected leaders have accepted both Chinese and Western technological investment in an attempt to balance their geopolitical interests. Finally, in countries with strong checks and balances and democratic oversight, such as in Western Europe, the effects of the DSR have been more neutral. That said, some surveillance technologies pose an inherent risk to civil liberties, from which even established liberal democracies are not wholly immune.

China served as an exemplar for Iranian digital repression long before the advent of the DSR. Following the Chinese model, a May 2001 decree centralised Iran's internet connections through state-controlled international gateways.[60] Over time, the authorities increased their control over the internet by banning high-speed connections for the masses, blocking material that allegedly threatened national security or public morals, and suppressing digital activism and other online political activity by students and marginalised groups.

After Western firms withdrew from the Iranian market in response to the government's violent crackdown on peaceful protesters in 2009, the state-owned Telecommunication Company of Iran purchased electronic surveillance systems from Huawei and ZTE, including a deal that was later found to be in violation of US export controls.[61] Huawei engineers reportedly helped the Iranian authorities to block text messages and the Skype communications app during the 2009 demonstrations.[62] In 2021, the two countries signed a 25-year cooperation agreement that set out plans for 5G development and digitalisation.[63]

Tehran has also copied China's legal and technical tactics for controlling the web. The Iranian government has used a draconian Computer Crimes Law, passed in 2009, to imprison countless journalists, activists, executives and ordinary citizens.[64] Most foreign social-media platforms are blocked, while domestic versions are heavily censored for any content that is deemed to threaten national security or public morals.[65] Officials have enlisted the help of Chinese companies to build a 'national information network' modelled on the Great Firewall.[66] All domestic services must be transferred to servers based within the country to allow for greater cooperation with Iran's unaccountable security agencies.

When mass protests erupted in Iran in November 2019 over an increase in fuel prices, officials ordered service providers to block social media and online news outlets for six days while keeping hospitals, banks and other services online.[67] During the nationwide blackout, the authorities managed to reduce the circulation of images and videos of the brutal police crackdown on protesters, thus maintaining control over the media narrative. The national information network was proven to be effective for repression without the social and economic costs of shutting down the internet, and was made possible with the help of Chinese companies.

Kazakhstan has also followed China's path towards digital authoritarianism. The two countries signed a comprehensive strategic partnership agreement in 2015, the same year that Kazakhstan unveiled a landmark plan to digitalise the economy, develop internet infrastructure and boost e-government.[68] Since then, officials have increasingly partnered with Chinese firms such as Hikvision and Dahua.[69] After a visit to Hikvision's corporate headquarters in Hangzhou in 2019, President Kassym-Jomart Tokayev expressed his enthusiasm for their products: 'You click on the screen, data on a person comes out … when he graduated from university, where he goes in his free time, what loans he has outstanding, and so on … We need to go in this direction.'[70] More recently, Dahua has partnered with local companies to supply thousands of surveillance cameras for the country's capital, Astana.[71]

Like Iran, Kazakhstan's government has tested its own version of China's Great Firewall, dubbed the National Security Certificate.[72] This root certificate would undermine encrypted data connections for all users and entities based in the country, allowing mass surveillance by security agencies. Parliamentarians have also called for platforms to store data about local users on servers located in the country, following China's model of data localisation.[73] The government has resorted to more draconian measures to control information flows during national crises – in January 2022, for example, after cuts to fuel subsidies sparked protests and riots in several cities, the internet was shut down for five days.[74]

Civil-rights organisations in Kazakhstan have expressed concern not only over the state's new schemes for online censorship and surveillance but also about Beijing's influence in the country.[75] The authorities, however, have also used digital repression in response to public criticism of China – in April 2021, for example, officials shut down internet connections in a district of Almaty, the country's largest city, where there had been a demonstration against the transfer of 120,000 hectares of land to Chinese entities for the construction of factories.[76]

In Uganda, the authorities have sought Chinese surveillance technologies at least partly to confront a mounting opposition movement against President Yoweri Museveni and his National Resistance Movement (NRM), in power since 1986. In 2017 Museveni reportedly ordered the chief of the national police to approach the Chinese government for assistance in expanding digital surveillance; soon afterwards, Uganda concluded a cyber-security agreement with CEIEC that included the technical capability to monitor social media.[77] In 2018, officials procured a Huawei Safe City project for a reported US$126m, established a police unit devoted to cyber operations and enlisted Huawei technicians for further training on surveillance. In 2019, Huawei was reportedly involved in building 11 monitoring centres for law enforcement, while the government was building a new US$30m command centre connecting over 5,000 Huawei-made surveillance cameras enabled with facial-recognition technology. Security officials enlisted the help of Huawei engineers to gain access to the electronic communications of Bobi Wine, who later lost the January 2021 presidential election to Museveni in a contested outcome. Wine had been organising a political rally with members of the opposition through encrypted communication apps. Using intelligence collected from a WhatsApp group, police were able to go to the location of the rally to arrest participants and organisers.[78]

The January election was marred by mass detentions, disinformation and draconian censorship. Wine's political party claimed 3,000 of its supporters had been held or forcibly disappeared.[79] Meta (formerly Facebook) reported that fake and duplicate accounts linked to the Ministry of Information had been engaged in 'coordinated inauthentic behavior' around the election.[80] Days before the vote, the government restricted access to Facebook, Instagram, Telegram, Twitter, WhatsApp and other platforms, before shutting down the internet altogether. After the election, the EU and US threatened to impose sanctions over human-rights abuses and political interference, while China's top diplomat, Yang Jeichi, congratulated Museveni on his victory.[81]

In contrast to such use of digital technology to entrench existing authoritarianism, those in power in some fragile democracies and partly free states have used it to impose or re-impose restrictions and controls, with mixed success. Zambia, for example, began to see increased Chinese tech investment after 2012, when Huawei and ZTE sponsored a visit to China by a delegation of Zambian officials.[82] In 2017 Huawei completed the first phase of the government's 'Smart Zambia' project, including a US$75m data centre funded by concessional loans from Chinese state-owned banks, and embarked on phase II, which includes an e-government platform, a national fibre-optic network and an e-customs platform similar to China's Golden Gate project.[83] In 2019 the government reportedly received help from Huawei engineers to spy on the phones and social-media accounts of government critics, and Zambian officials confirmed that they had worked with Chinese experts at Huawei to locate and detain a team of pro-opposition bloggers.[84] Ahead of the August 2021 presidential election, Beijing's ambassador to Lusaka signalled China's preference for the re-election of Edgar Lungu.[85] On election day Zambia's telecoms regulator cut access to Facebook,

Messenger, Twitter and WhatsApp, before a high-court decision forced a reversal two days later.[86] Despite these moves, long-time opposition leader Hakainde Hichilema beat Lungu with almost 60% of the vote. Though there is considerable disquiet in Zambia over increasing Chinese involvement in the country, the election of Hichilema, who had been charged with treason in 2017 and questioned by police in 2018 after speaking about Chinese activities in the local timber industry, appears to offer an example of a fragile democracy pushing back against Chinese economic and political influence.[87]

Similar dynamics are apparent in Ecuador, where Rafael Correa (president from 2007 to 2017) pursued greater state intervention in the economy and strengthened relations with countries such as Belarus, China, Iran and Russia, including a comprehensive strategic partnership with China, while distancing the country from the US.[88] The populist president's tenure was marked by attacks against the media and civil society, as well as any institutional checks on his power.[89] Ecuadorian officials observed China's surveillance system during the 2008 Beijing Olympics and subsequently commissioned CEIEC and Huawei to develop the US$200m ECU 911 public-security and emergency-services platform, which proved relatively ineffective against crime but was used by security and intelligence agencies to target Correa's political opponents.[90]

Ecuador's judicial and electoral systems, however, prevented further democratic backsliding. Correa was ineligible to stand for re-election in 2017, having served two terms, despite a movement to amend the constitution to allow him a third. He was succeeded by his former vice-president Lenín Moreno. In 2020 Correa was sentenced in absentia to eight years in prison for corruption while president and banned from political office for 25 years.[91] His successors have sought to rebalance the country's relations with the US and China. In January 2021, the Moreno administration signed a US$3.5bn deal with the US International Development Finance Corporation to refinance its external debt in exchange for banning Chinese companies from Ecuador's telecommunications networks.[92] Moreno's successor Guillermo Lasso, who defeated a Correa protégé in the 2021 presidential election, signalled that the country would seek even closer relations with the US.[93] In 2022, Freedom House upgraded Ecuador from 'Partly Free' to 'Free', stating that the previous year's elections 'did not suffer from the types of abuses' seen during previous polls.[94]

In Malaysia, where leaders have long cultivated close ties with the CCP in view of its economic and military power, then-prime minister Najib Razak participated in the inauguration in 2016 of a Huawei centre of excellence, and the following year his deputy announced plans for the company to build an intelligent surveillance system in 200 'hotspots' throughout the country.[95] Cooperation later extended to the municipal level, with Chinese firm Yitu providing Kuala Lumpur police with AI-powered facial-recognition glasses in 2018.[96] Ahead of the 2018 general election, however, Razak faced accusations of selling out the country to China.[97] He reportedly procured surveillance technology from an Israeli cyber-security start-up, Senpai, rather than a Chinese firm, to spy on his domestic opponents.[98] Razak lost the election and was later sentenced to 12 years in prison on charges of abuse of power, money laundering and breach of trust for his role in a massive corruption scandal related to the country's sovereign wealth fund.[99] China and Malaysia continue to cooperate on technology investments, but in 2021 Kuala Lumpur awarded a US$2.6bn 5G-infrastructure contract to Ericsson rather than Huawei.[100]

Serbia, despite being a candidate for EU accession, has pursued close economic, military and healthcare cooperation with China, including through a comprehensive strategic partnership.[101] President Aleksandar Vucic has gone to great lengths to flatter Chinese officials, for example kissing the Chinese flag during the arrival in Serbia of Chinese medical supplies and COVID-19 experts in March 2020 (a video of this went viral), and marking the 100th anniversary of the CCP in July 2021 with a video message praising the accomplishments of 'Socialism with Chinese characteristics'.[102] Since 2019, Serbian and Chinese police have conducted joint patrols in Serbian cities, ostensibly to monitor Chinese tourists but in practice often in areas that are home to significant Chinese investment projects.[103] As part of a Safe City project in Belgrade, Huawei has installed over 1,000 cameras equipped with facial-recognition technology. The company also has built a regional innovation centre and data centre in the capital.[104]

Vucic has used Serbia's close relations with Beijing as a counterweight to the more conditional relationship with Brussels and Washington. At the same time, however, Belgrade has shown a willingness to cooperate with the US, often to the dismay of Chinese diplomats. In September 2020, Vucic signed an economic-normalisation agreement with Kosovo that included US financing for several high-level projects in both countries in exchange for a commitment to refrain from using 'untrusted vendors' in 5G equipment.[105] The following week, Vucic reassured the Chinese ambassador that Serbia would continue to cooperate with China in various fields, including telecommunications.[106] Some observers believe the Serbian president may decide to invite bids from European firms for 5G while continuing to pursue deals with Huawei over smart cities, surveillance cameras and the maintenance of existing telecommunications networks.[107]

In established liberal democracies, on the other hand, Chinese technological investments have sparked public debate and pushback, with a strong civil society and independent agencies serving as bulwarks against creeping digital repression. In 2017, for example, Huawei gave the French city of Valenciennes a €2m surveillance centre and hundreds of cameras in exchange for it using the Safe City system as a showcase for potential European buyers.[108] Opposition politicians, media outlets and civil-society organisations immediately raised objections. In 2019, local human-rights organisations created a new coalition, Technopolice, to 'resist the proliferation of automated video-surveillance and predictive policing technologies'.[109] The French National Commission for Information Technology and Liberties (CNIL) warned city officials in 2020 that parts of the system, which included smart image analysis and the automated reading of vehicle-registration plates, violated French data-protection law.[110] In August 2021 the CNIL report was made public and the mayor announced that the city would cease using Huawei cameras, although he claimed it was due not to the controversy but to the fact that the Chinese company was leaving the European market.[111]

In 2021, Italy became the first EU member state to introduce a moratorium on the use of video systems equipped with facial-recognition technology by private entities, while Germany's new coalition government committed to banning facial-recognition systems in public areas.[112] The EU is debating a draft Artificial Intelligence Act that would place some limits on 'high risk' applications of AI, including for surveillance. The European Parliament went even further, calling for a ban on indiscriminate AI surveillance in public spaces, the use of facial-recognition databases by law enforcement, and so-called predictive-policing systems.[113]

## Stalling the rise of digital authoritarianism

There is a global trend towards greater state surveillance and use of digital technologies to monitor citizens. The pervasive recording of individuals' speech and behaviour through the internet has made it easier for those in power to find evidence on which to base the prosecution of political opponents. In 2021, the authorities in a record number of countries arrested individuals for non-violent online political speech.[114] Even in places with relatively strong democratic institutions, these tools can be abused to target legitimate speech.[115] Systems designed to tackle violent crime and terrorism can be repurposed to suppress non-violent protests and build databases of known dissidents. Emerging technologies also present novel risks to the administration of good governance, given the prospect of over-reliance on technological solutions to address deep-seated social issues. With digital surveillance now extending beyond written communication into mapping people's movements, gestures and personal networks, governments will have in their hands an unprecedented amount of data for drawing connections that flag citizens for suspicion. The coronavirus pandemic has also accelerated the uptake of digital technologies, with governments around the world having justified the uptake of intrusive biometric surveillance tools in the name of public health.[116]

China's large-scale export of digital technologies, most recently branded as the DSR, contributes to the alarming aspects of this trend both directly and indirectly. Many Western firms also sell surveillance technology to authoritarian regimes, making it hard to quantify the DSR's normative effects precisely. But the export of the same technologies that China uses to suppress its own populace – without any of the safeguards or transparency measures that some Western firms claim for their own products – is likely to erode civil liberties even further in authoritarian states, and to prove threatening in states where institutions or regulations remain fragile. Even in liberal democracies, such technology could prove a challenge to existing norms. And the DSR magnifies China's growing influence, prestige and economic leverage even if Chinese tech sales to some countries do not include surveillance technology. The support from developing states for China in international forums thereby contributes to a broader Chinese campaign in favour of cyber sovereignty: an internet under the control of repressive governments, rather than the open internet imbued with Western liberal values.

The DSR's effect on norms and civil liberties in participating countries will ultimately depend on each country's institutional framework and the types of technology imported. There is an obvious distinction between, on the one hand, governments that develop smart cities (especially technologies focused on public security) to protect themselves from their own populations, and on the other, those that incorporate emerging technologies in collaboration with local communities in a process characterised by transparency, oversight and accountability.

Few states, however, will match the scale of China's digital autocracy anytime soon, regardless of their intentions. Most states currently lack the resources and political capital to rapidly replicate the informatisation and social-governance measures that Chinese leaders have instituted over the decades. As the world's foremost surveillance state, China will remain in a league of its own for some time to come.

## CHAPTER SEVEN

# Balancing prosperity and security along the Digital Silk Road

**Scott Malcomson**

Huawei founder Ren Zhengfei used to tell the story of meeting Jiang Zemin in 1994 and urging on the president the view that switching-equipment technology, which was then Huawei's main product, was not just useful for communications but also a matter of national security. Lacking it, Ren said, was like lacking armed forces.[1] Security and prosperity overlapped, and securing domestic production of the best technology, including communications technology, was part of securing China. According to Ren, Jiang agreed.

What happens, however, when Chinese ICT companies such as Huawei go abroad? Does their security mission end at the border, or does it extend overseas? This is a question each destination country, not just China, would have to assess for itself, balancing the economic benefits of engagement with Chinese tech companies against the potential use of those companies for purposes that serve Chinese security but perhaps not the recipient's. Not surprisingly, the ways in

**Scott Malcomson** is a principal at Strategic Insight Group.

which individual countries have balanced security and prosperity with regard to Chinese technologies have depended on how much they thought they already had of each. How do the Chinese perceive the main markets for their companies' technologies, and how do those countries themselves understand this balance?

Positions have evolved since Ren met Jiang. The CCP's hands-off policy in many (but not all) tech sectors has changed into one of intense party anxiety about ensuring state control, in part because Chinese tech giants potentially threaten the party's monopoly of power at the commanding heights of the economy. Outside China, wealthier countries' distrust of Chinese technology has tended to increase due to their fear for the future of their own tech sovereignty. Latin American and African countries, peripheral markets for most Western and non-Chinese East Asian tech companies, have accepted Chinese technology and now possess the basic infrastructure – though perhaps not the capital – to grow their own tech sectors. Middle Eastern, North African and Central Asian states have been more thoroughly brought within the Chinese tech sphere of influence, public and private. Central Europe has been the willing focus of DSR initiatives that were as much about Chinese diplomatic strategy towards the EU as about commercial interests. But deep fears of foreign surveillance and control, as well as a backlash against China by core EU states, have weakened China's position in the former Soviet bloc. India, always wary of China on security grounds but needing it for investment, has executed a remarkable strategy of balancing the US and China in what amounts to virtual non-alignment. Somewhat similarly, Southeast Asia (China's economic near abroad) has found ways to work closely with Chinese tech companies while preserving considerable local autonomy and a great diversity of national tech-development strategies.

The gradually increasing global wariness about Chinese tech-nology suggests that China's remarkable successes through the DSR have left it more exposed, in terms of the future prospects of its multinationals and its own tech sector, than it expected to be. When China began advocating internet sovereignty, it should have been careful what it wished for. The technology of 5G and other radio-based systems reinforces such sovereignty because these systems require large land-based computing power physically nearby in order to function well. But even apart from the technological imperative, states that might once have envisioned a free and open internet now often seek to protect their internet sovereignty not just from Western tech companies but also from China itself. In both authoritarian and democratic states, if for somewhat different reasons, the trend is towards controlling citizens' data and building auton-omous, even protected, tech sectors. China's tech companies are thrown back onto the domestic market and those poorer foreign markets where they found their first successes over-seas. That is a difficult position from which to compete on a global scale. The great vulnerability of the Chinese tech sector has always been its dependence, in many different ways, on the Chinese state. If the Chinese state continues to tighten its control over Chinese technology, Chinese companies will struggle to grow their market share, with eventual negative repercussions in China itself.

## The DSR in the rich world

Among wealthier industrialised countries, the balance between security and prosperity led informally to two camps. In one were Australia, Japan, New Zealand, South Korea, Taiwan and the US, all of which decided to exclude Chinese technology from a number of commercial sectors, most visibly from late 2018 onwards but in many cases much earlier. The US had long focused on telecommunications-network providers Huawei and ZTE as potential threats. The initial context, for both the US and China, was more commercial than geopolitical: as early as 2003 the US technology firm Cisco accused Huawei of stealing source code. Multiple such accusations, some vindicated in court settlements, followed, culminating in the US House Intelligence Committee's decision in 2012 to recommend exclusion of Huawei and ZTE from US markets.[2] By mid-2020, the White House was seeking to exclude most Chinese technology from the US market and any other markets it could convince to go along. For China's most technologically advanced neighbours plus the US, this appeared to be a choice of security over prosperity, as the economic benefits of cheaper inputs and products were outweighed by fears of network infiltration and technological dependence.

The other camp, comprising European countries and Canada, tended towards the view that the risks from Chinese technology companies were manageable, the counterweight to US companies desirable and the commercial gains worth the risks. German, Czech, British and other intelligence agencies publicly acknowledged that there were dangers, but these did not greatly affect policy until 2020.[3] By that time, US strategy had evolved to weaken Chinese technology companies' supply chains by categorising the companies as unreliable vendors. The root of the problem, from the official US point of view, was that Chinese technology as such could not be trusted to be independent from the needs and desires of the CCP, so it hardly mattered how transparent a Chinese technology company might be. The CCP's ambition to have a state-backed world-dominating technology sector was itself the problem; and for that the only acceptable solution from Washington's perspective was for Beijing to abandon the ambition. There was no means for remediation, apart perhaps from opening the Chinese market to free competition by non-Chinese companies (not something the CCP appeared ready to contemplate) or the demise of the CCP itself. With the problem implicitly framed in this way, and with strong commitments from India, Japan, South Korea, Taiwan and the US – a quarter of the global population and a third of global GDP (in purchasing-power-parity terms) – the Chinese position weakened in a very short time. Europe's limited decoupling from Chinese technology further expanded that part of the global economy that chose security over prosperity. This shift was not always wholly related to direct security concerns; for example, US measures against Huawei convinced the UK that, leaving actual security questions to one side, Huawei would be unable to supply high-quality components over time.

## The DSR as development project

Within the less developed markets, the DSR, *avant la lettre*, was identifiably a type of development project: a foreign power sometimes subsidising companies to provide products and services the market alone would not. But it was not simply a matter of cheap state-supplied capital. Chinese ICT firms, unlike their Western counterparts, avoided expensive initiatives in new markets such as Latin America, instead adopting lower-cost and lower-risk strategies.[4] Their forward operating teams succeeded first in small infrastructure contracts which enabled them to build up their presence in a new market. Only then did they move to sales of products such as mobile phones, routers, modems and other devices.

Established suppliers such as Ericsson, Nokia and Samsung did not consider these markets sufficiently lucrative to justify competing with Chinese companies on price. For Chinese companies, however, with relatively low domestic labour costs, a vast captive market at home and financial support from state banks, wiring poor countries and introducing them to online financial and other OTT services, newly available through mobile internet access, was a worthwhile endeavour. Companies also received political credit at home for contributing to the BRI, and they gained experience at corporate management on a global scale. For the investee countries, the choice between prosperity and security was relatively easy. They knew they could not guarantee the security of their own networks in any case; Chinese companies offered a chance to enter the twenty-first century, a chance that was not being offered by anyone else at a price that seemed affordable and without political conditionality. Opting for prosperity was straightforward.

China's modest and incremental approach was applied in Africa as well, although there the Chinese state often played a more visible role than in Latin America. Chinese interest in securing resources had earlier led it to make major investments in Angola, Nigeria and Zambia, and it was these countries which saw the first telecommunications projects led by Chinese tech companies in the early 2000s. But the Chinese state also helped its tech companies in countries like Ethiopia and Kenya that were not rich in resources. Unlike the US and the EU, China has not tried to dissuade states from playing a large role in ICT development. For example, Western donors would not accept Ghana's desire for its internet backbone to be state-owned, but China did. Moreover, China did not dissuade states from spending on tech projects that might seem imprudent or unwise, such as Nigeria's satellite programme.[5]

That does not mean Chinese projects are always deferential to the host state or even likely to increase its power. The parallel development of telecoms and the internet in Africa since the mid-1990s has been extremely variable and fluid, with mixed-nership models quite common, and the relative shares of private national players, multinationals and states changing frequently. Mobile investments across borders were dominated by eight multinational companies in the mid-2000s, only two of which (MTN and Vodacom) had major African participation, in both cases from South Africa.[6] Kenya's government once famously declared the internet illegal, banning government employees from using it until 1999. The unpredictability of practices and roles in Africa's tech markets proved to be an advantage for China and its companies, whose own experience of economic development had often been in open contradiction of Western norms: Chinese expectations were low and flexible. And the Chinese government was ready to support its companies abroad, prioritising foreign-policy goals over market forces.[7]

In Latin America, some telecommunications initiatives have been driven by China's political affinities (for Venezuela under Hugo Chávez and Ecuador under Rafael Correa) and its expanding demand for food imports (from Argentina, Brazil and Peru), minerals (Chile and Peru) and energy (Brazil, Guyana and Venezuela), all of which are served by investments loosely under the BRI.[8] State-owned ZTE, which specialises in smart-city systems, has set up surveillance networks in Argentina, Bolivia, Ecuador, Uruguay and Venezuela.[9] For private Chinese companies, however, the main interest has been commercial: providing services to whichever markets might prosper, regardless of political affiliation. Tencent has invested in fintech companies in Brazil (Nu) and Argentina (Ualá). Baidu has invested in local e-commerce companies, Meituan-Dianping and Didi Chuxing in mobility companies. Tech has had a rising share in China's foreign direct investment (FDI) in Latin America, as have tech-adjacent sectors like finance and other services.[10] Brazil has been especially popular as a destination for Chinese tech investment, one reason why even the right-leaning, US-oriented government of Jair Bolsonaro kept the door open to Huawei despite strong US pressure. Ironically perhaps, the US, which often criticises state subsidisation of Chinese technology, was willing to pay Brazilian operators not to choose Huawei and continued its campaign against Huawei in Brazil without definitive success.[11] Although Huawei did not take part in Brazil's 5G auction in November 2021, it was expected to partner with successful local bidders in the 5G build-out.

The end goal in Africa is not very different from in Latin America, although there has been a bit more caution, as shown by lower equity investment by Chinese companies in African start-ups. A fascinating exception is Transsion, which reached the dominant position in Africa's smartphone market competing against South Korean and Chinese rivals (mainly Huawei). African consumers knew that Transsion's Tecno was not an iPhone, but the iPhone was out of reach for many, and Tecno kept improving its product in response to consumer demands as well as setting up manufacturing in Africa. By 2019 it was investing in a UK-based, Africa-focused fintech start-up, PalmPay, together with China's NetEase and Taiwan's MediaTek.[12] But on the whole, China-based tech equity investment in Africa has been modest. Tencent failed to get traction with its WeChat product, though it has had more luck with its overseas music service Joox, which it launched in South Africa in partnership with DSTV. (At the time, Tencent and DSTV were both owned in part by Naspers, a South African company with roots in the white-supremacist media of the apartheid years.)[13] Alibaba has yet to make a real mark, though it has struck a partnership with the UK's Vodaphone for e-commerce in East and South Africa.

In both Latin America and Africa, the Chinese government helped subsidise the construction of telecommunications networks in poor countries, which, as a result, now have markets large enough to be more attractive to Chinese companies' competitors and to offer opportunities to local start-ups. China made the market but does not own it. Unlike in some other parts of the world (such as Southeast Asia and Central Asia), Chinese tech companies have not been able to dominate these markets for themselves except, to a degree, in Latin America (through equity investments rather than direct sales). This investment strategy is striking, and one from which Western tech multinationals have been learning. American tech companies have long wrestled with the trend towards localisation in data terms (data sovereignty) and in ownership terms (through start-ups or other equity investments rather than seeking market share for their own brands). Their Chinese counterparts faced the same problems but have shown, at times, an impressive ability to adjust their products to local markets and, relatedly, to accept local equity ownership.[14]

## The DSR as security-led development

There is a set of countries whose understanding of 'security' broadly aligns with that of the CCP: they see networks as tools of state control as well as means for economic development. The fear of Chinese infiltration of their communications networks is a much lesser concern. For these states, therefore, the trade-off between security and prosperity is less stark, and the Chinese model allows them to take advantage of tech developments while ensuring their continued ability to censor and surveil their populations. A Chinese network is preferable in that Chinese companies can offer integrated domestic surveillance services complementary to improved telecommunications and OTT services that are economically beneficial. This is the interlocking model that Beijing pioneered for China itself.

The Middle East and North Africa (MENA) is home to many of these countries. Relationships between Chinese tech companies, the Chinese state and MENA governments were not especially strong prior to the Arab Spring of 2010–12. Even China's January 2016 'Arab Policy Paper' said very little about ICTs, excluding any mention of the DSR or information technology. It did, however, vow to 'encourage hi-tech Chinese enterprises to innovate, start businesses and establish R&D centres in Arab States'.[15] The main technological aim was to integrate MENA into China's *Beidou* satellite navigation system. There was much discussion of the BRI, but largely within the context of energy issues, the CCP's regional focus at the time.

The Arab Spring showed MENA governments that they had ICT vulnerabilities that could not be resolved through simply shutting off the internet. It also became clear that internet access, in particular mobile access, was necessary for economic advancement and desired by the public. Chinese tech companies were ideally suited to provide ICT infrastructure oriented towards both surveillance and internet access, which can be seen as complementary. In 2017, Egypt, Saudi Arabia, Turkey and the United Arab Emirates (UAE) agreed to join a China-led Digital Economy International Cooperation Initiative, while in 2021 the Arab League agreed to a joint data-security initiative with China.[16] Whatever substance there might have been to such initiatives, they served as reminders that MENA governments shared China's basic view of the relationship between state security and digital security.

The DSR expansion in MENA was driven by Huawei and ZTE, although Alibaba was also active in the region, as were smaller surveillance companies such as Hikvision and SenseTime, and Hangzhou's Jollychic became a leading e-commerce firm.[17] Since the late 1990s, Huawei and ZTE had played an important role in helping Iran create a telecommunications network that would be able to keep Iranians online but unable to communicate with the outside world without at least the possibility of government knowledge. Among Arab countries, Huawei's longest relationship is with Egypt, beginning in 1999, but most of the company's regional presence came later. Huawei Marine laid fibre-optic cable from Tunisia to Italy in 2009 and from Libya to Greece in 2010.[18] In 2017 in Dubai, Huawei launched its first Middle East store and its first OpenLab – a centre for local training and the development of tailored tech solutions to serve the Gulf countries. The second OpenLab premiered the following year in Egypt to serve North Africa. Huawei opened its first regional cloud data centre in Egypt in 2019 and continued to push cloud development in the region.[19]

The Dubai OpenLab project had three tech priorities, based on consultation with local partners: public safety (including the use of Huawei's wireless networks, integrated with cloud computing, to enable facial and licence-plate recognition and the identification of 'public opinion analysis solutions'); smart cities; and oil-and-gas communications and security solutions.[20] That set of concerns resonates across the region. Despite being punished by Algeria in a 2012 bribery case, Huawei and ZTE continued to provide infrastructure for the country, a source of Chinese oil imports.[21] Huawei has been deeply involved in various high-profile tech projects in Morocco, including 5G. In Libya, Huawei won the contract to install the first phase of Tripoli's fibre-optic cable in 2008 and worked with ZTE on building out the country's digital phone system. The two companies stayed on through the overthrow of Muammar Gadhafi and the subsequent civil war. ZTE won a major contract in Tunisia in 2004, prior to the Arab Spring; Huawei contracted to build an LTE network there in 2020.[22] Egypt's IT minister met in 2019 with representatives of ten Chinese ICT companies, several of them deeply involved in surveillance tech and on the US Entity List; the next year it signed a three-year deal with blacklisted iFlytek.[23] Huawei remains strong in the Gulf countries, especially the UAE, which is the regional telecoms hub and has ambitious plans for the fourth industrial revolution.[24] Huawei and ZTE built much of the telecoms infrastructure in Iraq. ZTE is a major presence in Turkey's ICT market, and Huawei has recently raised its profile there. As of January 2022, no MENA country had agreed to ban Huawei, and it has been a vendor for many of the 5G networks launched in the region since 2018.[25]

The same accommodation between domestic security and prosperity found in MENA is also dominant in former Soviet Central Asia.[26] China has a strategic interest in Kazakhstan, Kyrgyzstan and Tajikistan, all of which share long borders with China's restive Xinjiang region and have Uighur populations living across those borders. Together with Uzbekistan, these three Central Asian states were the core members, along with Russia and China, of the security-oriented Shanghai Cooperation Organisation when it was founded in 2001. Chinese ICT companies arrived in Central Asia in the early 2000s. ZTE, for example, began mobile service in Tashkent, Uzbekistan's capital, in 2003, and built a fixed-line network for Tajikistan in 2005.[27] China took an intense interest in Central Asia well before Xi visited Kazakhstan to announce the 'new Silk Road' in 2013. By 2010 there were already over 300 Sino-Kyrgyz enterprises in manufacturing, construction, mining and hydropower, and China dominated FDI into the country.[28] Kazakhstan, the most important market in the region, also enjoyed strong investment from China in the pre-BRI period.[29] Throughout former Soviet Central Asia, Chinese investment focused on mineral resources and construction, including rail lines to Europe, and was led by the major heavy-infrastructure SOEs, but Huawei, ZTE and China Mobile were also early investors.[30]

Although China's capture of the political economy of post-Soviet Central Asia has met popular resistance on many occasions over the past two decades, it is unlikely to change. The region's economies depend on resource extraction led by Chinese companies. The DSR presence has been security-heavy and includes numerous companies on the US Entity List.[31] After some early dabbling with Western investors and ICT companies, Central Asian ICT markets are now dominated by small local oligarchies with political connections and by states themselves. After various experiments with private capital, Uzbekistan's telecoms and internet sector is now almost entirely state-owned. Uzbek President Shavkat Mirziyoyev's trip to the 2019 BRF resulted in as much as US$1bn in investment commitments, with at least US$300m going to DSR projects including surveillance systems.[32] Huawei is updating similar systems in Tajikistan's capital and has been running the core network of mobile provider Babilon for over a decade, while ZTE owns another telecoms company in the country.[33] Kyrgyzstan's ICT network is dominated by state-owned MegaCom, which selected Huawei and ZTE to perform an upgrade in 2011. The only partial exception to this pattern is Kazakhstan, where both Nokia and Ericsson have been active.[34]

A final member of this group of security-minded states is Serbia, which is an interesting outlier in Central Europe and the Balkans with its pro-Russia and pro-China stance. The first relationship is an old one, the second quite new, but both fit into the political frame of Serbian bargaining with the EU, which Serbia hopes one day to join. Serbia has cooperated closely with the Chinese armed forces as well as with Huawei on smart-city projects and other types of surveillance.[35] Huawei regards Serbia as its launch pad for all of the Balkans. Serbia's political lean towards China, repeatedly demonstrated in recent years, may increase its attractiveness for Chinese firms as Huawei and its DSR companions face greater obstacles in much of the rest of Europe.

This otherwise quite disparate group of countries in MENA, Central Asia and the Balkans is united by having relatively authoritarian governments and a willingness to be dependent on Chinese technology. These countries see the China tech connection as reducing their vulnerability to Western countries and political institutions which might otherwise seek to endanger their hold on power, as indeed happened when Western technology companies and governments made informal common cause during the Arab Spring and other 'colour revolutions'. The paramount consideration for these countries, as for China (and Russia), is ensuring their security against domestic disturbances, including those perceived to be encouraged by Western powers and tech firms. Prosperity is a secondary goal. Chinese technology allows them to pursue both.

**The DSR as political leverage**
The countries of Central and Southeast Europe initially viewed Chinese technology investments as both a way to energise more rapid development and a demonstration of the benefits of being a crossroads between the rich West and a rising East. But they have had a disappointing experience in terms of prosperity, while growing concerns about compromised security have been exacerbated by China's accommodation of Russia's invasion of Ukraine and its close technological relationship with Russia more generally. The DSR in Central Europe evolved in the framework of the '16+1' initiative begun by China in 2011, with its first regional summit in 2012. (It became 17+1 with the addition of Greece in April 2019.) The most active participants, with the status of Chinese 'strategic partners', were the Czech Republic, Hungary, Poland and Serbia.[36] Overall, Chinese FDI has not been very large, and Hungary has been the leading

recipient, followed by Poland and the Czech Republic. Those countries were also the main recipients of Chinese investment in new production facilities, which began in the 2000s with a focus on electronics manufacture and telecommunications; Huawei and ZTE were early arrivals, along with Hisense, TCL and Lenovo.[37]

While much of the promised BRI heavy infrastructure in the region has been very slow to materialise, the record with regard to DSR investments is better, especially in Hungary.[38] Poland's DSR-related inward investments (TCL, Huawei, ZTE) have also been rising, including investment from Nuctech, a maker of security-screening machines.[39] Romania, the third-largest recipient of inward Chinese investment in the Balkan sub-region, received early investment from ZTE (2002) and Huawei (2003), and those two continued to invest in ICT in subsequent years.[40] Huawei has created hundreds of jobs in Romania, including through the company's fourth (after China, India and Mexico) Global Services Center. The company has mostly employed Romanian engineers and has established research ties with Romanian universities.[41]

The early entry of Huawei and ZTE into Central and Southeast Europe was consistent with their policy of establishing themselves in ICT markets where their rivals might be less able to compete on price. But unlike in Central Asia, for example, Chinese tech has not crowded out rivals. European national champions Nokia and Ericsson continue to be strong presences, including in Hungary and Serbia.[42] At the same time, there has been growing disillusionment in the region about the promises of Chinese investment, alongside increasing worries about China in digital-security terms and a realisation that China will only marginally decrease the region's dependence on trade and investment from other European states.[43] In addition, EU attitudes towards China have been hardening since

2018, giving Central European, Southeast European and the Baltic states less cover to expand ties with China on sensitive issues. The Czech Republic, Estonia, Greece, Latvia, Poland and Romania have all looked to non-Chinese vendors for their 5G development.[44] Lithuania's defence ministry even looked at banning some Chinese-manufactured mobile phones.[45] Though the region remains warily open to Chinese investment (and tourism), its interest in the DSR is waning, while the determination on the part of civil society to resist any 'surveillance society' is impressively durable. The utility of the region to Beijing's EU policy could wear thin, leaving Chinese tech companies to make what use they can of the region's markets without reference to any larger diplomatic scheme.

**The DSR as regional policy**

As globalisation and global trade weakened after 2008 and the industrialised states entered a prolonged period of slow growth, Southeast Asia and China grew increasingly dependent on each other for growth, particularly given China's looming demographic slowdown. Southeast Asian countries were increasingly unable to imagine economic prosperity without China, but also recognised that China needed them as well. With Australia, Japan, New Zealand, South Korea and Taiwan firmly in the Western security camp, and with vibrant, technologically advanced economies of its own, Southeast Asia was a natural focal point for Chinese tech companies.

By the same token, the Southeast Asian countries already knew China in ways that other neighbours, such as the countries of Central Asia, did not. The country that has most obdurately resisted the DSR is the one whose political system most closely resembles China's: Vietnam's defence ministry chose to build its own 5G system rather than accept a Chinese one.[46] But aside from Vietnam, there is a spectrum of regional acceptance of the DSR, which can be illustrated by looking at Cambodia, Malaysia and Singapore.

Cambodia grew closer to China after co-premier Hun Sen's 1997 coup, in the face of pressure from the US and Europe to adopt a less authoritarian form of government. Hun Sen's banning of the opposition in 2017, when he was prime minister, followed by a questionable election in 2018 and the effective establishment of a one-party state, led the EU to threaten Cambodia with tariffs. This provided China with an opportunity to increase its patronage (Chinese companies were already the principal foreign investors in Cambodian industry) and the DSR formed part of that initiative.[47] Hun Sen's government developed a belated digitalisation plan in March 2019, and he took it to the second BRF the following month in Beijing. Among the agreements he brought home was one to have Huawei build Cambodia's 5G network. In 2021 Huawei became the first officially authorised provider of cloud-computing services in Cambodia.[48]

While Huawei had been in Cambodia since 1999, this did not prompt particular economic dynamism. Though the country did have a high mobile-phone connection rate, internet adoption lagged well behind even that in Laos and Myanmar.[49] The government's start-up digitalisation fund, created in mid-2019, had its spending capped at only US$5m per year. In June 2020, Cambodia's national bank was still making only slow progress towards a digital payments system.[50] The CEO of Huawei Cambodia announced in 2020 that the company would give Cambodia's telecoms ministry 'a data centre facility, video conference system, a piece of fibre-to-the-office equipment and Huawei laptops', which does not suggest a high level of digital development.[51] Cambodia's decision to go all in with the DSR, and in particular with Huawei, was a political one, reflecting the country's dependence on Beijing.

More prosperous and populous, Malaysia had a broader set of DSR options. Its mobile-telecoms market was fragmented but with three strong players: Malaysian businessman Ananda Krishnan's Maxis; state-controlled Axiata; and Norway's Telenor, which owned 49% of Malaysia's DiGi and was also a major provider in Bangladesh, Myanmar and Thailand. Malaysia had excellent international cable connections early on, financed by broad consortiums, although Huawei Marine built the Malaysia–Cambodia–Thailand undersea cable (Cambodia's first), launched in 2017. Huawei entered Malaysia in 2001, eventually making Kuala Lumpur its regional hub and helping to roll out mobile broadband in 2008 and opening a major data centre in 2015.[52] It secured the 5G contract with Maxis in October 2019. ZTE entered Malaysia in 2004 and went on to build 2G, 3G and 4G networks for DiGi, becoming a main supplier for Telekom Malaysia. Malaysian economic development has long been guided by the state, underpinned by the desire to create an indigenous (i.e., non-Chinese and non-Indian) middle class. Huawei and ZTE both emphasised working with the government to achieve its aims, including ethnic ones, demonstrating their ability to align with local policies even if those include employment discrimination against ethnic Chinese.[53]

The most important firm for the DSR in Malaysia, however, has been Alibaba. Malaysia has long sought to become a logistics and transport hub, and Alibaba has been able to offer the country expertise in both e-commerce and logistics through Lazada (an Amazon-like company, begun with mostly European venture financing in Singapore, in which Alibaba bought a controlling interest in 2016) and web-based logistics subsidiary Cainiao. The company also led in bringing e-banking to Malaysia, through Alipay, and Alibaba's smart-city City Brain project, honed in Hangzhou, held considerable appeal as a way to decongest traffic in Kuala Lumpur.[54] The Malaysia Digital Economy Corporation's Digital Free Trade Zone project, launched in 2017, provided an ideal home for Alibaba's integrated product offerings.[55] Alibaba's success in Malaysia was driven by superior, cost-competitive products and energetic government support. It is noteworthy that the DSR expanded in Malaysia when the government grew much closer to Beijing, but that DSR companies managed to adjust when Malaysian politics shifted, in early 2018, to a more suspicious attitude towards the possibility of absorption into China's economic sphere. This required flexibility on the part of the key Malaysian DSR partners and a willingness among Chinese tech companies to localise their products and processes, including training and hiring.[56] Nonetheless, after Malaysia decided to concentrate its 5G network under a single, government-backed operator, it awarded the contract to build the network to Ericsson.[57]

Singapore serves as Southeast Asia's tech hub. It is well suited to the fourth industrial revolution: with so little land, it is dependent on virtual geography for growth and to protect its high position in the value chain. China is its largest export and import market, the US being third or fourth. Its digital economy is highly diverse and attracts investments by both Chinese and Western firms. Alibaba, Baidu, ByteDance, Tencent, JD.com, China Mobile and other Chinese companies all have large presences in Singapore and use it as a gateway to Southeast Asia, more or less in the same way that Google and Amazon do.[58] The DSR has been just one of the many tech streams to flow through Singapore.

Such diversity might be threatened by escalating tensions between Washington and Beijing. The US took Singapore's decision in June 2020 to award its principal 5G roll-outs to Nokia and Ericsson as proof of the rising tide of disillusionment with the CCP.[59] Singapore is certainly well aware of the many dangers posed by China, including in cyber security. In February 2019 it added 'digital defence' to the five pillars of its 'Total Defence' model (military, civil, economic, social and psychological), which had not been altered since its introduction in 1984. Nonetheless, Huawei continues to have a large presence in Singapore, and the city-state signed eight MoUs with Shenzhen in mid-2020 as part of a smart-city initiative to strengthen ties between their small and medium enterprises.[60]

Southeast Asia has been a vibrant region for global growth in the aftermath of the 2008 recession. Its choice has been for prosperity, and it has managed the security challenge posed by its northern neighbour by constantly nurturing a diverse technological and investment base that spreads risk, maintaining open capital markets, encouraging local tech entrepreneurship, and otherwise embracing the confident globalisation that has gone out of fashion among many larger powers.

### The DSR as neo-imperialism

The complexities and ambivalences of India's relations with China are thoroughly reflected in its seesaw relationship with Chinese technology. India seeks security and prosperity equally; it often ends up veering far towards one, then reversing just as far back towards the other.

In the late 1990s and 2000s, India attempted to develop its domestic technology sector. It succeeded in pharmaceuticals and chemistry-related technology, as well as in IT-enabled services (such as outsourcing) and software exports, but it did not develop ICT industries remotely comparable to those emerging in China in the same period. In particular, it did not manufacture hardware.[61] The country's 3G and 4G networks were built by Nokia, Ericsson, Samsung, Huawei and ZTE. India was well aware that this created an economic vulnerability.[62] It also created a security vulnerability.

India first blocked the use of Chinese telecoms equipment in 2010, on suspicion of spying; the unofficial ban was lifted after Chinese companies agreed to new safeguards. By 2012, Huawei and ZTE had 35% of India's wireless-infrastructure business and 65% of wired broadband. The next year, India's telecommunications ministry was investigating Huawei and ZTE kit for spyware and eavesdropping software. The National Security Council's Intelligence Bureau considered Huawei and ZTE to be part of a PLA-led effort aimed at 'dominating the world telecom scene and strengthening its electronic warfare capabilities'.[63] When Tencent's app WeChat began to gain market share in India in 2013, rumours circulated that there was a security risk in using it; WeChat's product shortcomings might have doomed it anyway, but the security worries accelerated its fall.[64] All of this was before the launch of the BRI, towards which India has been consistently cool. The official Telecom Equipment and Services Export Promotion Council, established to nurture exports of Indian telecoms products and services, urged a ban on purchases from Huawei, ZTE and Fiberhome in 2018, citing security concerns.[65] The embrace of Chinese ICT networks by neighbouring Nepal, Pakistan and Sri Lanka, as part of the DSR, only increased the sense of strategic threat.

India's ICT sector was upended in 2016 with the entrance of Mukesh Ambani's Reliance Jio into direct competition with India's incumbent telecoms companies. Aided by a deft touch with regulators as well as a massive war chest, Reliance Jio boldly proposed to connect most of India wirelessly to the internet.[66] Within six months India became the biggest mobile-data consumer in the world. Costs plummeted and the telecommunications industry consolidated into three major players. The question became: who would exploit this vast new market?

The previous year, Facebook had suffered a spectacular political and economic failure in India in trying to establish its Internet.org (or 'Free Basics') service in partnership with Reliance Mobile, run by Ambani's brother, Anil. India's tech sector teamed up with political activists and politicians to identify Facebook as the second coming of the East India Company, against which Indians should embrace the self-reliance that had been such a distinct feature of Indian resistance to colonialism in past decades. Facebook was repulsed, and Free Basics was withdrawn in February 2016.[67]

Chastened by the WeChat and Facebook rejections, major Chinese tech players took a new approach in India, buying local tech companies and growing them. Beginning in 2014 and peaking in 2017, with a later burst in 2019, Alibaba (buying into e-commerce companies Paytm, Snapdeal and BigBasket, among others) and Tencent (Ola, Flipkart) acquired tech companies across the Indian landscape. In just a few years, Chinese tech investors became central to India's development of its own tech sector.[68] Equity investments into start-ups had also served as their model in Latin America and Southeast Asia, though less so elsewhere. It was not an approach that US tech companies had attempted in India, although US corporates did play catch-up. The US equivalents of Alibaba and Tencent arrived, with Facebook buying nearly 10% of Reliance Jio and Amazon reportedly looking for a share of Jio's main remaining rival, Bharti Airtel, which just five years earlier had received a huge loan from Chinese banks to fund a 4G build-out involving Huawei, ZTE and China Mobile. In August 2020, Amazon and Bharti Airtel agreed a strategic partnership in cloud computing to counter Jio's similar deal with Microsoft.[69]

It was in this context that a formal ban on use of Huawei or ZTE for the build-out of India's 5G networks was considered, following the India–China Himalayan border skirmish in June 2020. Long-time advocates of such a move enjoyed some vindication.[70] On 29 June 2020, 59 Chinese apps were banned from India on national-security grounds. Google soon bought its own large stake in Jio, as did other US investors, effectively wiping out the US$20bn of debt that Jio had taken on to finance its massive push to dominate Indian telecommunications.[71] While Chinese firms have not been formally banned, Indian telecoms companies do not want to be caught out, and none have done deals with Huawei or ZTE. In May 2021, India's Department of Telecommunications limited 5G trials to non-Chinese companies.[72] By September 2021, India had joined Australia, Japan and the US in a tech alliance clearly aimed at countering the Chinese government and Chinese tech companies.[73]

India's swing away from Chinese technology was not just about India. By reaching into its geopolitical traditions to pioneer a single-state digital non-aligned movement, India was highlighting the replicability of the Chinese model of digital development from an impoverished base. India's technology sector is positioning itself to expand into frontier and emerging markets just as China's champions are being hobbled by US policy and their own indifferent record at selling online services, as distinct from subsidised infrastructure, into those same markets.[74] China will face increased competition in those less prosperous markets that used to give Chinese tech companies a more or less open field, just when those companies are finding it harder to thrive because they are also getting shut out of the richer markets.

## Security or prosperity

The global adventure of the DSR has been rich in ironies. The Chinese state subsidised the building of global telecommunications infrastructure as a deposit on future digital earnings, but it is unclear whether its companies will actually reap the long-term rewards. Chinese companies have benefited from the imperial colouring of American mega-platforms, but China inspires no more trust than the US and often a good deal less, so its image in certain countries has gone from anti-colonial to imperial. This provoked a backlash in record time, as seen in almost parable form in India.[75] China's mega-platforms borrowed from the playbook of America's but somehow thought they would not experience the same local resentments at their attempt to hold out a bright future and then quickly claim possession of it. China pushed hard for internet sovereignty, apparently without considering that the idea might be embraced as a defence against China itself.

For much of the world, the expansion of Chinese tech companies overseas was a boon: it brought the benefits of the internet closer to hundreds of millions of people. It simultaneously brought the 'surveillance model' (which is not intrinsically capitalist, state-socialist or authoritarian) to those same places. That is not simply a matter of telecommunications infrastructure (or of politics). Alibaba, for example, is not a surveillance company, but it was able to develop its e-finance business, now one of the world's largest, because Chinese consumers needed credit and wanted to participate in e-commerce. Their personal information, including social-media habits and much else, was online for the taking. Once aggregated and structured, it provided what had been missing: the content for credible individual credit profiles and an ongoing record of how those individuals' online lives were working out financially. Alipay spread outside China on the back of this experience. The technology had solved the problem of an unbankable poor citizenry through surveillance technology of a kind. WeChat did much the same thing with a different business model, but then so had Google and Facebook. All mega-platforms that provide internet services take in consumer information and then try to hoard it to protect their commercial advantages and create new ones.

Ideally, there would not have to be a choice between security and prosperity. Unfortunately, the speed of data transmission over the internet means that any large network – whether GooglePay or Alipay, Alibaba Cloud or AWS – can exfiltrate large amounts of data across any border. In theory and in engineering reality, data flows freely across borders, but it does not flow instantly, particularly when it is travelling over radio waves rather than fibre-optic cables. There is a time lag, or latency; and the services that are driving adoption of the mobile internet, in particular video streaming, require a lot of computing power and therefore make the time lag worse. The computing power – or 'compute', in the jargon – is geographically bound. The closer it is to the consumer, the better, because mobile signals travel over radio waves and there is an upper limit to how fast that can be. This is even true, to a degree, of fixed-line transmission. China has struggled to get its tech sector, concentrated in the eastern cities, to embrace data centres in the west of the country.[76]

The result is both more communication crossing international borders and a greater localisation of human-to-server interaction. Data transmission is global but heavy computing remains stubbornly tied to land, and therefore vulnerable to claims by sovereign states. The implication for the DSR is that Chinese tech companies will have to situate much of their compute outside China in order to compete. When the data is on another nation's soil it becomes more vulnerable to local demands. The appeal of 5G systems, for example, is more data at higher speeds, which means more compute – which means more local control or data sovereignty. That in turn leads to a loss of leverage by the central server in Shenzhen or Mountain View and a loss of leverage by the corresponding central state in Beijing or Washington DC.

The good outcome would be for data to become more diffused, innovation globally decentralised (as local start-up ecologies benefit from a degree of subsidy and protection) and technical standards non-aligned. Whether the CCP and the US will be able to give up that level of monopoly control – to choose prosperity, by sharing markets, over the security of exclusive markets – is the central question. For now, both appear to be going in the opposite direction. But if the diverse ways in which other countries have faced that same choice themselves over the past 20 years are indicative, then even in great-power conflict other countries do sometimes get a vote, as in the US–China balancing acts in Europe, India, Brazil and Southeast Asia. The great majority will choose prosperity, but only up to a point. It is to Beijing's and Washington's ultimate advantage not to force the world beyond that point and require other states to choose definitively, on a security basis, which tech camp to join, because that kind of division would dampen the prosperity prospects for all. Nonetheless, current political-economic trends do mostly point in that direction.[77]

CONCLUSION

## David Gordon and Meia Nouwens

The DSR has already improved the connectivity of millions of people across the globe. More importantly, it is positioned to dramatically expand that impact. In 2021, almost half the world's population was still not connected to the digital domain, just as the coronavirus pandemic was increasing the importance of such connectivity.[1] China's major tech companies have grown from domestic start-ups in the late 1990s to become key actors in global digitalisation. The advent of the DSR both reflected and accelerated this change. Indeed, by 2021, China's BATs (Baidu, Alibaba, Tencent) had begun to rival the US FANGs (Facebook, Amazon, Netflix, Google) for dominance in third-country markets, offering services and platforms in physical as well as cloud-based form, from brick-and-mortar data centres to e-commerce, e-government and fintech software solutions and smartphone applications. Chinese giants Huawei and ZTE have hard-wired much of the globe overland through various generations of telecommunications networks, and undersea through the laying of submarine cables connecting countries and continents. In outer space, Chinese private-sector and state-owned companies are building the next generation of small satellites, to broaden access to satellite communications, while China's *Beidou* network offers alternatives to the US GPS, the Russian GLONASS and the European *Galileo* satellite navigation systems. In cities, Chinese digitally connected sensor networks monitor levels of traffic and pollution – and also people – through smart and surveillance-based Safe City projects. And on smartphones the world over, Chinese apps offer everything from online payments systems to shopping and social media.

The debate about which technologies and projects should be included under the DSR rubric is itself a product of a much larger disagreement: whether the DSR is at its core a political or commercial endeavour. The perspective in this book is that it is both: it covers the commercial practices of Chinese technology companies investing in and exporting technology to third markets around the world, and it is a political slogan and geopolitical effort by Beijing to leverage Chinese commercial success for its own strategic and soft-power gains. Chinese companies have long been active players in the global telecommunications industry. Attributing the outbound investment trends of Chinese technology principally to the DSR would be giving the government in Beijing far too much credit.

But by coining the DSR metaphor in 2015 and including it in official BRI documentation, the Chinese government has signalled the importance it places on the commercial success of China's tech sector, especially abroad. While the DSR forms part of Xi's flagship BRI project to expand global connectivity and synergise development efforts while placing China at the heart of the globalisation process, the two differ in significant ways and should be seen for the most part as separate entities. Resistance to the BRI in recipient countries has had minimal effect on the DSR, and the success of the DSR is unlikely to reduce the challenges facing the BRI. The DSR covers projects that are by and large negotiated, promoted, carried out and funded without a significant role for the Chinese state. Unlike the BRI, the majority of DSR activities are initiated by private Chinese companies, with the participation of state-linked enterprises limited largely to physical telecommunications-network infrastructure.

Chinese investment in global digital infrastructure, however, is not just business for business's sake. Despite the best efforts of China's private tech companies to persuade the world that they are independent of CCP and government organs, a credibility gap remains. Geopolitics has gone digital, and the DSR and the private-sector companies that instrumentalise it will find it increasingly difficult to shake off political associations. The story of the DSR thus cannot be a simple one of commercial expansion and competition between technology companies. The rise of Chinese technology companies, and their global expansion, marks the unfolding of a Digital Great Game that encompasses strategic rivalries, competition between highly interdependent actors that rely on each other's supply chains, and a battle for dominance in an area of industry that is for the future what oil and currencies have been to the last century and a half. The DSR is already one of Beijing's most significant foreign-policy endeavours.

## China's ambitions and the response of the West

Since Xi signalled the end of Beijing's 'hide and bide' approach to the outside world, the BRI has become the centrepiece of China's drive to become a leading global power. The launch of the DSR and the elevation of the BRI to constitutional status provide context for the growing concern in the US, other Western countries and many other Asian states around Chinese technology developments that began to intensify in 2018.

After the second BRF in April 2019, the BRI entered a period of consolidation that was reinforced by the toll on economic growth from China's domestic struggle with COVID-19. But in his keynote speech to the November 2020 Asia-Pacific Economic Cooperation summit, Xi took the opportunity to highlight Beijing's continued commitment to the BRI: 'China will further harmonise policies, rules and standards with [BRI] partners, and deepen effective cooperation with them on infrastructure, industry, trade, science and technological innovation, public health and people-to-people exchanges.'[2] And in a speech at the China–ASEAN Expo in Nanning a few days later, Xi specifically highlighted his commitment to 'build a digital Silk Road' with ASEAN.[3]

Despite widespread Chinese and Western media coverage stressing China's innumerable technological achievements, the US is still the only global technology superpower, as Marcus Willett argues in his chapter. While Chinese tech companies are on the leading edge of the Chinese private sector in terms of global competitiveness, they still lag behind those from the US and other Western countries and, most significantly, remain dependent upon Western inputs, especially the most advanced microprocessor chips, for their operations.

Huawei, China's most important technology firm, which has led Beijing's bid to bring 5G to the world, is the focal point of US efforts to push back against China's technological rise. In 2019 and 2020 the US moved to ensure that the Chinese national champion would not be capable of attaining its global goals. Huawei has been vulnerable because parts of the semiconductor supply chain, especially electronic-design-automation software and microchip-manufacturing plants, are critical bottlenecks as the US enforces its expanded export controls and related rules. China's leading domestic chipmaker, Semiconductor Manufacturing International Corporation (SMIC), is three to five years and multiple technology generations behind the global cutting edge.[4] The Trump administration was able to take advantage of this leverage in a way that neither Huawei nor the Chinese political leadership could effectively fend off.

The point of Deng's cautionary injunction to hide and bide was precisely to prevent such an outcome. Although to return openly to hide and bide would involve tremendous loss of face and thus is not an option for Xi, even if he would consider it, China appears to be more open to the prospect of decoupling its economy from that of the US. China's initial response to the Trump administration's rhetoric about decoupling was similar to that of much of the Western business world: the level of interdependence made such an outcome impossible. But in 2019, as US efforts escalated, Beijing embraced at least partial decoupling, a signal that it was revising its long-standing assessment that the global context was conducive to China's continued rise. China's 2020 dual-circulation economic strategy put more emphasis on domestic drivers of growth and sought to enhance strategic autonomy. But this strategy actually walked back from decoupling by opening up more space in the Chinese economy for foreign financial and technology firms, a sign of renewed Chinese anxiety around the possibility of a 'China-less' Western tech economy.

It is hard to argue that China's greater technological assertiveness, through Made in China 2025 and the DSR, has worked out well for its quest for greater global acceptance. Chinese national champions, especially Huawei, find themselves shackled and restrained in strategically important parts of the world. A 2020 Pew Research Center poll of 14 major countries (nine in Europe, plus Australia, Canada, Japan, South Korea and the US) found a dramatic deterioration in public sentiment towards China, which coincided with the emergence of US–China technological competition as well as the coronavirus pandemic.[5] And China's previously improving bilateral relations with at least five important countries – Australia, India and Japan in the Pacific, and Germany and the UK in Europe – have deteriorated since 2019. In all these cases, part of the reason for the deterioration has been concern over Chinese technology. All of this makes countries participating in the DSR – where such pushback is much less evident – more important both for the Chinese state and for Chinese tech companies.

## Balancing commerce with state loyalty

One of the most important ways in which the DSR is distinct from the other elements of the BRI is that private-sector companies are significant drivers and shapers of the entire enterprise, not just tools for implementing it. As Paul Triolo and Damien Ma point out in their chapters, the role of the Chinese private sector in the DSR has been commercially motivated. But that is not to say that government actions have been marginal to shaping the opportunity–risk environment that Chinese companies have faced. The launch of the DSR coincided with Beijing's imposition of restrictions on foreign investments by Chinese companies in an effort to combat capital flight and to gain more influence over the private sector. But Chinese tech companies were given extensive support in the form of the DSR and a much freer hand than their non-tech counterparts over a much wider range of markets, which the companies themselves saw as their major targets for expansion.

The main political obstacle to Chinese tech companies' outward expansion has been the US government. If there is no breakthrough for Huawei with the Biden administration, the company will need to refocus back to China and use second-best chips in the developing world, where Xi's continued support for the DSR means 5G is still a fruitful long-term investment for the company. China's huge domestic market will almost certainly enable the company to remain afloat.

But the question of trust, which had been working against Washington after the 2013 revelations by Edward Snowden of the scope of US digital surveillance, has now shifted. Until 2019, even many US allies were looking to a cheaper, faster 5G roll-out with Huawei. But the world's advanced industrial economies are, with some exceptions, now looking to the Biden administration to collaborate with other Western countries to develop an alternative to China for the next generation of data technologies. Even Huawei's DSR investments could face difficulties; in many of their markets there is local talent and authorities who are looking for opportunities to support it (one reason why India chose Chinese social-media apps as the arena to push back against China's Himalayan provocations).

At the same time, the politics of the domestic regulatory environment facing major Chinese tech firms appear to be shifting. Like most policy arenas under Xi, regulation has been a black box to Chinese as well as foreign observers. The analytic assumption had been that the authorities are eager to support China's leading tech players. That is why the abrupt cancellation in early November 2020 of the dual IPO listings for the Ant Group, Alibaba's fintech spin-off, on the Shanghai and Hong Kong stock exchanges, just two days before trading was set to begin, was so startling for both domestic and international observers. For Xi the intervention was an assertion of political control after Jack Ma's public criticism of China's state banks and regulators a few days earlier. In Xi's China the private sector is expected to align behind the party's dictates. The IPO postponement signalled that tech champions are not excluded from this diktat.

What is becoming increasingly clear is the role that regulators played in the postponement. Over the past decade, Chinese internet giants have been serving small businesses and individuals in need of financial services denied to them by state-owned banks that only extend credit to established enterprises. Viewed as drivers of China's economic growth and innovative forces, these technology firms have been subject to less regulatory control than their banking-sector peers. But now that Ant has become a behemoth playing a systemically important financial role in China, the lines of what Beijing considers acceptable behaviour are shifting. The intervention is a sign that Chinese regulators are concerned first and foremost about financial stability. Ant is a leader in financial innovation, and the IPO would have demonstrated confidence in Chinese markets as US markets become less hospitable. But regulators have spent the past few years targeting financial risks in fintech, and, shortly before the IPO, the China Banking and Insurance Regulatory Commission and the PBoC proposed new caps on lending and leverage for online lenders. The Ant IPO raised flags for the central bank that the private sector might pre-empt its efforts to develop a digital currency, especially given its ongoing concerns about the use of digital currencies to circumvent capital controls and enable unidentifiable movement of funds offshore.

It now appears that Beijing is intent on imposing tighter controls on fintech companies to offset their growing popularity compared to formal banking institutions, and to limit their ability to develop cryptocurrencies that would compete with the central bank's 'public' effort. But the ubiquity in China of the Alibaba payments platform means that Ant, part of the Alibaba group, is not likely to be destroyed in the way Russia's most prominent private company, Yukos, was after its founder Mikhail Khodorkovsky fell into disfavour with President Putin. Nonetheless, Beijing has sent a message that other tech firms, and investors, will not ignore. For observers of the DSR, the assumption of a general overlap of interests between Chinese tech companies and the Beijing government will need re-examination.

## How recipient states view the DSR

Scott Malcomson points out in his chapter that the increasing global unease about Chinese technology leaves it more exposed than it expected to be, despite the many success stories in the DSR. He emphasises that the pushback against Chinese tech has been overwhelmingly from countries outside the DSR. This is critical. He highlights the countries in Central Asia, the Middle East and North Africa for which DSR projects have been more about enhancing domestic security than development per se. These mostly authoritarian regimes are natural partners for Beijing. But the DSR has also been effective in subsidising the expansion of telecoms networks in poor countries in a way that has created further opportunities for Chinese companies, firms from other countries and also local start-ups. As Malcomson puts it, 'China made the market but does not own it'. It is not surprising, then, that in sub-Saharan Africa and Latin America, even in countries where there has been domestic opposition to other BRI infrastructure projects, DSR activities are seen in a positive light. The simple fact is that controversies over land ownership, displacement and the presence of large numbers of Chinese labourers – the main sources of resentment against BRI projects – are not aspects of DSR projects. And the benefits, especially enhanced connectivity, are widely dispersed.

It is much harder to generalise about Southeast Asia. In Cambodia, Laos and Myanmar, for example, China has filled a soft-power vacuum in some of the world's poorest states, and they have become highly dependent on Beijing. But DSR activities are much more extensive in the region's richer countries, where Chinese companies face competition from Japanese, South Korean, European and American firms, as well as politically influential local aspirants. China is planning for the long term in Southeast Asia, and Chinese tech companies have fared better than some of their BRI counterparts in navigating the vagaries of the region's animated democratic politics.

Malcomson's broadly positive view of the impact of the DSR on recipients might appear to be inconsistent with our assessment that China's tech assertiveness has not facilitated greater geopolitical influence for Beijing. But the findings are not mutually exclusive. Malcomson believes that future technology trends will necessitate a far greater degree of localisation: 'Chinese tech companies will have to situate much of their compute outside China in order to compete. When the data is on another nation's soil it becomes more vulnerable to local demands.' Chinese companies in the DSR could find themselves squeezed between a Beijing regime wanting greater political influence over Chinese tech projects and local governments that are also gaining leverage.

**The future of the DSR**
How the DSR evolves will substantially affect what our world looks like at mid-century. Will it be more open, competitive and globalised, with technology diversified even further beyond the current stakeholders? Or will the tech world have bifurcated, making countries choose between allegiance to China or the West? Might a middle path emerge? Will standards be dominated by the few or the many? And will global norms and values be governed by rules of censorship and cyber sovereignty, or continue to operate in the current, more open model?

There is no evidence to suggest that China has a fully planned-out road map to 2049. Certainly, as Ma points out in his chapter, Beijing has a strategic aim to return China to global centre stage as a great power by that year. But 2049 is simply too far in the future for serious analytic foresight, especially on technology-related issues. It does appear that Beijing has a series of intermediate goals towards which it is actively planning, and which provide a framework for measuring success: to become a high-tech manufacturing superpower by 2025, a global AI powerhouse by 2030, and an international standards-setter for new technologies by 2035. The extent to which Beijing achieves these intermediate goals will signal whether China is on a trajectory to becoming a global great power by mid-century. How might the DSR play a role in meeting these three deadlines, and what factors might affect the DSR's overall trajectory in the next ten to 15 years?

The interface between the DSR and Xi's dual-circulation economic strategy will be especially important. At the core of this concept is a bifurcated economy with one realm ('external circulation') integrated with the rest of the world, but increasingly overshadowed by a second realm ('internal circulation') that will cultivate domestic demand, capital and ideas. The goal of dual circulation is ultimately to increase China's self-reliance by diversifying its supply chains, allowing it to access technology and know-how without being bullied by the US. To accomplish this, Beijing will seek to make other countries more dependent on China, thereby converting its external economic links into global political power. The DSR will be a major instrument in the latter effort, while being itself strengthened by domestic technological gains generated by dual circulation.

The prospect of greater global pushback against the DSR, and the availability of competitive alternatives to it, could potentially slow its momentum. So far, global pushback has had more impact on the supply side of the DSR than on the demand side. The biggest obstacle raised to Beijing's plans has been Washington's sanctioning of Chinese companies linked to the PLA and its prohibition of exports to China of core technologies designed or manufactured in the US. A shortage of supplies of core components will force countries to make technical-based assessments that are likely to lead to more countries excluding Chinese tech from their digital ecosystems. Greater pushback in key Western and like-minded markets could do even more to temporarily halt the DSR's momentum and degrade the global reputation of Chinese firms. This is a real risk for such companies. As Marcus Willett argues in his chapter, the only thing Chinese companies can do to regain their reputation in the West and like-minded states is to stop being Chinese. However, Western countries are not commercially important to the DSR. The good news for Beijing is that the vast bulk of the developing world retains its interest in Chinese technology.

Viable alternatives to Chinese technology will be fundamental if the DSR is to be challenged in the near future. While groups of countries have been discussing ways to decrease dependencies on Chinese technology through forums such as the D-10 ('Democracies 10'), the Clean Network initiative and the Open RAN ('O-RAN') Alliance, at mid-2022 these remained nascent, with operational concepts yet to be fully crystallised and coordinated. Developing and emerging economies facing the largest connectivity gaps will not pause in their efforts to link into global markets, so alternative solutions will need to be developed and delivered, at low cost, if Chinese tech companies' advantages are to be challenged. For Beijing, sustaining DSR markets will be facilitated by the dual-circulation strategy's financing of the development of higher-quality Chinese core components, which will create an opportunity to hone skills and develop cutting-edge products into the future.

But the future of the DSR also will depend on how the relationship between the Chinese government and private sector evolves. While dual circulation seeks to promote tech innovation, the irony is that Beijing's recent policy choices are becoming more interventionist towards big tech companies and disincentivise the growth of the private sector. Fearful of running afoul of regulators, other tech companies have cancelled their own plans for IPOs. The more interventionist Beijing becomes, the more Chinese firms will be seen as instruments of the state, and the greater the pushback against Chinese tech, and the DSR, may be. Moreover, the more Beijing tries to constrict decision-making in the boardrooms of Chinese tech giants, the less likely such companies are to continue innovating and serving as market leaders in their fields. And the more Beijing stifles innovation, the less likely it is that the DSR and Chinese tech can be leveraged as a successful foreign-policy tool. To a great extent, the CCP's policies at home will determine the DSR's future abroad.

## What DSR success might look like

The emerging picture, then, is one of major obstacles in China's path to meeting its interim technology goals abroad over the next 15 years, but betting that the DSR will fail might not be the most prudent strategy. Perhaps it is more useful to consider what would constitute success for the DSR from Beijing's perspective, and what that would mean for the rest of the world. Would it necessarily imply a fundamental bifurcation of global technology?

Washington's efforts to deny Chinese tech companies access to markets have been mostly unsuccessful outside the US, Europe and a handful of countries in Northeast Asia and Australasia. States participating in the BRI are unlikely to exclude Chinese technologies. The real battlegrounds for the DSR are those strategic and growing economies that are somewhat but not fully connected to China in terms of infrastructure, and home to large, young and tech-savvy populations. Southeast Asia will initially dominate this middle ground, which is why the region has been such a focal point for Beijing's digital efforts. Latin American countries may follow. Especially in the former, Chinese companies are well positioned to win the battle for access to infrastructure projects and the provision of digital services, as well as to successfully compete in the OTT-platform market.

But even if Chinese tech companies come to dominate Southeast Asian markets, the prospect of a full tech bifurcation, while not inconceivable, appears unlikely. While poor mainland Southeast Asian states such as Cambodia, Laos and Myanmar may be drawn fully into a China-centric tech agglomeration, the more advanced economies in the South China Sea archipelago are likely to remain strongly committed to a range of commercial and technological partnerships. Chinese success in Southeast Asia will contribute to Beijing's momentum elsewhere, especially in Latin America, but Western Hemisphere states are even more likely to resist being drawn into an exclusive Chinese technology sphere, especially given the strength of civil society and legal institutions that will look sceptically on Chinese notions of internet sovereignty.

Limited decoupling will continue in the developed world's foundries as the production of core-critical components will be diverted out of and away from Chinese supply chains, and China's reliance on foreign core technology components will remain its greatest vulnerability. Chinese companies have been clearly instructed by Beijing to step up their innovation and development of core technologies following the US ban on exporting critical microchips and semiconductors to China. This call will inevitably lead to a spurt of indigenous development, but success will depend on smart resource allocation and collaboration with global experts in technology, which also militates against full tech bifurcation. Current signs suggest that Beijing is taking a somewhat different approach to this challenge than in previous innovation initiatives. While foreign experts continue to share their technical expertise with China's own technology R&D community, Beijing is, in an effort to remove duplication of effort and combat corruption, trying to discourage the possibility of hundreds of Chinese companies (ranging from tech firms to restaurants and cement factories) producing microchips.

Beijing also has ways to increase the cost to the West of cutting off China from global semiconductor supply chains. China could retaliate against US-aligned chip producers by cutting off their supply of the rare-earth minerals that are required to manufacture those chips. A precedent has already been set: in 2010, Beijing briefly used access to rare earths as a stick against Tokyo during a territorial dispute in the East China Sea. In 2009, China accounted for 95% of global rare-earth production.[6] Since then, China's share has been declining as countries such as the US have begun to diversify their rare-earth supply chains: it was down to a little over 60% by 2019.[7] Between 2014 and 2017 the US imported 80% of its rare earths from China, but recognising this Achilles' heel, Washington has in recent years sought to diversify its supply chains, and Beijing's use of this tool is likely to be cautious so as not to further encourage these efforts.[8]

A successful DSR would probably promote a further bifurcation of the governing norms and values in cyberspace. This would take the form of content censorship and blocks on data privacy and data flows. The indigenisation of technology and components in China will impact the software that runs over them. As the head of the UK's National Cyber Security Centre, Ciaran Martin, said in 2020, it is looking less likely that the open 'Californian' model of the internet will survive.[9] However, a bifurcation of rules and norms would be unlikely to drive bifurcation across the entire technology spectrum. Instead, an increasingly complex global system defined by overlapping regional, national and international patchworks of legal and normative frameworks might emerge.

As Adrian Shahbaz argues in his chapter, the integration of Chinese digital technology – particularly surveillance technology – abroad will not immediately result in the replication of Chinese-style digital authoritarianism in recipient countries. The degree of influence that Chinese technologies could have on norms and civil liberties in recipient countries through the DSR 'will ultimately depend on each country's institutional framework and the types of technology imported'. Shahbaz further highlights how the DSR 'magnifies China's growing influence, prestige and economic leverage' and could contribute to greater support from developing states for China's campaign for cyber sovereignty in international forums. Digital borders might be delineated by the edges of multiple blocs of governance, rather than between just two spheres. How many countries, and which ones, might join its bloc would determine China's degree of success. In such a scenario, neither China nor the US would be able to claim a total victory.

China currently faces three major barriers to a successful DSR: pushback in (mostly) Western markets, exclusion from critical supply chains, and the increasingly uncertain relationship between its private tech sector and the government. But these difficulties need not spell doom for the DSR or for China's ability to achieve its 2035 goals. China is not alone in facing challenges; its global competitors do not form a cohesive tech bloc, and so far they lack a strategy for countering the DSR. The US and other liberal democracies will need to bridge their own differences. Alliances and collective agreements on security, defence and intelligence-sharing will need broadening to include commercial policies and competitiveness. As the example of the EU has shown, gaining consensus to act strategically will not be easy. Western companies have complex relationships both with the government in Beijing and with Chinese firms. Beijing's road to expanding the DSR may face a bumpy few years ahead, but reconfiguration could still allow Beijing to achieve substantial success in the longer term.

China has shown the world both its strengths and its weaknesses through its handling of the DSR. On the one hand, Beijing has had the strategic foresight to grasp an opportunity and leverage the strengths of the most entrepreneurial element of its private sector to gain prominence in the world's digital ecosystem. It has the potential to sustain this political and technological prominence into the future. On the other hand, aggressively acting on this opportunity has backfired spectacularly, raising alarm in key economies around the world at the prospect of Beijing seeking to leverage tech to achieve its goals for 2035, and ultimately 2049. While Beijing projects a narrative of absolute strength, technological prowess and benign intentions, this has been called into question by China's own policy choices and is deemed disingenuous by foreign powers. To complete China's rise to great-power status and global centrality, Beijing might ultimately need to change tack. In a phrase widely attributed to Xi in China, 'only innovators enter, only innovators are strong, only innovators win'. While this is usually applied to domestic innovation in high-tech fields, it might be just as applicable to China's approaches to foreign policy. How Beijing innovates in further rolling out Chinese tech across the world, and what the DSR will then look like, will have far-reaching impacts on global economics, politics and security.

# APPENDIX

## Official BRI members, BRI or BRI-like participation, and DSR participation by country

| Country | BRI | BRI-like | DSR |
|---|---|---|---|
| **Asia-Pacific** | | | |
| Afghanistan | | ● | ● |
| Australia | | | ● |
| Bangladesh | ● | ● | ● |
| Brunei | ● | ● | ● |
| Cambodia | ● | ● | ● |
| Cook Islands | ● | ● | |
| Federated States of Micronesia | ● | ● | |
| Fiji | ● | ● | ● |
| India | | | ● |
| Indonesia | ● | ● | ● |
| Japan | | | ● |
| Kiribati | ● | ● | |
| Laos | ● | ● | ● |
| Malaysia | ● | ● | ● |
| Maldives | ● | | ● |
| Mongolia | ● | ● | ● |
| Myanmar | ● | ● | ● |
| Nepal | ● | ● | ● |
| New Zealand | | ● | ● |
| Niue | ● | ● | |
| North Korea | | | ● |
| Pakistan | ● | ● | ● |
| Papua New Guinea | ● | ● | ● |
| Philippines | ● | ● | ● |
| Samoa | ● | ● | ● |
| Singapore | ● | ● | ● |
| Solomon Islands | ● | ● | ● |
| South Korea | | | ● |
| Sri Lanka | ● | ● | ● |
| Taiwan | | | ● |
| Thailand | ● | ● | ● |
| Tonga | ● | ● | |
| Vanuatu | ● | ● | ● |
| Vietnam | ● | ● | ● |
| | | | |
| **Europe** | | | |
| Albania | ● | ● | ● |
| Andorra | | | ● |
| Austria | ● | ● | ● |
| Belgium | | ● | ● |
| Bosnia-Herzegovina | ● | ● | ● |
| Bulgaria | ● | ● | ● |
| Croatia | ● | ● | ● |
| Cyprus | ● | ● | |
| Czech Republic | ● | ● | ● |
| Denmark | | | ● |
| Estonia | ● | ● | ● |
| Faroe Islands | | | ● |
| Finland | | | ● |
| France | | | ● |
| Germany | | ● | ● |

| | | | |
|---|---|---|---|
| Greece | ● | ● | |
| Hungary | ● | ● | |
| Iceland | | | ● |
| Italy | ● | ● | ● |
| Latvia | ● | ● | ● |
| Lithuania | ● | ● | ● |
| Luxembourg | ● | ● | ● |
| Moldova | ● | ● | ● |
| Monaco | | | ● |
| Montenegro | ● | ● | ● |
| Netherlands | | | ● |
| North Macedonia | ● | ● | |
| Norway | | | ● |
| Poland | ● | ● | ● |
| Portugal | ● | ● | ● |
| Romania | ● | ● | ● |
| San Marino | | | ● |
| Serbia | ● | ● | ● |
| Slovakia | ● | ● | ● |
| Slovenia | ● | ● | ● |
| Spain | | | ● |
| Sweden | | | ● |
| Switzerland | | | ● |
| United Kingdom | | | ● |
| **Latin America and the Caribbean** | | | |
| Antigua and Barbuda | ● | ● | ● |
| Argentina | | ● | ● |
| Bahamas | | | ● |
| Barbados | ● | ● | ● |
| Belize | | | ● |
| Bolivia | ● | ● | ● |
| Brazil | | ● | ● |
| Chile | ● | ● | ● |
| Colombia | | ● | ● |
| Costa Rica | ● | ● | ● |
| Cuba | ● | ● | ● |
| Dominica | ● | ● | |
| Dominican Republic | ● | ● | ● |
| Ecuador | ● | ● | ● |
| El Salvador | ● | ● | ● |
| Grenada | ● | ● | |
| Guatemala | | | ● |
| Guyana | ● | ● | ● |
| Haiti | | | ● |
| Honduras | | | ● |
| Jamaica | ● | ● | ● |
| Mexico | | ● | ● |
| Nicaragua | | | ● |
| Panama | ● | ● | ● |
| Peru | ● | ● | ● |
| Suriname | ● | ● | ● |
| Trinidad and Tobago | ● | ● | ● |
| Uruguay | ● | ● | ● |
| Venezuela | ● | ● | ● |
| **Middle East and North Africa** | | | |
| Algeria | ● | ● | ● |
| Bahrain | ● | ● | ● |
| Iran | ● | ● | ● |
| Iraq | ● | ● | ● |
| Israel | | ● | ● |

| | | | |
|---|:---:|:---:|:---:|
| Jordan | | ● | ● |
| Kuwait | ● | ● | ● |
| Lebanon | ● | ● | ● |
| Libya | ● | ● | ● |
| Malta | ● | ● | |
| Morocco | ● | ● | ● |
| Oman | ● | ● | ● |
| Qatar | ● | ● | ● |
| Saudi Arabia | ● | ● | ● |
| Syria | | | ● |
| Tunisia | ● | ● | ● |
| Turkey | ● | ● | ● |
| United Arab Emirates | ● | ● | ● |
| Yemen | ● | ● | |
| | | | |
| **North America** | | | |
| Canada | | | ● |
| Greenland | | | ● |
| United States | | | ● |
| | | | |
| **Russia and Eurasia** | | | |
| Armenia | ● | ● | ● |
| Azerbaijan | ● | ● | ● |
| Belarus | ● | ● | ● |
| Georgia | ● | ● | ● |
| Kazakhstan | ● | ● | ● |
| Kyrgyzstan | ● | ● | ● |
| Russia | | ● | ● |
| Tajikistan | ● | | ● |
| Turkmenistan | | ● | ● |
| Ukraine | ● | ● | ● |
| Uzbekistan | ● | ● | ● |
| | | | |
| **Sub-Saharan Africa** | | | |
| Angola | ● | ● | ● |
| Benin | ● | ● | ● |
| Botswana | ● | ● | ● |
| Burkina Faso | ● | ● | ● |
| Burundi | ● | ● | ● |
| Cameroon | ● | ● | |
| Cape Verde | ● | ● | ● |
| Central African Republic | ● | ● | |
| Chad | ● | ● | ● |
| Comoros | ● | ● | |
| Côte d'Ivoire | ● | ● | ● |
| Democratic Republic of the Congo | ● | ● | ● |
| Djibouti | ● | ● | ● |
| Egypt | ● | ● | ● |
| Equatorial Guinea | ● | ● | |
| Eritrea | ● | ● | ● |
| Ethiopia | ● | ● | ● |
| Gabon | ● | ● | |
| The Gambia | ● | ● | ● |
| Ghana | ● | ● | ● |
| Guinea | ● | ● | |
| Guinea-Bissau | ● | ● | ● |
| Kenya | ● | ● | ● |
| Lesotho | ● | ● | ● |
| Liberia | ● | ● | ● |
| Madagascar | ● | ● | ● |
| Malawi | | ● | ● |
| Mali | ● | ● | ● |

| Country | | | |
|---|---|---|---|
| Mauritania | ● | ● | ● |
| Mauritius | | ● | ● |
| Mozambique | ● | ● | ● |
| Namibia | ● | ● | ● |
| Niger | ● | ● | ● |
| Nigeria | ● | ● | ● |
| Republic of Congo | ● | ● | |
| Rwanda | ● | ● | ● |
| São Tomé and Príncipe | ● | ● | |
| Senegal | ● | ● | ● |
| Seychelles | ● | ● | ● |
| Sierra Leone | ● | ● | ● |
| Somalia | ● | ● | ● |
| South Africa | ● | ● | ● |
| South Sudan | | ● | ● |
| Sudan | ● | ● | ● |
| Tanzania | ● | ● | ● |
| Togo | ● | ● | ● |
| Uganda | ● | ● | ● |
| Zambia | ● | ● | ● |
| Zimbabwe | ● | ● | ● |

Source: IISS China Connects dataset, September 2022

Note: BRI-like and DSR participation are determined using the maximalist definitions employed by China Connects. Countries with no BRI or DSR participation are omitted.

NOTES

## Introduction

1 Pang Zhongying, *From Tao Guang Yang Hui to Xin Xing: China's Complex Foreign Policy Transformation and Southeast Asia* (Singapore: ISEAS–Yusof Ishak Institute, 2020), https://www.iseas.edu.sg/wp-content/uploads/2020/04/TRS7_20.pdf.

2 'Wang Yi: Building a New Type of International Relations with Win–Win Cooperation as the Core', Embassy of the People's Republic of China in the Republic of Liberia, 20 June 2013, https://www.mfa.gov.cn/ce/celr/chn/zgyw/t1376135.htm.

3 White House, 'United States Strategic Approach to the Peoples Republic of China', May 2020, https://trumpwhitehouse.archives.gov/wp-content/uploads/2020/05/U.S.-Strategic-Approach-to-The-Peoples-Republic-of-China-Report-5.24v1.pdf.

4 'EU–China – A Strategic Outlook', Joint Communication to the European Parliament, the European Council and the Council, JOIN(2019) 5 final, Strasbourg, 12 March 2019, https://ec.europa.eu/info/sites/default/files/communication-eu-china-a-strategic-outlook.pdf.

5 Constitution of the People's Republic of China, 20 November 2019, http://www.npc.gov.cn/englishnpc/constitution2019/201911/1f65146fb6104dd3a2793875d19b5b29.shtml.

6 Xi Jinping, 'Secure a Decisive Victory in Building a Moderately Prosperous Society in All Respects and Strive for the Great Success of Socialism with Chinese Characteristics for a New Era', address to the 19th National Congress of the Communist Party of China, 18 October 2017, https://www.mfa.gov.cn/ce/cels/eng/sgdt/t1507686.htm.

7 'Xi Jinping Says China "Will Not Seek to Dominate"', BBC News, 18 December 2018, https://www.bbc.co.uk/news/world-asia-china-46601175.

## Chapter One

1   See, for example, Nicholas Davis, 'What Is the Fourth Industrial Revolution?', World Economic Forum, 19 January 2016, https://www.weforum.org/agenda/2016/01/what-is-the-fourth-industrial-revolution/.

2   Defined as excluding fintech and e-commerce, and derived from the 2021 *Fortune* Global 500 Index.

3   See, for example, Alexander Klimburg, *The Darkening Web* (London: Penguin, 2017), p. 324.

4   Greg Austin, *Cyber Policy in China* (Cambridge: Polity, 2014), p. 1.

5   Sixty per cent of the Chinese population equates to about 880m internet users, compared with circa 90% or 300m in the US. Wan Lin, 'China's Internet Users Reach 900 Million, Live-streaming Ecommerce Boosting Consumption: Report', *Global Times*, 28 April 2020, https://www.globaltimes.cn/content/1187036.shtml; and 'Individuals Using the Internet (% of Population) – China, United States', World Bank database, 2020, https://data.worldbank.org/indicator/IT.NET.USER.ZS?locations=CN-US.

6   Katharin Tai and Yuan Yi Zhu, 'A Historical Explanation of Chinese Cybersovereignty', *International Relations of the Asia-Pacific*, 25 January 2022, https://academic.oup.com/irap/article/22/3/469/6514983, pp. 8, 14.

7   Taylor Fravel, *Active Defence: China's Military Strategy Since 1949* (Princeton, NJ: Princeton University Press, 2019), pp. 183–5.

8   *Ibid.*, p. 223.

9   Wang Jun and Yang Liuqing (eds), *Xìnxīhuà zuòzhàn guīlǜ* [Rules of Informatised Warfare] (Beijing: National Defense University Press, 2006). There is no word for 'cyber' in Chinese, where the concept is instead covered by the term 'informatisation'.

10  James Ball, Julian Borger and Glenn Greenwald, 'Revealed: How US and UK Spy Agencies Defeat Internet Privacy and Security', *Guardian*, 6 September 2013, https://www.theguardian.com/world/2013/sep/05/nsa-gchq-encryption-codes-security.

11  See 'Xi Jinping: Bǎ wǒguó cóng wǎngluò dàguó jiànshè chéngwéi wǎngluò qiángguó' [Xi Jinping: Transforming Our Country from a Cyber Power into a Cyber Superpower], Xinhua, 27 February 2014, http://www.xinhuanet.com//politics/2014-02/27/c_119538788.htm.

12  Greg Austin, *Cybersecurity in China: The Next Wave* (Cham: Springer International Publishing, 2018), p. 45. There is no clear indication of what Xi meant by 'core internet technologies', but they presumably involve both hardware and software.

13  According to the US National Science Board, in 2017 China spent US$496bn on digital R&D, not far behind the United States' US$549bn. China secured 58,990 international patents compared with the United States' 57,840, according to the World International Patent Office.

14  Evelyn Cheng, 'China Says It Now Has Nearly 1 Billion Internet Users', CNBC, 4 February 2021, https://www.cnbc.com/2021/02/04/china-says-it-now-has-nearly-1-billion-internet-users.html.

15  For further details and discussion of these advances, see Marcus Willett,

*On Offensive Cyber* (Abingdon: Routledge for the IISS, forthcoming).

16  Sean O'Connor, 'How Chinese Companies Facilitate Technology Transfer from the United States', Staff Research Report, US–China Economic and Security Review Commission, 6 May 2019, https://www.uscc.gov/sites/default/files/Research/How Chinese Companies Facilitate Tech Transfer from the US.pdf.

17  Huawei surpassed US firm Apple in 2019, and then Samsung, briefly, in 2020. It has since fallen out of the top five, mostly due to the US ban in August 2020 on the use of US microchips in Huawei technology.

18  'Personal Computer (PC) Vendor Market Share Worldwide from 2006 to 2021', Statista, 23 February 2022, https://www.statista.com/statistics/267018/global-market-share-held-by-pc-vendors/.

19  Rei Nakafuji, 'TikTok Overtakes Facebook as World's Most Downloaded App', Nikkei Asia, 9 August 2021, https://asia.nikkei.com/Business/Technology/TikTok-overtakes-Facebook-as-world-s-most-downloaded-app; John Koetsier, 'Here Are the 10 Most Downloaded Apps of 2020', *Forbes*, 7 January 2021, https://www.forbes.com/sites/johnkoetsier/2021/01/07/here-are-the-10-most-downloaded-apps-of-2020/; and John Koetsier, 'Top 10 Most Downloaded Apps and Games of 2021', *Forbes*, 27 December 2021, https://www.forbes.com/sites/johnkoetsier/2021/12/27/top-10-most-downloaded-apps-and-games-of-2021-tiktok-telegram-big-winners/. Prior to Prime Minister Narendra Modi's move to ban them in the wake of the June 2020 border clash with China, six of the ten most downloaded apps in India were Chinese. Rajesh Roy and Shan Li, 'India Bans TikTok, Dozens of Other Chinese Apps After Border Clash', *Wall Street Journal*, 30 June 2020, https://www.wsj.com/articles/india-blocks-dozens-of-chinese-apps-including-tiktok-following-border-clash-11593447321.

20  'Xi Jinping Picks Top Lieutenant to Lead China's Chip Battle Against U.S.', Bloomberg, 17 June 2021, https://www.bloomberg.com/news/articles/2021-06-17/xi-taps-top-lieutenant-to-lead-china-s-chip-battle-against-u-s.

21  'China Forecast to Fall Far Short of Its "Made in China 2025" Goals for ICs', IC Insights, 6 January 2021, https://www.icinsights.com/news/bulletins/China-Forecast-To-Fall-Far-Short-Of-Its-Made-In-China-2025-Goals-For-ICs/.

22  Shannon Tiezzi, 'New Report Highlights China's Cybersecurity Nightmare', *Diplomat*, 18 February 2015, https://thediplomat.com/2015/02/new-report-highlights-chinas-cybersecurity-nightmare/.

23  Bureau of Industry and Security, 'Addition of Entities to the Entity List', *Federal Register*, 21 May 2019, 84 FR22961, https://www.federalregister.gov/documents/2019/05/21/2019-10616/addition-of-entities-to-the-entity-list.

24  Chief, Public Safety and Homeland Security Bureau, 'In the Matter of Protecting Against National Security Threats to the Communications Supply Chain Through FCC Programs – Huawei Designation', Federal Communications Commission DA 20-690, 30 June

2020, https://docs.fcc.gov/public/
attachments/DA-20-690A1.pdf.

25 'US Designates Huawei, Four Other
Chinese Tech Firms National Security
Threats', Reuters, 13 March 2021,
https://p.dw.com/p/3qa0Q; and Karen
Freifeld, 'Biden Administration
Adds New Limits on Huawei's
Suppliers', Reuters, 11 March 2021,
https://www.reuters.com/article/
us-usa-huawei-tech-idUSKBN2B3336.

26 David Shepardson, 'US FCC Votes
to Advance Proposed Ban on
Huawei, ZTE Gear', Reuters, 18
June 2021, https://www.reuters.com/
technology/us-fcc-votes-launch-
further-crackdown-huawei-zte-
equipment-2021-06-17.

27 Semiconductor Industry Association,
'Statement on Export Control Rule
Changes', 17 August 2020, https://
www.semiconductors.org/sia-
statement-on-export-control-rule-
changes-2/.

28 Tiezzi, 'New Report Highlights
China's Cybersecurity Nightmare'.

## Chapter Two

1 China's Ministry of Commerce
has posted the full text at http://
www.mofcom.gov.cn/article/i/
dxfw/jlyd/201601/20160101243342.
shtml. An official English
translation is available at 'Full
Text: Action Plan on the Belt and
Road Initiative', State Council of
the People's Republic of China, 30
March 2015, http://english.gov.cn/
archive/publications/2015/03/30/
content_281475080249035.htm. For
the sake of linguistic and grammatical
accuracy, the author's translation of
this and other Chinese documents in
this chapter may differ in places from
their official English versions.

2 Ibid.

3 Liu Jia and Gao Shuang,
'China, EU to Promote Digital
Silk Road', China Daily, 7 July
2015, https://www.chinadaily.
com.cn/silkroad/2015-07/07/
content_21238887.htm.

4 EU–China summit joint
statement, 29 June 2015, https://
www.consilium.europa.eu/en/
press/press-releases/2015/06/29/
eu-china-statement/.

5 Liu and Gao, 'China, EU to Promote
Digital Silk Road'.

6 Lu Wei, 'Shaping an Interconnected
World, Sharing a China–EU Common
Dream', ChinaEU, 17 January 2015,
https://www.chinaeu.eu/shaping-
an-interconnected-world-sharing-a-
china-eu-common-dream-lu-wei/.

7 Zhao Huanxin, 'Digital Silk Road
Linked to "Net Plus"', China
Daily, 8 September 2015, https://
www.chinadaily.com.cn/business
/2015chinaarabforum/2015-09/08/
content_21823512.htm.

8 He Yini, 'Zhanjiang Declaration
Wraps Up 15th Forum on Internet
Media of China', 17 July 2015, http://
www.chinadaily.com.cn/business/
fourmoninternet/2015-07/17/
content_21314789.htm.

9 State Council-edited posting of
Zhao, 'Digital Silk Road Linked to
"Net Plus"', http://english.www.

gov.cn/news/top_news/2015/12/24/
content_281475259901640.htm.

10  National Development and Reform
Commission, 'Wǒwěi děng yǒuguān
bùmén guīfàn 'Yídài Yílù' chàngyì
Yīngwén yìfǎ' [Relevant Organs
(Including the NDRC) to Standardise
the English Translation of the Belt
and Road Initiative], https://web.
archive.org/web/20180325171248/
http://www.ndrc.gov.cn/gzdt/201509/
t20150921_751695.html.

11  State Council-edited posting of Zhao,
'Digital Silk Road Linked to "Net
Plus"'. To this day, official English-
language documents issued by the
Chinese authorities tend to avoid
proper-noun phrasing and spell the
DSR with a lower-case 'd'.

12  World Internet Conference,
'Infographic: Achievements of
the 2nd WIC', 21 December 2015,
http://www.wuzhenwic.org/2015-
12/21/c_48309.htm.

13  Yi Chen, '"Shùzì Sīlù" ràng
Zhōngguó yǔ shìjiè gòngxiǎng xìnxī
chéngguǒ' ['Digital Silk Road' to
Enable China and the World to
Share the Fruits of Informatisation],
Huanqiu.com, 18 December 2015.

14  Liu and Gao, 'China, EU to Promote
Digital Silk Road'.

15  ZTE Corporation, 'ZTE CEO Shi
Lirong Shares M-ICT Vision at WIC
in Wuzhen', 18 December 2015,
https://mp.weixin.qq.com/s?__biz=
MjM5NTMzNTc4NQ==&mid=401
561245&idx=1&sn=022795cb0c348a
08172b1cdbf69bae7c&scene=0#wec
hat_redirect.

16  'Right Time for a Smooth Information
Silk Road: Shi Lirong', China Daily,
16 December 2015, http://www.
chinadaily.com.cn/china/2015-12/16/
content_22727337.htm.

17  'China Revises 2016 GDP Slightly
Lower, Keeps 6.7 Percent Growth
Unchanged', Reuters, 4 January 2018,
https://www.reuters.com/article/
us-china-economy/china-revises-
2016-gdp-slightly-lower-keeps-
6-7-percent-growth-unchanged-
idUSKBN1EU08E.

18  'China to Curb "Irrational" Overseas
Investment by Domestic Firms in
"Belt and Road" Projects', South China
Morning Post, 18 August 2017,
https://www.scmp.com/news/china/
economy/article/2107336/china-
curb-irrational-overseas-investment-
domestic-firms-belt-and.

19  Zhōngguó Gòngchǎndǎng Zhāngchéng
[Charter of the Communist Party
of China], revised 24 October 2017,
http://www.12371.cn/2017/10/28/
ARTI1509191507150883.shtml.
A version in English, entitled
'Constitution of the Communist Party
of China', is available at http://www.
xinhuanet.com//english/download/
Constitution_of_the_Communist_
Party_of_China.pdf.

20  Zhōngyāng Jìwěi Jiānchábù
Wǎngzhàn, 'Zhōngyāng
Xuānchuánbù yuán fùbùzhǎng,
Zhōngyāng Wǎngxìnbàn yuán
zhǔrèn Lǚ Wěi yánzhòng wěijì
bèi kāichú dǎngjí hé gōngzhí'
[Central Commission for Discipline
Inspection, 'Lü Wei – Former Deputy
Minister of the Publicity Department
of the Communist Party of China and
Former Director of the Cyberspace
Administration of China – Is
Found to Be in Severe Violation of
Discipline, and Has Been Dismissed
as a Party Member and Civil
Servant'], Xinhua, 13 February 2018,
http://www.xinhuanet.com/2018-
02/13/c_1122415614.htm.

21  Hong Shen, 'Building a Digital Silk Road? Situating the Internet in China's Belt and Road Initiative', *International Journal of Communication,* vol. 12, 2018, p. 2687, https://ijoc.org/index.php/ijoc/article/view/8405.

22  *Ibid.*, p. 2686.

23  Xi Jinping, 'Working Together to Deliver a Brighter Future for Belt and Road Cooperation', 26 April 2019, http://www.beltandroadforum.org/english/n100/2019/0426/c22-1266.html. A version in Chinese is available at http://vn.china-embassy.org/chn/sghkt/t1658356.htm.

24  The Second Belt and Road Forum for International Cooperation, 'List of Deliverables of the Second Belt and Road Forum for International Cooperation', 27 April 2019, http://www.beltandroadforum.org/english/n100/2019/0427/c36-1312.html; and 'Dì Èr Jiè "Yídài Yílù" Guójì Hézuò Gāofēng Lùntán Chéngguǒ Qīngdān' [The List of Deliverables for the Second 'Belt and Road' Forum for International Cooperation], http://www.beltandroadforum.org/n100/2019/0427/c24-1310.html.

## Chapter Three

1  Belt and Road Forum for International Cooperation, 'Full Text of President Xi's Speech at the Opening of Belt and Road Forum', 14 May 2017, http://2017.beltandroadforum.org/english/n100/2018/0306/c25-1038.html.

2  Ministry of Foreign Affairs of the People's Republic of China, 'Remarks by H.E. Xi Jinping, President of the People's Republic of China at the Opening Ceremony of the 17th China–ASEAN Expo and China–ASEAN Business and Investment Summit', 27 November 2020, available at https://web.archive.org/web/20210702052719/https://www.fmprc.gov.cn/mfa_eng/zxxx_662805/t1836117.shtml.

3  Mao Qian, 'ZTE Expands CDMA Presence in India's BSNL', *ZTE Technology,* vol. 9, no. 12, 2007, https://res-www.zte.com.cn/mediares/magazine/publication/tech_en/pdf/200712.pdf; 'MegaFon Opts for Huawei', CommsUpdate, 25 June 2003, https://www.commsupdate.com/articles/2004/03/26/etc-orders-will-network-from-huawei/; Ou Yangjian, 'ZTE Equipment Serves 2004 Athens Olympics', ZTE, 31 January 2004, https://www.zte.com.cn/global/about/magazine/zte-technologies/2004/1/en_251/161279.html; John Blau, 'China's Huawei Wins First 3G Contract in Europe', IT World Canada, 14 December 2004, https://www.itworldcanada.com/article/chinas-huawei-wins-first-3g-contract-in-europe-2/37646; and Wang Guan, 'Rìběn Ruǎnyín, Zhōngguó Huáwéi, Zhōngxīng, liánshǒu kāifā "4.5G"' [Japan's SoftBank, China's Huawei and ZTE Jointly Develop '4.5G'], Huanqiu Wang, 14 July 2015, https://tech.huanqiu.com/article/9CaKrnJNlAf.

4  Steven Feldstein, 'Testimony Before the US–China Economic and Securing Review Commission Hearing on

China's Strategic Aims in Africa', 8 May 2020, https://www.uscc. gov/sites/default/files/Feldstein_ Testimony.pdf.

5 Paul Adepoju, 'Huawei Wins Major Optic Fiber Contract in Togo', 2 April 2015, https://innovation-village. com/huawei-wins-major-optic-fiber-contract-in-togo/; and 'ZTE Supports Smartfren Launch 4G LTE-advanced Service in Indonesia', TelecomTV, 26 August 2015, https://www.telecomtv. com/content/5g/zte-supports-smartfren-launch-4g-lte-advanced-service-in-indonesia-18041/.

6 Zhang Erchi, 'In Depth: Huawei's Plan to Snatch Alibaba's Cloud Crown', *Nikkei Asia*, 16 July 2021, https://asia.nikkei.com/Spotlight/ Caixin/In-depth-Huawei-s-plan-to-snatch-Alibaba-s-cloud-crown.

7 World Bank, 'Belt and Road Economics: Opportunities and Risks of Transport Corridors', 18 June 2019, p. 108, https://www. worldbank.org/en/topic/regional-integration/publication/belt-and-road-economics-opportunities-and-risks-of-transport-corridors.

8 David Gordon, Haoyu Tong and Tabatha Anderson, 'China's BRI: The Development-finance Dimension', IISS Research Report, 30 March 2020, https://www.iiss. org/blogs/research-paper/2020/03/ beyond-the-myths-of-the-bri.

9 'Ukrtelecom Begins Three-year Modernisation Project with Huawei', CommsUpdate, 12 April 2016, https://www.commsupdate.com/ articles/2016/04/12/ukrtelecom-begins-three-year-modernisation-project-with-huawei/.

10 *Ibid.*

11 'Russia's Megafon Signs $600 mln Loan Agreements with China Development Bank', Reuters, 4 December 2015, https://www. reuters.com/article/russia-megafon-china-loans/russias-megafon-signs-600-mln-loan-agreements-with-china-development-bank-idUKR4N13Q00L20151204; and Lee Jones and Shahar Hameiri, 'Debunking the Myth of "Debt-trap Diplomacy"', Chatham House, 19 August 2020, https:// www.chathamhouse.org/2020/08/ debunking-myth-debt-trap-diplomacy/4-sri-lanka-and-bri.

12 Institute of Developing Economies, Japan External Trade Organization, 'China in Africa: The Role of China's Financial Institutions', October 2009, https://www.ide.go.jp/English/Data/ Africa_file/Manualreport/cia_11.html.

13 'Alibaba CEO Zhang Tells Employees: "We Must Absolutely Globalize"', Alizila, 14 May 2015, https://www. alizila.com/alibaba-ceo-zhang-tells-employees-we-must-absolutely-globalize/.

14 Wade Shepard, 'Is China's Belt and Road Already in Retreat?', *Forbes*, 30 January 2020, https://www.forbes. com/sites/wadeshepard/2020/01/30/ is-chinas-belt-and-road-already-in-retreat/.

15 Alexander Neill, 'Indonesia', in Meia Nouwens et al., 'China's Digital Silk Road: Integration into National IT Infrastructure and Wider Implications for Western Defence Industries', IISS Research Paper, 11 February 2021, pp. 14–20, https://www.iiss.org/blogs/ research-paper/2021/02/china-digital-silk-road-implications-for-defence-industry.

16 Lingling Wei, 'China's New Power Play: More Control of

Tech Companies' Troves of Data', *Wall Street Journal*, 12 June 2021, https://www.wsj.com/articles/chinas-new-power-play-more-control-of-tech-companies-troves-of-data-11623470478.

[17] Li Yuan, 'Why China Turned Against Jack Ma', *New York Times*, 24 December 2020, https://www.nytimes.com/2020/12/24/technology/china-jack-ma-alibaba.html.

[18] Austin Carr and Coco Liu, 'The China Model: What the Country's Tech Crackdown Is Really About', Bloomberg, 27 July 2021, https://www.bloomberg.com/news/articles/2021-07-27/china-tech-crackdown-xi-charts-new-model-after-emulating-silicon-valley.

[19] US Department of State, 'The Clean Network', https://web.archive.org/web/20201201213632/https://www.state.gov/the-clean-network/; and US Embassy and Consulates in Brazil, 'Under Secretary Keith Krach's Remarks on Economic Security', 11 November 2020, https://br.usembassy.gov/under-secretary-keith-krachs-5g-policy-remarks-in-brazil/.

[20] Annabelle Liang, 'Canada to Ban China's Huawei and ZTE from Its 5G Networks', BBC News, 20 May 2022, https://www.bbc.com/news/business-61517729; and 'Huawei and ZTE Left Out of India's 5G Trials', BBC News, 5 May 2021, https://www.bbc.co.uk/news/business-56990236.

[21] 'Huawei Is Taking Sweden to Court After the Country Banned Its 5G Products', Euronews, 31 January 2022, https://www.euronews.com/next/2022/01/31/huawei-is-taking-sweden-to-court-after-the-country-banned-its-5g-products; and UK Department for Digital Culture, Media and Sport, National Cyber Security Centre and The Rt Hon Oliver Dowden CBE MP, 'Huawei to Be Removed from UK 5G Networks by 2027', 14 July 2020, https://www.gov.uk/government/news/huawei-to-be-removed-from-uk-5g-networks-by-2027.

[22] 'Keeping Many Eyes on Traffic in Poland', Hikvision, https://www.hikvision.com/en/newsroom/success-stories/traffic/keeping-many-eyes-on-traffic-in-poland/.

[23] Scott Malcomson, 'Poland', in Nouwens et al., 'China's Digital Silk Road: Integration into National IT Infrastructure and Wider Implications for Western Defence Industries', pp. 41–4.

# Chapter Four

1   See Huang Yong, 'Construction of Digital Silk Road Lights Up BRI Cooperation', *People's Daily Online*, 24 April 2019, http://en.people.cn/n3/2019/0424/c90000-9571418.html.

2   Email exchanges in August and September 2020 with officials at large Chinese tech companies and with China-based technology consultants.

3   Li Bo, 'The Digital Belt and Road Program Yields Fruits amid the Coronavirus Pandemic', *Beijing Review*, 11 May 2020, http://www.bjreview.com/World/202005/t20200511_800203964.html; and personal email communications with Li Bo, August 2020.

4   Inspur Group is actively cooperating with local companies in Ethiopia and Ghana to build cloud data centres and is sharing 'mature' Chinese informatisation practices such as smart cities, smart education and smart agriculture with African countries. It is also training African IT talent – the firm has held several international seminars on cloud computing and big data in China, involving nearly 10,000 technical experts from Egypt, Ethiopia, Ghana, South Africa and other African countries. See Kangling Chen and Bo Li, *Gòngjiàn Shùzì 'Yídài Yílù' yǔ qǐyè quánqiúhuà xīn móshì* [Constructing the Digital 'Belt and Road' and a New Model for Enterprise Globalisation], 2019 Digital Belt and Road Annual Research Report (Fudan: Fudan University Institute of Belt and Road and Global Governance, 2019). English abstract available at https://brgg.fudan.edu.cn/en/articleinfo_484.html.

5   Jevens Nyabiage and Jodi Xu Klein, 'Years Before China's Belt and Road Plan Got Its Name, Huawei Was Driven to Seek Emerging-market Contracts', *South China Morning Post*, 16 April 2020, https://www.scmp.com/business/companies/article/3080076/years-chinas-belt-and-road-plan-got-its-name-huawei-was-driven.

6   A virtual power plant (VPP) is a cloud-based distributed power plant that aggregates the capacities of heterogeneous distributed energy resources (DER) for the purposes of enhancing power generation and trading or selling power on the electricity market.

7   Paul Triolo and Kevin Allison, 'The Geopolitics of Semiconductors', Eurasia Group, September 2020, https://www.eurasiagroup.net/files/upload/Geopolitics-Semiconductors.pdf.

8   See, for example, Alibaba Cloud, 'Alibaba Cloud Launches Second Data Center in Indonesia, Doubling Capacity', 9 January 2019, https://www.alibabacloud.com/press-room/alibaba-cloud-launches-second-data-center-in-indonesia-doubling-capacity.

9   See, for example, 'E-commerce Giant Alibaba Makes Cambodia Its Regional Logistics Hub', *Capital Cambodia*, 22 March 2019, https://capitalcambodia.com/e-commerce-giant-alibaba-makes-cambodia-its-regional-logistics-hub/; 'Alibaba Aims to Grow Five Times Bigger in Myanmar by mid-2019', *Nation*, 24 October 2018, https://www.nationthailand.com/noname/30357101; 'INET

Brings Alibaba Cloud Services to Thailand', *Nation*, 23 January 2020, https://www.nationthailand.com/business/30380947; Alibaba Cloud, 'Alibaba Cloud Establishes Philippines Ecosystem Alliance to Accelerate Digital Transformation', 2 July 2020, https://www.alibabacloud.com/press-room/alibaba-cloud-establishes-philippines-ecosystem-digital-transformation; and 'Alibaba Cloud Doubles Down on ASEAN Region', Digital News Asia, 1 October 2019, https://www.digitalnewsasia.com/business/alibaba-cloud-doubles-down-asean-region.

10  Ma Si, 'SenseTime Deal to See Construction of the First AI Park in Malaysia', *China Daily*, 30 April 2019, http://global.chinadaily.com.cn/a/201904/30/WS5cc7a224a3104842260b93ed.html.

11  When asked about Huawei's role in Malaysia in May 2019, against the backdrop of increasing global scrutiny of the company, Mahathir dismissed espionage concerns with the rhetorical question 'What is there to spy on in Malaysia?' See Anna Maria Romero, '"What Is There to Spy in Malaysia? We Are an Open Book." Dr Mahathir on the Possibility of Huawei Spying on the Country', Independent News & Media, 31 May 2019, http://theindependent.sg/what-is-there-to-spy-in-malaysia-we-are-an-open-book-dr-mahathir-on-the-possibility-of-huawei-spying-on-the-country/.

12  P Prem Kumar, 'Malaysia Delays 5G by 12 Months as Spectrum Allocations Nullified', Nikkei Asian Review, 4 June 2020, https://asia.nikkei.com/Business/Telecommunication/Malaysia-delays-5G-by-12-months-as-spectrum-allocations-nullified.

13  Jeremy Goldkorn, 'Another Huawei Restriction from U.S. Commerce Department', SupChina, 17 August 2020, https://supchina.com/2020/08/17/another-huawei-restriction-from-u-s-commerce-department/; and Paul Triolo and Allison Sherlock, '"New Infrastructure" – China's Race for 5G and Networked Everything Has a New Catchphrase', SupChina, 1 July 2020, https://supchina.com/2020/07/01/new-infrastructure-chinas-race-for-5g-and-networked-everything-has-a-new-catchphrase/.

14  See 'Thailand AIS Speeds Up 5G Investment with Huawei Among Core Network Builders', Disruptive Tech Asia, 20 July 2020, https://disruptivetechasean.com/big_news/thailand-ais-speeds-up-5g-investment-with-huawei-among-core-network-bidders/.

15  Sunsuke Tabeta, 'China's 5G Network to Reach 2m Base Stations This Year', Nikkei Asia, 2 March 2022, https://asia.nikkei.com/Spotlight/5G-networks/China-s-5G-network-to-reach-2m-base-stations-this-year.

16  Dan Swinhoe, 'Alibaba Opens South Korean Data Center in Seoul', Data Center Dynamics, 30 March 2022, https://www.datacenterdynamics.com/en/news/alibaba-opens-south-korean-data-center-in-seoul.

17  See Alibaba Cloud, 'Alibaba Cloud and Sena Traffic Systems to Build a Smart Traffic Solution', 23 May 2019, https://www.alibabacloud.com/press-room/alibaba-cloud-and-sena-traffic-systems-to-build-a-smart-traffic-solution.

18  Katrin Hille, Liu Qianer and

Kiran Stacey, 'Huawei Focuses on Cloud Computing to Secure Its Survival', *Financial Times*, 30 August 2020, https://www.ft.com/content/209aa050-6e9c-4ba0-b83c-ac8df0bb4f86.

19 Huawei announced in June 2020 that it had digitalised the 5G-powered AI Lab launched the previous year and created a Virtual AI Academy. See Huawei, 'Huawei Launches New Virtual AI Academy in Singapore to Accelerate Training and Upskilling of ICT Professionals', 23 June 2020, https://www.huawei.com/en/news/2020/6/huawei-virtual-ai-academy-singapore.

20 See 'Thailand AIS Speeds Up 5G Investment with Huawei Among Core Network Builders'.

21 Apornrath Phoonphongphiphat, 'Top Thai Telecom Urges Factories to Adopt 5G for Robots and AI', Nikkei Asia, 21 August 2020, https://asia.nikkei.com/Spotlight/5G-networks/Top-Thai-telecom-urges-factories-to-adopt-5G-for-robots-and-AI.

22 Miriam Wangui, 'Huawei to Develop Konza Data Centre and Smart City', Kenyan Wall Street, 19 April 2019, https://kenyanwallstreet.com/huawei-to-develop-konza-data-centre%EF%BB%BF-and-smart-city/.

23 Aarav Ghosh, 'China Reinforces Blockchain Connection with BRI Countries', Namecoin News, 5 December 2019, https://www.namecoinnews.com/china-reinforces-blockchain-connection-with-bri-countries/.

24 Nick Stockton, 'China Launches National Blockchain Network in 100 Cities', IEEE Spectrum, 20 March 2020, https://spectrum.ieee.org/computing/software/china-launches-national-blockchain-network-100-cities.

25 See 'Jiédiǎn yùnxíng qíngkuàng' [Node Operation], Blockchain-based Service Network, https://www.bsnbase.com/p/main/serviceNetworkDesc?type=RunningCondition; and David Pan, 'China Aims to Be the World's Dominant Blockchain Power – With Help from Google, Amazon and Microsoft', CoinDesk, 30 July 2020, https://www.coindesk.com/china-aims-to-be-the-worlds-dominant-blockchain-power-with-help-from-google-amazon-and-microsoft.

26 See, for example, Mikk Raud, 'Knowledge Base: Blockchain-based Service Network (BSN, Qūkuàiliàn Fúwù Wǎngluò)', DigiChina, 2 July 2021, https://digichina.stanford.edu/work/knowledge-base-blockchain-based-service-network-bsn-区块链服务网络/.

27 Personal communications with RedDate officials, September 2021.

28 UDPN White Paper, working draft, provided to author in August 2021.

29 Personal communications with RedDate officials, August 2021 to April 2022.

30 For example, FISCO BCOS, developed by Tencent with the participation of Huawei, is one of the major blockchain protocols that the BSN allows developers to build on, and is reportedly integral to the BSN's infrastructure. However, Huawei plays no public role in the BSN. See David Pan, 'China's Blockchain Infrastructure Launches Website for Global Devs', CoinDesk, 11 August 2020, https://www.coindesk.com/chinas-blockchain-infrastructure-launches-website-for-global-devs.

31  All domestically hosted protocols must incorporate Beijing-approved encryption. Therefore, while foreign PCNs can in theory host Ethereum and the EOS permissionless blockchains, because both protocols have structures/encryption that are contrary to Chinese laws, they cannot be hosted on Chinese PCNs. See 'China's BSN Announces Support for Six More Public Chains', Decrypt, 22 July 2020, https://decrypt.co/36327/chinas-bsn-announces-support-for-six-more-public-chains.

32  Jonathan Cheng, 'China Rolls Out Pilot Test of Digital Currency', *Wall Street Journal*, 20 April 2020, https://www.wsj.com/articles/china-rolls-out-pilot-test-of-digital-currency-11587385339.

33  Hung Tran and Barbara C. Matthews, 'China's Digital Currency Electronic Payment Project Reveals the Good and the Bad of Central Bank Digital Currencies', Atlantic Council, 24 August 2020, https://www.atlanticcouncil.org/blogs/new-atlanticist/chinas-digital-currency-electronic-payment-project-reveals-the-good-and-the-bad-of-central-bank-digital-currencies/; and Martin Chorzempa, 'China's Pursuit of Leadership in Digital Currency. Testimony Before the US–China Economic and Security Review Commission', Peterson Institute for International Economics, 15 April 2021, https://www.piie.com/commentary/testimonies/chinas-pursuit-leadership-digital-currency.

34  Matt Sheehan, Marjory Blumenthal and Michael R. Nelson, 'Three Takeaways from China's New Standards Strategy', Carnegie Endowment for International Peace, 28 October 2021, https://carnegieendowment.org/2021/10/28/three-takeaways-from-china-s-new-standards-strategy-pub-85678.

35  Paul Triolo, 'The Telecommunications Industry in US–China Context: Evolving Toward Near-complete Bifurcation', National Security Report, Johns Hopkins Applied Physics Laboratory, 2020, https://jhuapl.edu/Content/documents/Triolo-Telecomms.pdf.

36  Matteo Giovannini, 'The Digital Silk Road's Growing Strategic Role During the Epidemic', CGTN, 10 June 2020, https://news.cgtn.com/news/2020-06-10/The-Digital-Silk-Road-s-growing-strategic-role-during-the-epidemic-RbN21gC6xW/index.html.

37  See, for example, US Department of State, 'The Clean Network', https://web.archive.org/web/20210116201551/https://www.state.gov/the-clean-network/.

38  White House, 'A Declaration for the Future of the Internet', 28 April 2022, https://www.whitehouse.gov/wp-content/uploads/2022/04/Declaration-for-the-Future-for-the-Internet_Launch-Event-Signing-Version_FINAL.pdf.

39  White House, 'Fact Sheet: United States and 60 Global Partners Launch Declaration for the Future of the Internet', 28 April 2022, https://www.whitehouse.gov/briefing-room/statements-releases/2022/04/28/fact-sheet-united-states-and-60-global-partners-launch-declaration-for-the-future-of-the-internet/.

40  US Department of State, 'Digital Briefing with Deputy Secretary of State, Wendy Sherman', 6 May

2022, https://www.state.gov/digital-briefing-with-deputy-secretary-of-state-wendy-sherman/.

41  White House, 'Fact Sheet: President Biden and G7 Leaders Launch Build Back Better World (B3W) Partnership', 12 June 2021, https://www.whitehouse.gov/briefing-room/statements-releases/2021/06/12/fact-sheet-president-biden-and-g7-leaders-launch-build-back-better-world-b3w-partnership/.

42  'Huawei Invests $60m in Angola Technological Centers', *China Daily*, 17 June 2021, https://www.chinadaily.com.cn/a/202106/17/WS60caf9d0a31024ad0bac9c23.html.

## Chapter Five

1  Avery Goldstein, 'China's Grand Strategy under Xi Jinping: Reassurance, Reform, and Resistance', *International Security*, vol. 45, no. 1, Summer 2020, pp. 164–201.

2  Damian Ma, 'Can Xi Pivot from China's Disruptor-in-Chief to Reformer-in-Chief?', *World Politics Review*, 15 November 2016, https://www.worldpoliticsreview.com/articles/20460/can-xi-pivot-from-china-s-disrupter-in-chief-to-reformer-in-chief.

3  Orville Schell and John Delury, *Wealth and Power: China's Long March to the Twenty-first Century* (New York: Random House, 2014).

4  Michael Pillsbury, *The Hundred-year Marathon: China's Secret Strategy to Replace America as the Global Superpower* (New York: St Martin's Griffin, 2016).

5  Wen Yang, '"Tāoguāngyǎnghuì" wéishénme huì chéngwéi chángqī guócè?' [Why Has 'Hide and Bide' Become a Long-term National Strategy?], *Guancha*, 25 August 2014, https://www.guancha.cn/WenYang/2014_08_25_259913.shtml.

6  Estimates of when China will surpass the US in total GDP vary, depending on assumptions of growth rates, exchange rates and inflation. But according to the World Bank's purchasing-power-parity calculations, China became the world's largest economy in 2017, at $19.6trn compared to the US economy's $19.5trn. See World Bank Group, 'Purchasing Power Parities and the Size of World Economies', 2020, p. 3, https://openknowledge.worldbank.org/bitstream/handle/10986/33623/9781464815300.pdf.

7  'Wǔ nián lái, Xí Jìnpíng zhèyàng duōcì chǎnshù Zhōngguómèng' [Over Five Years and on Many Occasions, Xi Jinping Has Elaborated on the Chinese Dream in This Way], *People's Daily*, 29 November 2017, http://cpc.people.com.cn/xuexi/n1/2017/1129/c385474-29673705.html.

8  'Full Text of Resolution on Amendment to CPC Constitution', Xinhua, 24 October 2017, available at https://web.archive.org/web/20180128134830/http://www.xinhuanet.com/english/2017-10/24/c_136702726.htm. The changes were formally enshrined in the constitution at the 13th National People's Congress in 2018.

9    The World Bank defines (as of 1
     July 2022) high-income countries as
     those with per capita gross national
     income of more than US$13,205.
     China is currently considered an
     'upper-middle-income' country by
     this definition. See The World Bank,
     'World Bank Country and Lending
     Groups', https://datahelpdesk.
     worldbank.org/knowledgebase/
     articles/906519-world-bank-country-
     and-lending-groups.
10   David M. Lampton, *The Three Faces
     of Chinese Power: Might, Money, and
     Minds* (Berkeley and Los Angeles, CA:
     University of California Press, 2008).
11   See 'Xín Jìnpíng: Zài jīngjì shèhuì
     lǐngyù zhuānjiā zuòtánhuì shàngde
     jiǎnghuà' [Xi Jinping: Speech at a
     Forum of Experts in the Economic
     and Social Fields], Xinhua, 24
     August 2020, http://www.xinhuanet.
     com/politics/leaders/2020-
     08/24/c_1126407772.htm.
12   Katsuji Nakazawa, 'Xi Jinping
     Sends Shock Waves with His 2035
     Manifesto', Nikkei Asia, 6 August
     2020, https://asia.nikkei.com/
     Editor-s-Picks/China-up-close/
     Xi-Jinping-sends-shock-waves-
     with-his-2035-manifesto. For the
     value of BRI investments in 2017–27,
     see Organisation for Economic
     Co-operation and Development, 'The
     Belt and Road Initiative in the Global
     Trade, Investment and Finance
     Landscape', in *OECD Business and
     Finance Outlook 2018* (Paris: OECD
     Publishing, 2018), https://doi.
     org/10.1787/bus_fin_out-2018-6-en.
13   Wang Jisi, '"Xī Jìn", Zhōngguó
     dìyuán zhànluè de zàipínghéng'
     ['March West': China's Geostrategic
     Rebalancing], *Global Times*, 17
     October 2012, https://opinion.

     huanqiu.com/article/9CaKrnJxoLS
     (English version available
     at https://brill.com/view/
     book/edcoll/9789004273917/
     B9789004273917_008.xml). Yun
     Sun of Brookings provided further
     analysis of Wang's concept: see
     Yun Sun, 'March West: China's
     Response to the US Rebalancing',
     Brookings Institution, 31 January
     2013, https://www.brookings.edu/
     blog/up-front/2013/01/31/march-
     west-chinas-response-to-the-u-s-
     rebalancing/.
14   Herbert S. Yee, 'The Three World
     Theory and Post-Mao China's Global
     Strategy', *International Affairs*, vol. 59,
     no. 2, 1983, pp. 239–49.
15   Hongying Wang, 'A Deeper Look
     at China's "Going Out" Policy',
     Center for International Governance
     Innovation, 8 March 2016, https://
     www.cigionline.org/publications/
     deeper-look-chinas-going-out-policy.
16   See 'Xín Jìnpíng: Zài qǐyèjiā
     zuòtánhuì shàngde jiǎnghuà' [Xi
     Jinping: Speech at the Entrepreneur
     Forum], Xinhua, 21 July 2020, http://
     www.xinhuanet.com/politics/
     leaders/2020-07/21/c_1126267575.
     htm.
17   'Zěnme kàn "liùyìrén měiyuè
     shōurù zhǐyǒu yìqiān yuan"' [How
     to Interpret the '600 Million Have
     a Monthly Income of Just 1,000
     Yuan'], Xinhua, 22 June 2020, http://
     www.xinhuanet.com/politics/2020-
     06/22/c_1126144559.htm.
18   'Translation: 14th Five-year Plan
     for National Informatization –
     Dec. 2021', DigiChina, Stanford
     University, 24 January 2022, https://
     digichina.stanford.edu/work/
     translation-14th-five-year-plan-for-
     national-informatization-dec-2021/.

19 Michael Stott, 'China Cleans Up in Latin America as US Flounders over Coronavirus', *Financial Times*, 8 August 2020, https://www.ft.com/content/741e72ed-e1db-4609-b389-969318f170e8.

20 Jonathan Cheng, 'China Rolls Out Pilot Test of Digital Currency', *Wall Street Journal*, 20 April 2020, https://www.wsj.com/articles/china-rolls-out-pilot-test-of-digital-currency-11587385339.

21 Aditi Kumar and Eric Rosenbach, 'Could China's Digital Currency Unseat the US Dollar?', *Foreign Affairs*, 20 May 2020, https://www.foreignaffairs.com/articles/china/2020-05-20/could-chinas-digital-currency-unseat-dollar.

22 Jie Xiong and Sajda Qureshi, 'The Quality Measurement of China High-technology Exports', 2013 International Conference on Information Technology and Quantitative Management, https://core.ac.uk/download/pdf/81168066.pdf.

23 Steve McCaskill, 'Huawei: We Make It Cheaper and Simpler to Deploy 5G', TechRadar, 22 February 2019, https://www.techradar.com/news/huawei-we-make-it-cheaper-and-simpler-to-deploy-5g.

24 Weihai Wu, 'Xīnjījiàn "shí sì wǔ" guī huà jià gòu yǔ wǔ dà yíng lì mó shì' [14th Five-year Plan New Infrastructure Framework and Five Profit Models], Sohu, 7 April 2020, https://www.sohu.com/a/386012032_728291.

25 Derek Scissors, 'China's Global Investment in 2019: Going Out Goes Small', American Enterprise Institute, January 2020, https://www.aei.org/wp-content/uploads/2020/01/Chinas-global-investment-in-2019-1.pdf.

26 James Thorne, 'China's VC Industry Bounces Back After Coronavirus-induced Winter', PitchBook, 2 April 2020, https://pitchbook.com/news/articles/chinas-vc-industry-bounces-back-after-coronavirus-induced-winter.

27 David Ackerman et al., 'Market Share Analysis: IaaS and IUS, Worldwide, 2018', Gartner, 5 July 2019, https://www.gartner.com/en/documents/3947169/market-share-analysis-iaas-and-ius-worldwide-2018.

28 'Three Represents', *China Daily*, 10 July 2007, https://www.chinadaily.com.cn/china/2007-07/10/content_6142053.htm.

29 '2018 nián Zhōngguó Gòngchǎndǎng dǎng nèi tǒngjì gōngbào' [Chinese Communist Party 2018 Internal Statistics Report], Organization Department of the CCP, available at http://www.12371.cn/2019/06/30/ARTI1561860413392572.shtml.

30 Jude Blanchette, 'Against Atrophy: Party Organisations in Private Firms', *Made in China Journal*, 18 April 2019, https://madeinchinajournal.com/2019/04/18/against-atrophy-party-organisations-in-private-firms/.

31 Henny Sender, 'China's Tech Giants Grapple with Threats at Home and Abroad', *Financial Times*, 24 August 2020, https://www.ft.com/content/259b64b3-9974-464e-b0bb-8b27cebe65a9.

32 Yan Xiaojun and Jie Huang, 'Navigating Unknown Waters: The Chinese Communist Party's New Presence in the Private Sector', *China Review*, vol. 17, no. 2, June 2017, pp. 37–63.

33 *The Economist* found in 2020 that roughly 10% of publicly listed companies in mainland China

praised Xi and the CCP in their annual reports. See 'Xi Jinping Is Trying to Remake the Chinese Economy', *The Economist*, 15 August 2020, https://amp.economist.com/briefing/2020/08/15/xi-jinping-is-trying-to-remake-the-chinese-economy.

34  Jun Maand Xuan He, 'The Chinese Communist Party's Integration Policy Towards Private Business and Its Effectiveness: An Analysis of the Ninth National Survey of Chinese Private Enterprises', *Chinese Journal of Sociology*, vol. 4, no. 3, 2018, pp. 422–49.

35  Ma Huateng's seven suggestions to the NPC were posted on Tencent's official WeChat account on 18 May 2020: see 'Qǐng kàn, Mǎ Huàténg dàibiǎo de qīfèn jiànyì' [Tencent, Please See Seven Recommendations by Representative Pony Ma], https://mp.weixin.qq.com/s/OCBNZcG8UCAAybBpXjUlag.

36  Alibaba, 'Jiànshè 21 Shìjì Shùzì Sīchóu Zhīlù: Ālǐ Bābā de Jīngjì Shíjiàn' [Building the 21st-century Digital Silk Road: Alibaba's Economic Practices], April 2019, http://www.199it.com/archives/868119.html.

37  Tin Hinane El Hadi, 'The Promise and Peril of the Digital Silk Road', Chatham House, 6 June 2019, https://www.chathamhouse.org/expert/comment/promise-and-peril-digital-silk-road.

38  Jane Li, 'How Alibaba and Tencent Are Divvying Up India's Unicorns', Quartz, 16 December 2019, https://qz.com/india/1767741/how-chinas-alibaba-and-tencent-are-divvying-up-indias-unicorns/.

39  Aditya Kalra and Munsif Vengattil, 'Exclusive: China's ByteDance Says India TikTok Ban Causing $500,000 Daily Loss, Risks Jobs', Reuters, 23 April 2019, https://www.reuters.com/article/us-tiktok-india-exclusive/exclusive-chinas-bytedance-says-india-tiktok-ban-causing-500000-daily-loss-risks-jobs-idUSKCN1RZ0QC.

40  See 'International Relations in Asia: Culture, Nation, and State', speech delivered by Lucian W. Pye, Sigur Center for Asian Studies, April 1998, p. 9, https://www2.gwu.edu/~sigur/assets/docs/scap/SCAP1-Pye.pdf.

41  Isabel Reynolds and Emi Urabe, 'Japan to Fund Firms to Shift Production Out of China', Bloomberg, 8 April 2020, https://www.bloomberg.com/news/articles/2020-04-08/japan-to-fund-firms-to-shift-production-out-of-china?sref=LbhqoV4I.

# Chapter Six

1    Elsa Kania, 'Seeking a Panacea: The Party-state's Plans for Artificial Intelligence (Part 2)', Center for Advanced China Research, 15 November 2017, https://www.ccpwatch.org/single-post/2017/11/15/seeking-a-panacea-the-party-state-s-plans-for-artificial-intelligence-part-2.

2    Jane Wakefield, 'AI Emotion-detection Software Tested on Uyghurs', BBC News, 26 May 2021, https://www.bbc.co.uk/news/technology-57101248.

3    Freedom House, 'China', 'Freedom on the Net 2021', 21 September 2021, https://freedomhouse.org/country/china/freedom-net/2021.

4    John Perry Barlow, 'A Declaration of the Independence of Cyberspace', Electronic Frontier Foundation, 1996, https://www.eff.org/cyberspace-independence.

5    Joseph Reagle Jr, 'W3C Activities Related to the US "Framework for Global Electronic Commerce"', W3C, 1997, https://www.w3.org/TR/NOTE-framework-970706.

6    George P. Shultz, 'New Realities and New Ways of Thinking', *Foreign Affairs*, vol. 63, no. 4, Spring 1985, p. 716.

7    'Clinton's Words on China: Trade Is the Smart Thing', *New York Times*, 9 March 2000, https://www.nytimes.com/2000/03/09/world/clinton-s-words-on-china-trade-is-the-smart-thing.html.

8    Information Office of the State Council of the PRC, 'The Internet in China: Protecting Internet Security', June 2010, http://china.org.cn/government/whitepaper/2010-06/08/content_20207978.htm.

9    James Griffiths, *The Great Firewall of China* (London: Zed Books, 2019), p. 246.

10   Lucy Hornby, 'China Paper Slams U.S. for Cyber Role in Iran Unrest', Reuters, 24 January 2010, https://www.reuters.com/article/us-china-us-internet/china-paper-slams-u-s-for-cyber-role-in-iran-unrest-idUSTRE60N0V320100124.

11   Eva Dou, 'China's Xi Jinping Opens Tech Conference with Call for "Cyber Sovereignty"', *Wall Street Journal*, 16 November 2016, https://www.wsj.com/articles/chinas-xi-jinping-opens-tech-conference-with-call-for-cyber-sovereignty-1479273347.

12   Lu Wei, 'Cyber Sovereignty Must Rule Global Internet', *Huffington Post*, 15 December 2014, https://www.huffpost.com/entry/china-cyber-sovereignty_b_6324060.

13   Ye Zheng, 'Thoughts on Internet Sovereignty', CPCNews, 20 July 2015, http://theory.people.com.cn/n/2015/0720/c386965-27332547.html.

14   See, for example, Max Seddon, 'Russia's Chief Internet Censor Enlists China's Know-how', *Financial Times*, 26 April 2016, https://www.ft.com/content/08564d74-0bbf-11e6-9456-444ab5211a2f; and Andrei Soldatov and Irina Borogan, 'Putin Brings China's Great Firewall to Russia in Cybersecurity Pact', *Guardian*, 29 November 2016, https://www.theguardian.com/world/2016/nov/29/putin-china-internet-great-firewall-russia-cybersecurity-pact.

15   Nathan Hodge and Mary Ilyushina, 'Putin Signs Law to Create an Independent Russian Internet', CNN, 1 May 2019, https://edition.cnn.

com/2019/05/01/europe/vladimir-putin-russian-independent-internet-intl/index.html.

16  Adrian Shahbaz and Allie Funk, 'The Pandemic's Digital Shadow', Freedom House, 2020, https://freedomhouse.org/report/freedom-net/2020/pandemics-digital-shadow.

17  Adrian Shahbaz, Allie Funk and Andrea Hackl, 'User Privacy or Cyber Sovereignty', Freedom House, 2020, https://freedomhouse.org/report/special-report/2020/user-privacy-or-cyber-sovereignty.

18  'TikTok Threatens Legal Action Against Trump US Ban', BBC News, 7 August 2020, https://www.bbc.com/news/business-53660860.

19  See Yarosalv Trofimov, Drew Hinshaw and Kate O'Keeffe, 'How China Is Taking Over International Organizations, One Vote at a Time', Wall Street Journal, 29 September 2020, https://www.wsj.com/articles/how-china-is-taking-over-international-organizations-one-vote-at-a-time-11601397208. After Fang Liu stepped down as secretary general of the International Civil Aviation Organization in 2021, the remaining three agencies headed by Chinese nationals were the Food and Agriculture Organization, the ITU and the United Nations Industrial Development Organization.

20  Ted Piccone, 'China's Long Game on Human Rights at the United Nations', Brookings Institution, September 2018, https://www.brookings.edu/wp-content/uploads/2018/09/FP_20181009_china_human_rights.pdf.

21  John Feng, 'China Backed by 65 Nations on Human Rights Despite Xinjiang Concerns', Newsweek, 23 June 2021, https://www.newsweek.com/support-chinas-human-rights-polices-doubles-among-un-members-1603246.

22  Trofimov, Hinshaw and O'Keeffe, 'How China Is Taking Over International Organizations, One Vote at a Time'.

23  Piccone, 'China's Long Game on Human Rights at the United Nations'.

24  Samantha Hoffman, 'Managing the State: Social Credit, Surveillance, and the Chinese Communist Party's Plan for China', in Artificial Intelligence, China, Russia, and the Global Order (Montgomery, AL: Air University Press, 2019), p. 49.

25  Rogier Creemers, 'The International and Foreign Policy Impact of China's Artificial Intelligence and Big-Data Strategies', in Artificial Intelligence, China, Russia, and the Global Order (Montgomery, AL: Air University Press, 2019), p. 129; and 'The Internet Timeline of China 1986–2003', CNNIC, 28 June 2012, https://web.archive.org/web/20220315205701/http://www.cnnic.com.cn/IDR/hlwfzdsj/201306/t20130628_40563.htm.

26  Greg Walton, 'Corporate Complicity in the Development of Surveillance Technology', Human Rights in China, 17 June 2002, https://www.hrichina.org/en/content/4598.

27  Xu Xu, 'To Repress or to Co-opt? Authoritarian Control in the Age of Digital Surveillance', American Journal of Political Science, 7 April 2020, https://doi.org/10.1111/ajps.12514.

28  Central Party School International Research Institute (ed.), Research

*on National Security with Chinese Characteristics* (Beijing: Central Party School Press, 2016), p. 144; and Katherine Atha et al., 'China's Smart Cities Development', SOSi, January 2020, https://www.uscc.gov/research/chinas-smart-cities-development.

29 Freedom House, 'Freedom on the Net 2022', 18 October 2022, https://freedomhouse.org/report/freedom-net/2022/countering-authoritarian-overhaul-internet.

30 Xu, 'To Repress or to Co-opt? Authoritarian Control in the Age of Digital Surveillance'.

31 Liu Caiyu, 'Villages Gain Public Security Systems', *Global Times*, 2 April 2018, https://web.archive.org/web/20180402180631/http://www.globaltimes.cn/content/1096361.shtml.

32 Charles Rollet, 'China Public Video Surveillance Guide: From Skynet to Sharp Eyes', IPVM, 14 June 2018, https://ipvm.com/reports/sharpeyes.

33 Paul Bischoff, 'Surveillance Camera Statistics: Which Cities Have the Most CCTV Cameras?', Comparitech, 22 July 2020, https://www.comparitech.com/vpn-privacy/the-worlds-most-surveilled-cities/.

34 Hoffman, 'Managing the State: Social Credit, Surveillance, and the Chinese Communist Party's Plan for China'; Qian Gang, 'China Under the Grid', China Media Project, 7 December 2008, https://chinamediaproject.org/2018/12/07/china-under-the-grid/; and Lucy Hornby, 'China Reverts to "Grid Management" to Monitor Citizens' Lives', *Financial Times*, 3 April 2016, https://www.ft.com/content/bf6a67c6-940e-11e5-bd82-c1fb87bef7af.

35 'Community Grid System Helps China Fight Virus', *Global Times*, 5 February 2020, https://www.globaltimes.cn/content/1178528.shtml.

36 SCMP Graphics, 'Europe's Coronavirus Lockdown Nightmare', *South China Morning Post*, 26 March 2020, https://multimedia.scmp.com/infographics/news/world/article/3077057/europe-coronavirus/index.html. This claim is supported by academic research: see Yujun Wei et al., 'COVID-19 Prevention and Control in China: Grid Governance', *Journal of Public Health*, vol. 43, no. 1, March 2021, pp. 76–89, https://academic.oup.com/jpubhealth/article/43/1/76/5911705.

37 William Zheng, 'Grass-roots Officials Take Lead Role on the Front Line of Wuhan's Grid-by-grid Battle Against Coronavirus', *South China Morning Post*, 17 March 2020, https://www.scmp.com/news/china/society/article/3075453/grass-roots-officials-take-lead-role-front-line-wuhans-grid-grid.

38 Atha et al., 'China's Smart Cities Development'.

39 *Ibid.*

40 *Ibid.*

41 Julianna Wu, 'Tech Panorama', KrASIA, 17 July 2020, https://kr-asia.com/tech-panorama-how-chinas-four-tigers-of-ai-tech-torn-between-hyped-valuation-and-profitability-dilemma.

42 Chris Buckley and Paul Mozur, 'How China Uses High-tech Surveillance to Subdue Minorities', *New York Times*, 22 May 2019, https://www.nytimes.com/2019/05/22/world/asia/china-surveillance-xinjiang.html.

43 Adrian Zenz and James Leibold, 'Xinjiang's Rapidly Evolving Security State', *China Brief*, vol. 17, no. 4, Jamestown Foundation, 14

March 2017, https://jamestown.org/program/xinjiangs-rapidly-evolving-security-state/.

44  Human Rights Watch, 'China's Algorithms of Repression', 1 May 2019, https://www.hrw.org/report/2019/05/01/chinas-algorithms-repression/reverse-engineering-xinjiang-police-mass; and Buckley and Mozur, 'How China Uses High-tech Surveillance to Subdue Minorities'.

45  Wilber Ross, 'Commerce Department Adds Eleven Chinese Entities Implicated in Human Rights Abuses in Xinjiang to the Entity List', US Department of Commerce, 20 July 2020, https://2017-2021.commerce.gov/news/press-releases/2020/07/commerce-department-adds-eleven-chinese-entities-implicated-human.html.

46  Buckley and Mozur, 'How China Uses High-tech Surveillance to Subdue Minorities'; and Charles Rollet, 'Hikvision Markets Uyghur Ethnicity Analytics, Now Covers Up', IPVM, 11 November 2019, https://ipvm.com/reports/hikvision-uyghur.

47  Paul Mozur, 'One Month, 500,000 Face Scans: How China Is Using A.I. to Profile a Minority', *New York Times*, 14 April 2019, https://www.nytimes.com/2019/04/14/technology/china-surveillance-artificial-intelligence-racial-profiling.html.

48  Freedom House, 'Iran', 'Freedom on the Net 2018', October 2018, https://freedomhouse.org/report/freedom-net/2018/rise-digital-authoritarianism.

49  Steven Feldstein, 'The Global Expansion of AI Surveillance', Carnegie Endowment for International Peace, 17 September 2019, https://carnegieendowment.org/2019/09/17/global-expansion-of-ai-surveillance-pub-79847; and Sheena Chestnut Greitens, 'Dealing with Demand for China's Global Surveillance Exports', Brookings Institution, April 2020, https://www.brookings.edu/research/dealing-with-demand-for-chinas-global-surveillance-exports/.

50  Atha et al., 'China's Smart Cities Development', p. 59.

51  *Ibid.*

52  Greitens, 'Dealing with Demand for China's Global Surveillance Exports', p. 2; and Jonathan Hillman and Maesea McAlpin, 'Watching Huawei's "Safe Cities"', Center for Strategic and International Studies, 4 November 2019, p. 1, https://www.csis.org/analysis/watching-huaweis-safe-cities.

53  See CEIEC, 'Digital Identity', https://www.ceiec.com/solution/publicSecurity/IdentityInformatization/.

54  Griffiths, *The Great Firewall of China*, p. 294.

55  Feldstein, 'The Global Expansion of AI Surveillance'.

56  'Golden Projects', CNET, 27 June 1997, https://www.cnet.com/news/golden-projects/.

57  Liza Lin and Josh Chin, 'U.S. Tech Companies Prop Up China's Vast Surveillance Network', *Wall Street Journal*, 26 November 2019, https://www.wsj.com/articles/u-s-tech-companies-prop-up-chinas-vast-surveillance-network-11574786846; and Dan Strumpf and Liza Lin, 'Blacklisting of Chinese Firms Rattles American Supply Chains', *Wall Street Journal*, 21 July 2020, https://www.wsj.com/articles/blacklisting-

of-chinese-firms-rattles-american-supply-chains-11595343494.

58 PwC, 'Building the Smart City of Prague', https://www.pwc.com/c1/future-of-government-cee/smart-city-prague.html; and NEC, 'Start-up of Data Utilization-type Smart Cities', https://www.nec.com/en/global/techrep/journal/g18/n01/180102.html.

59 Privacy International, 'Hacking Team's Global License Revoked by Italian Export Authorities', 8 April 2016, https://privacyinternational.org/blog/1042/hacking-teams-global-license-revoked-italian-export-authorities.

60 Freedom House, 'Iran', 'Freedom on the Net 2009', 1 April 2009, https://www.refworld.org/docid/49d47592c.html.

61 Steve Stecklow, Farnaz Fassihi and Loretta Chao, 'Chinese Tech Giant Aids Iran', *Wall Street Journal*, 27 October 2011, https://www.wsj.com/articles/SB10001424052970204644504576651503577823210; 'IRGC Gives Up Stake in Telecommunications Possibly to Avoid Sanctions', Radio Farda, 24 October 2018, https://en.radiofarda.com/a/iran-irgc-gives-up-stake-in-telecommunications/29561856.html; Steve Stecklow, 'Special Report: Chinese Firm Helps Iran Spy on Citizens', Reuters, 22 March 2012, https://www.reuters.com/article/us-iran-telecoms/special-report-chinese-firm-helps-iran-spy-on-citizens-idUSBRE82L0B820120322; Office of Public Affairs, United States Department of Justice, 'ZTE Corporation Agrees to Plead Guilty and Pay Over $430.4 Million for Violating U.S. Sanctions by Sending U.S.-origin Items to Iran', 7 March 2017, https://www.justice.gov/opa/pr/zte-corporation-agrees-plead-guilty-and-pay-over-4304-million-violating-us-sanctions-sending; and David J. Lynch, Simon Denyer and Heather Long, 'U.S. Reaches Deal with China's ZTE That Includes $1 Billion Fine, Commerce Secretary Says', *Washington Post*, 7 June 2018, https://www.washingtonpost.com/business/economy/us-reaches-deal-with-chinas-zte-that-includes-1-billion-fine-commerce-secretary-says/2018/06/07/ccffa4b0-6a52-11e8-9e38-24e693b38637_story.html.

62 Stecklow, Fassihi and Chao, 'Chinese Tech Giant Aids Iran'.

63 Golnaz Esfandiari, 'Iran to Work with China to Create National Internet System', Radio Free Europe/Radio Liberty, 4 September 2020, https://www.rferl.org/a/iran-china-national-internet-system-censorship/30820857.html; and Farnaz Fassihi and Steven Lee Myers, 'Defying U.S., China and Iran Near Trade and Military Partnership', *New York Times*, 11 July 2020, https://www.nytimes.com/2020/07/11/world/asia/china-iran-trade-military-deal.html.

64 Freedom House, 'Iran', 'Freedom on the Net 2009'.

65 Freedom House, 'Iran', 'Freedom on the Net 2021', 21 September 2021, https://freedomhouse.org/country/iran/freedom-net/2021.

66 Center for Human Rights in Iran, 'China to Help Iran Implement Its Closed National Internet', 21 January 2014, https://www.iranhumanrights.org/2014/01/china-iran-internet/; and Article 19, 'Part 1: The National Internet Project', in *Tightening the Net: Internet Security and Censorship in Iran*, 2016, p. 12, https://www.

article19.org/data/files/The_National_Internet_AR_KA_final.pdf.

67  Freedom House, 'Iran', 'Freedom on the Net 2020', 14 October 2020, https://freedomhouse.org/country/iran/freedom-net/2020.

68  People's Republic of China, Ministry of Foreign Affairs, 'Joint Declaration on New Stage of Comprehensive Strategic Partnership Between the People's Republic of China and the Republic of Kazakhstan (Full Text)', 31 August 2015, https://digitalkz.kz/wp-content/uploads/2020/03/ГП ЦК на англ 03,06,2020.pdf.

69  Sergey Sukhankin, 'Taking the Digital Component of the BRI in Central Asia, Part Two: Developments in Kazakhstan', China Brief, vol. 21, no. 9, Jamestown Foundation, 7 May 2021, https://jamestown.org/program/tracking-the-digital-component-of-the-bri-in-central-asia-part-two-developments-in-kazakhstan/.

70  Zhanbolat Mamyshev, 'Tokayev poruchil perenyat' u Kitaya opyt cifrovizatcii grazhdan' [Tokayev Instructed to Adopt the Experience of Digitalisation of Citizens from China], Kursiv, 10 August 2019, https://kursiv.kz/news/obschestvo/2019-10/tokaev-poruchil-perenyat-u-kitaya-opyt-cifrovizacii-grazhdan; and Asemgul Mukhitkyzy, 'It Even Recognizes People in Masks – Does Kazakhstan Need Hikvision Cameras', Radio Azattyq, 10 October 2019, https://rus.azattyq.org/a/kazakhstan-china-survelliance-camera/30210035.html.

71  Bradley Jardine, 'China's Surveillance State Has Eyes on Central Asia', Foreign Policy, 15 November 2019, https://foreignpolicy.com/2019/11/15/huawei-xinjiang-kazakhstan-uzbekistan-china-surveillance-state-eyes-central-asia/.

72  Catalin Cimpanu, 'Kazakhstan Government Is Intercepting HTTPS Traffic in Its Capital', ZDNet, 6 December 2020, https://www.zdnet.com/article/kazakhstan-government-is-intercepting-https-traffic-in-its-capital/; and Nicole Perlroth, 'Kazakhstan Moves to Tighten Control of Internet Traffic', New York Times, 3 December 2015, https://bits.blogs.nytimes.com/2015/12/03/kazakhstan-moves-to-tighten-control-of-internet-traffic/.

73  Freedom House, 'Kazakhstan', 'Freedom on the Net 2021', 21 September 2021, https://freedomhouse.org/country/kazakhstan/freedom-net/2021.

74  Katia Patin, 'Kazakhstan Shut Down Its Internet. These Programmers Opened a Backdoor', Coda, 27 January 2022, https://www.codastory.com/authoritarian-tech/kazakhstan-shut-down-its-internet-these-programmers-opened-a-backdoor/.

75  Kanat Altynbaev, 'Kitayskaya tekhnika v gorodakh Kazakhstana vyzvala opaseniya iz-za vozmozhnoy shpionskoy slezhki' [Chinese Equipment in Cities of Kazakhstan Raised Concerns over Possible Spy Surveillance], Central Asia News, 11 December 2019, https://central.asia-news.com/ru/articles/cnmi_ca/features/2019/12/11/feature-01.

76  'Sotni chelovek vyshli na miting Dempartii v Almaty' [Hundreds Protest in Almaty at a Democratic Party Rally], Vlast.kz, 24 April 2021, https://vlast.kz/novosti/44711-sotni-celovek-vysli-na-miting-dempartii-v-almaty.html.

77  Yasin Mugerwa, 'China to Help

Uganda Fight Internet Abuse', *Daily Monitor*, 26 July 2017, https://www.monitor.co.ug/News/National/China-Uganda-Internet-Evelyn-Anite-Africa-Internet-Users/688334-4032626-u1l61r/index.html.

78  Joe Parkinson, Nicholas Bariyo and Josh Chin, 'Huawei Technicians Helped African Governments Spy on Political Opponents', *Wall Street Journal*, 15 August 2019, https://www.wsj.com/articles/huawei-technicians-helped-african-governments-spy-on-political-opponents-11565793017. Details about the national surveillance system are not public and it is unclear how much is yet to be completed.

79  Elias Biryabarema, 'Ugandan Opposition Say 3,000 of Their Supporters Seized Since November', Reuters, 2 February 2021, https://www.reuters.com/article/uk-uganda-election-idUSKBN2A222P.

80  'Uganda Bans Social Media Ahead of Presidential Election', Reuters, 12 January 2021, https://www.reuters.com/article/uk-uganda-election-idUKKBN29H17I; and Meta (formerly Facebook), 'January 2021 Coordinated Inauthentic Behavior Report', 9 February 2021, https://about.fb.com/news/2021/02/january-2021-coordinated-inauthentic-behavior-report/.

81  Jevans Nyabiage, 'China Sees Chance to Woo Uganda as West Mulls Sanctions for Bloody Election', *South China Morning Post*, 22 February 2021, https://www.scmp.com/news/china/diplomacy/article/3122668/china-sees-chance-woo-uganda-west-mulls-sanctions-bloody.

82  Sebastian Moss, 'Huawei's $75m Zambian Data Center Readies for Launch', DCD, 3 February 2017, https://www.datacenterdynamics.com/en/news/huaweis-75m-zambian-data-center-readies-for-launch/.

83  Huawei, 'New ICT Helps Build Smart Zambia', https://e.huawei.com/uk/case-studies/global/2017/201710091443; and Moss, 'Huawei's $75m Zambian Data Center Readies for Launch'.

84  Parkinson, Bariyo and Chin, 'Huawei Technicians Helped African Governments Spy on Political Opponents'.

85  'Zambia's Election Is Crucial, But It's Not a Fair Fight', *The Economist*, 7 August 2021, https://www.economist.com/leaders/2021/08/07/zambias-election-is-crucial-but-its-not-a-fair-fight.

86  Freedom House, 'Zambia', 'Freedom on the Net 2021', 21 September 2021, https://freedomhouse.org/country/zambia/freedom-net/2021.

87  Nicolas Germain, Roméo Langlois and Yi Song, 'Zambia: Under Chinese Influence', France24, 5 July 2021, https://www.france24.com/en/tv-shows/reporters/20210705-zambia-under-chinese-influence-full-length-version; 'Zambia Opposition Leader Hichilema Questioned Over "Anti-China" Remarks', Africanews, 21 November 2018, https://www.africanews.com/2018/11/21/zambia-opposition-leader-hichilema-questioned-over-anti-china-remarks/; and 'The Task Facing Zambia's New President, Hakainde Hichilema', *The Economist*, 21 August 2021, https://www.economist.com/middle-east-and-africa/2021/08/19/the-task-facing-zambias-new-president-hakainde-hichilema.

88  Carlos de la Torre, 'Latin America's

Shifting Politics: Ecuador After Correa', *Journal of Democracy*, vol. 29, no. 4, October 2018, pp. 77–88, https://muse.jhu.edu/article/705719; Ryan Dube, 'Ecuador's New Leader Needs Help from U.S., but China Will Stay Close', *Wall Street Journal*, 12 April 2021, https://www.wsj.com/articles/ecuadors-new-leader-needs-help-from-u-s-but-china-will-remain-close-11618266593; and People's Republic of China, Ministry of Foreign Affairs, 'Xi Jinping Holds Talks with President Rafael Correa of Ecuador – The Two Heads of State Agree to Establish China–Ecuador Comprehensive Strategic Partnership to Push Bilateral Relations for Greater Development Under New Situation', 18 November 2018, https://web.archive.org/web/20211028040900/https://www.fmprc.gov.cn/mfa_eng/topics_665678/XJPDEGDEBLZLJX GSFWBCXZBLLMJXDYTJHZZDESS CLDRFZSHY/t1417413.shtml.

89  de la Torre, 'Latin America's Shifting Politics: Ecuador After Correa'.

90  Paul Mozur, Jonah M. Kessel and Melissa Chan, 'Made in China, Exported to the World: The Surveillance State', *New York Times*, 24 April 2019, https://www.nytimes.com/2019/04/24/technology/ecuador-surveillance-cameras-police-government.html.

91  José María León Cabrera, 'Ecuador's Former President Convicted on Corruption Charges', *New York Times*, 7 April 2020, https://www.nytimes.com/2020/04/07/world/americas/ecuador-correa-corruption-verdict.html.

92  Gideon Long and Demetri Sevastopulo, 'US Development Bank Strikes Deal to Help Ecuador Pay China Loans',
*Financial Times*, 14 January 2021, https://www.ft.com/content/affcc432-03c4-459d-a6b8-922ca8346c14.

93  Gideon Long and Demetri Sevastopulo, 'Ecuador's Exporters Caught Between US and China After Debt Deal', *Financial Times*, 2 March 2021, https://www.ft.com/content/cc5f827a-e787-46cc-a9e9-43b19ba59299.

94  Freedom House, 'Ecuador', 'Freedom in the World 2022', 24 February 2022, https://freedomhouse.org/country/ecuador/freedom-world/2022.

95  Laili Ismail, '200 Hi-def CCTV Cameras for "Modern Policing" to Prevent Crimes – Deputy PM', *New Straits Times*, 9 November 2017, https://www.nst.com.my/news/nation/2017/11/301202/200-hi-def-cctv-cameras-modern-policing-prevent-crimes-deputy-pm.

96  CK Tan, 'Malaysian Police Adopt Chinese AI Surveillance Technology', Nikkei Asia, 18 April 2018, https://asia.nikkei.com/Business/Companies/Chinas-startup-supplies-AI-backed-wearable-cameras-to-Malaysian-police.

97  Liz Lee, 'Selling the Country to China? Debate Spills into Malaysia's Election', Reuters, 26 April 2018, https://www.reuters.com/article/us-malaysia-election-china-idUSKBN1HY076.

98  Tomer Ganon and Hagar Ravet, 'Israeli Cyber Startup Senpai Helped Malaysia's Corrupt Leader Spy on Opposition', CTech, 28 May 2020, https://www.calcalistech.com/ctech/articles/0,7340,L-3828013,00.html.

99  'Najib Razak: Malaysia Ex-PM Gets 12-year Jail Term in 1MDB Corruption Trial', BBC News, 28 July 2020, https://www.bbc.co.uk/news/world-asia-53563065.

100 Huawei, 'Cybersecurity Malaysia, Celcom and Huawei Malaysia Team Up to Explore Development of Malaysia's Cyber Security Capabilities Towards 5G', 30 March 2021, https://www.huawei.com/my/news/my/2021/cybersecurity-malaysia-celcom-huawei-malaysia-team-up-for-5g-cyber-security-test-lab; Huawei, 'Malaysia Prime Minister Launches Huawei's Customer Solution Innovation Center', 23 November 2021, https://www.huawei.com/en/news/2021/11/Huawei-Malaysia-Prime-Minister-CSIC; and P Prem Kumar, 'Malaysia Picks Ericsson Over Huawei to Build 5G Network', Nikkei Asia, 1 July 2021, https://asia.nikkei.com/Spotlight/5G-networks/Malaysia-picks-Ericsson-over-Huawei-to-build-5G-network.

101 Republic of Serbia, Ministry of Foreign Affairs, 'China', https://www.mfa.gov.rs/en/foreign-policy/bilateral-cooperation/china.

102 'Serbia President Kisses Chinese National Flag as Support Team Arrives', CGTN, YouTube, 23 March 2020, https://www.youtube.com/watch?v=om7UImD-hmE; and 'Serbia Ignores West's Concerns, Praises China's Marxism', Euractiv, 7 July 2021, https://www.euractiv.com/section/politics/short_news/serbia-ignores-wests-concerns-praises-chinas-marxism/.

103 Vuk Vuksanovic, 'Securing the Sino-Serbian Partnership', China Observers in Central and Eastern Europe, 12 November 2019, https://chinaobservers.eu/securing-the-sino-serbian-partnership/.

104 Stefan Vladisavljev, 'Surveying China's Digital Silk Road in the Western Balkans', War on the Rocks, 3 August 2021, https://warontherocks.com/2021/08/surveying-chinas-digital-silk-road-in-the-western-balkans/.

105 Majda Ruge and Stefan Vladisavljev, 'Serbia's 5G Deal with Washington: The Art of Muddling Through', European Council on Foreign Relations, 22 September 2020, https://ecfr.eu/article/commentary_serbias_5g_deal_with_washington_the_art_of_muddling_through/.

106 Zhang Hui, 'Serbia Vows to Deepen Telecommunication Cooperation with China Despite Agreement Signed in Washington', *Global Times*, 18 September 2020, https://www.globaltimes.cn/content/1201327.shtml.

107 Ruge and Vladisavljev, 'Serbia's 5G Deal with Washington: The Art of Muddling Through'.

108 John Honovich, 'Huawei Gives France Free City Surveillance', IPVM, 16 February 2017, https://ipvm.com/reports/huawei-france.

109 'Technopolice: Resisting the Total Surveillance of Our Cities and of Our Lives', La Quadrature du Net, 4 February 2020, https://www.laquadrature.net/en/2020/02/04/technopolice-resisting-the-total-surveillance-of-our-cities-and-of-our-lives/.

110 Anas Daif, 'Valenciennes: la Ville Mise en Garde par la CNIL sur l'Usage de Son Système de Vidéosurveillance Offert par Huawei', Franceinfo, 4 August 2021, https://france3-regions.francetvinfo.fr/hauts-de-france/nord-0/valenciennes/valenciennes-la-ville-mise-en-garde-par-la-cnil-sur-l-usage-de-son-systeme-de-videoprotection-offert-par-huawei-2203429.html.

111 'Valenciennes: la Mairie Va Abandonner Ses Caméras Huawei', *La Voix du Nord*, 5 August 2021, https://www.lavoixdunord. fr/1053487/article/2021-08-05/ cameras-chinoises-huawei-le-maire-va-changer-d-operateur.

112 EDRi, 'Italy Introduces a Moratorium on Video Surveillance Systems That Use Facial Recognition', 15 December 2021, https://edri.org/our-work/ italy-introduces-a-moratorium-on-video-surveillance-systems-that-use-facial-recognition/; and Oliver Noyan, 'New German Government to Ban Facial Recognition and Mass Surveillance', Euractiv, 26 November 2021, https://www.euractiv.com/ section/data-protection/news/new-german-government-to-ban-facial-recognition-and-mass-surveillance/.

113 Natasha Lomas, 'European Parliament Backs Ban on Remote Biometric Surveillance', TechCrunch, 6 October 2021, https://techcrunch. com/2021/10/06/european-parliament-backs-ban-on-remote-biometric-surveillance/.

114 Adrian Shahbaz and Allie Funk, 'The Global Drive to Control Big Tech', Freedom House, September 2021, https://freedomhouse. org/report/freedom-net/2021/ global-drive-control-big-tech.

115 Adrian Shahbaz and Allie Funk, 'Social Media Surveillance', Freedom House, November 2019, https://freedomhouse.org/ report/freedom-on-the-net/2019/ the-crisis-of-social-media/ social-media-surveillance.

116 Shahbaz and Funk, 'The Pandemic's Digital Shadow'.

## Chapter Seven

1 Nathaniel Ahrens, 'China's Competitiveness: Myth, Reality, and Lessons for the United States and Japan: Case Study: Huawei', Center for Strategic and International Studies, February 2013, pp. 5–6, https:// csis-website-prod.s3.amazonaws. com/s3fs-public/legacy_files/files/ publication/130215_competitiveness_ Huawei_casestudy_Web.pdf.

2 For a recent Chinese perspective focusing on Cisco, see the blog post by Wang Tao, 'Zhōng Měi kējì dàjuézhàn – xūyào duì Huáwéi shuōde xīnlǐhuà, Huáwéi zhōngjí píngjǐng zài nǎlǐ' [The China–US Technology Battle 6: What Needs to Be Said to Huawei? Where Is Its Real Bottleneck?], 13 June 2020, https://user.observersnews.com/ main/content?id=327432; Chuin-Wei Yap et al., 'Huawei's Yearslong Rise Is Littered with Accusations of Theft and Dubious Ethics', *Wall Street Journal*, 25 May 2019, https:// www.wsj.com/articles/huaweis-yearslong-rise-is-littered-with-accusations-of-theft-and-dubious-ethics-11558756858; and Mike Rogers and Dutch Ruppersberger, 'Investigative Report on the U.S. National Security Issues Posed by Chinese Telecommunications Companies Huawei and ZTE', US House of Representatives, 8 October 2012, http://republicans-intelligence. house.gov/sites/intelligence.house. gov/files/documents/Huawei-ZTE

Investigative Report (FINAL).pdf.

3    Björn Alexander Düben, 'The Souring Mood Towards Beijing from Berlin', Interpreter, 15 April 2019, https://www.lowyinstitute.org/the-interpreter/souring-mood-towards-beijing-berlin; and Miriam Rozen, 'EU Chides China and Others for IP Breaches – Again', Financial Times, 18 June 2020, https://www.ft.com/content/0d48a5dc-9362-11ea-899a-f62a20d54625.

4    Robert Evan Ellis, 'The Strategic Dimension of Chinese Activities in the Telecommunications Sector', Revista Científica General José María Córdova, vol. 11, no. 11, January–June 2013, https://revistacientificaesmic.com/index.php/esmic/article/view/207/507.

5    Roselyn Hsueh and Michael Bryon Nelson, 'Who Wins? China Wires Africa: The Cases of Angola and Nigeria', paper presented at NYU/Giessen Development Finance Conference, New York University School of Law, 9 April 2013; and Iginio Gagliardone, China, Africa, and the Future of the Internet (London: Zed Books, 2019), pp. 26–8.

6    Vivien Foster and Cecilia Briceño-Garmendia, Africa's ICT Infrastructure: Building on the Mobile Revolution (Washington DC: World Bank, 2011), pp. 95–8, https://openknowledge.worldbank.org/handle/10986/2325.

7    Muriuki Mureithi, 'The Internet Journey for Kenya: The Interplay of Disruptive Innovation and Entrepreneurship in Fueling Rapid Growth', in Bitonge Ndemo and Tim Weiss (eds), Digital Kenya: An Entrepreneurial Revolution in the Making (London: Palgrave Macmillan, 2017), pp. 27–53; and

Tokunbo Ojo, 'Political Economy of Huawei's Strategies in the Nigerian Telecommunication Market', International Communication Gazette, vol. 79, no. 2, January 2017, pp. 317–32. See also Gagliardone, China, Africa, and the Future of the Internet, pp. 49–50

8    On Guyana, see Mat Youkee, 'China Extends Its Reach into Guyana', Diálogo Chino, 28 January 2019, https://dialogochino.net/en/infrastructure/21419-china-extends-its-reach-into-guyana/.

9    Cassandra Garrison, '"Safe Like China": In Argentina, ZTE Finds Eager Buyer for Surveillance Tech', Reuters, 5 July 2019, https://www.reuters.com/article/us-argentina-china-zte-insight-idUSKCN1U00ZG.

10   United Nations Economic Commission for Latin America and the Caribbean, 'Foreign Direct Investment in Latin America and the Caribbean', pp. 75ff, https://www.cepal.org/sites/default/files/publication/files/47148.2/S2100318_en.pdf.

11   Otaviano Canuto, 'How Chinese Investment in Latin America Is Changing', Americas Quarterly, 12 March 2019, https://www.americasquarterly.org/article/how-chinese-investment-in-latin-america-is-changing/; Maurício Renner, 'Huawei Se Defende da Ameaça de Bolsonaro', Baguete, 24 June 2020, https://www.baguete.com.br/noticias/24/06/2020/huawei-se-defende-da-ameaca-de-bolsonaro; and Juan Pedro Tomás, 'U.S. Considers Financing for Brazilian Telcos Not Selecting Chinese Gear', RCR Wireless News, 24 June 2020, https://rcrwireless.com/20200624/

business/us-considers-financing-brazilian-telcos-not-selecting-chinese-gear.

12  Jake Bright, 'PalmPay Launches in Nigeria on $40M Round Led by China's Transsion', TechCrunch, 13 November 2019, https://techcrunch.com/2019/11/12/palmpay-launches-in-nigeria-on-40m-round-led-by-chinas-transsion/.

13  Joseph Cotterill, 'South African Media Group Naspers to Spin Off Pay-TV Unit', *Financial Times*, 17 September 2018, https://www.ft.com/content/759de15c-ba8c-11e8-94b2-17176fbf93f5; 'Tencent Eyes Africa for Streaming Music Growth', Tech Central, 6 April 2020, https://techcentral.co.za/tencent-eyes-africa-for-streaming-music-growth/175666/; and '#Declassified: Apartheid Profits – the Tap Root of the National Party', News24, 15 August 2017, https://www.news24.com/News24/declassified-apartheid-profits-the-tap-root-of-the-national-party-20170815.

14  Scott Malcomson, 'What Motivates China's Entrepreneurs? An Interview with Kai-fu Lee', *New York*, 10 October 2018, https://nymag.com/developing/2018/10/kai-fu-lee-scott-malcomson-chinese-entrepreneurship-global-tech.html.

15  'China's Arab Policy Paper', China.org.cn, 14 January 2016, http://www.china.org.cn/world/2016-01/14/content_37573547.htm.

16  Guo Yiming, 'Digital Economy Cooperation to Empower Belt, Road', China.org.cn, 4 December 2017, http://www.china.org.cn/world/2017-12/04/content_50083923.htm.

17  'JollyChic Brightens China–Middle East Online Silk Road', *China Daily*, 8 October 2018, https://www.chinadaily.com.cn/a/201810/08/WS5bbab42ca310eff303280f73.html; Archana Narayaran, 'World's Largest AI Startup SenseTime to Open Abu Dhabi Hub', Bloomberg, 23 July 2019, https://www.bnnbloomberg.ca/world-s-largest-ai-startup-sensetime-to-open-abu-dhabi-hub-1.1291495; and 'Hikvision Outlines Focus on Artificial Intelligence (AI) at Intersec', *Security Middle East*, 25 January 2020, https://www.securitymiddleeastmag.com/hikvision-ai-forum-leads-the-technology-trend-in-security-industry/.

18  Adel Abdel Ghafar and Anna L. Jacobs, *Beijing Calling: Assessing China's Growing Footprint in North Africa* (Washington DC: Brookings, 2019).

19  'Huawei Launches OpenLab in Dubai', SmartCitiesWorld, 2 May 2017, https://www.smartcitiesworld.net/news/news/huawei-launches-openlab-in-dubai-1633; 'Huawei Expands OpenLab Network to North Africa', ITP.net, 30 January 2018, https://www.itp.net/infrastructure/616415-huawei-expands-openlab-network-to-north-africa; 'Egypt, Huawei Sign MoU for Cloud Computing, AI Networks', *Egypt Independent*, 26 February 2019, https://egyptindependent.com/egypt-huawei-sign-mou-for-cloud-computing-ai-networks/; and Huawei Cloud, 'Middle East Huawei Cloud Summit Qatar', 31 May 2021, https://www.huaweicloud.com/intl/en-us/about/Middle_East_HUAWEI_CLOUD_SUMMIT_Qatar/.

20  'China's Huawei Opens First Middle East Store in Dubai', Gulf Business, 6 November 2017, https://gulfbusiness.com/chinas-huawei-

opens-first-middle-east-store-dubai/; and Alvin R. Cabral, 'Welcome to Huawei's OpenLab Dubai, a Haven for Geeks', *Khaleej Times*, 27 April 2017, https://www.khaleejtimes.com/local-business/welcome-to-huaweis-openlab-dubai-a-haven-for-geeks.

21 'Huawei and ZTE Fined in Algeria Bribery Case', CommsMEA, 12 June 2012, https://www.itp.net/commsmea/12336-huawei-and-zte-fined-in-algerian-bribery-case. Algerian and Chinese company officials were also given prison sentences.

22 'Huawei et le Ministère des Technologies de la Communication et de la Transformation Digitale: Une Future Coopération pour Faire Avancer la Stratégie Digitale 2025 en Tunisie', Leaders, 25 June 2020, https://www.leaders.com.tn/article/30166.

23 'ICT Ministry, China's iFlytek Sign Deal on Language Processing', *Egypt Today*, 20 July 2020, https://www.egypttoday.com/Article/3/89979/ICT-ministry-China-s-iFlytek-sign-deal-on-language-processing.

24 John Calabrese, 'The Huawei Wars and the 5G Revolution in the Gulf', Middle East Institute, 30 July 2019, https://www.mei.edu/publications/huawei-wars-and-5g-revolution-gulf; and Natasha Turak, 'America's Huawei Fight Is of No Concern to the UAE, Dubai A.I. Executive Says', CNBC, 2 May 2019, https://www.cnbc.com/2019/05/02/americas-huawei-fight-is-of-no-concern-to-the-uae-dubai-ai-exec.html.

25 Neil Halligan, 'Huawei Remains Strong in Middle East Despite US Restrictions', *Arabian Business*, 19 September 2019, https://www.arabianbusiness.com/technology/428314-huawei-remains-strong-in-middle-east-despite-us-restrictions; and 'Huawei, Controversial in the West, Is Going Strong in the Gulf', *Economic Times*, 25 February 2021, https://economictimes.indiatimes.com/news/international/business/huawei-controversial-in-the-west-is-going-strong-in-the-gulf/articleshow/81201665.cms.

26 The centrality of Chinese technology to Central Asian security is covered in Niva Yau, 'Chinese Governance Export in Central Asia', *Security and Human Rights*, 2 February 2022, https://doi.org/10.1163/18750230-bja10009.

27 ZTE, 'Uzbekistan CDMA Deal Confirms ZTE's Central Asian Leadership', 12 November 2004, https://www.zte.com.cn/global/about/magazine/zte-technologies/2004/15/en_301/161410.html; and 'ZTE to Build Tajikistan NGN', Light Reading, 27 July 2005, https://www.lightreading.com/ethernet-ip/zte-to-build-tajikistan-ngn/d/d-id/616277.

28 Jeffrey Reeves, *Chinese Foreign Relations with Weak Peripheral States: Asymmetrical Power and Insecurity* (London: Routledge, 2015), pp. 61–3.

29 Daniel C. O'Neill, 'Risky Business: The Political Economy of Chinese Investment in Kazakhstan', *Journal of Eurasian Studies*, vol. 5, no. 2, July 2014, pp. 145–6, https://doi.org/10.1016/j.euras.2014.05.007.

30 See Marlene Laruelle (ed.), *China's Belt and Road Initiative and Its Impact in Central Asia* (Washington DC: The George Washington University Central Asia Program, 2018), https://centralasiaprogram.org/wp-content/uploads/2017/12/OBOR_Book_.pdf;

and Nargis Kassenova and Brendan Duprey (eds), *Digital Silk Road in Central Asia: Present and Future* (Cambridge, MA: Davis Center for Russian and Eurasian Studies, 2021), https://daviscenter.fas.harvard.edu/sites/default/files/files/2021-06/Digital_Silk_Road_Report.pdf.

31 Bradley Jardine, 'China's Surveillance State Has Eyes on Central Asia', *Foreign Policy*, 15 November 2019, https://foreignpolicy.com/2019/11/15/huawei-xinjiang-kazakhstan-uzbekistan-china-surveillance-state-eyes-central-asia/.

32 'Mirziyoyev predlozhil Huawei zanyat'sya razvitiyem setey 5G v Uzbekistane' [Mirziyoyev Proposes That Huawei Engage in Development of 5G Networks in Uzbekistan], Fergana News Agency, 26 April 2019, https://fergana.agency/news/106944/; and Umida Hashimova, 'Before and Beyond 5G: Central Asia's Huawei Connections', *Diplomat*, 19 February 2020, https://thediplomat.com/2020/02/before-and-beyond-5g-central-asias-huawei-connections/.

33 Sarvinoz Ruhullo, 'V Dushanbe ulichnyye kamery nachnut raspoznavat' litsa' [In Dushanbe, Street Cameras Will Begin to Recognise Faces], Radio Ozodi, 17 June 2019, https://rus.ozodi.org/a/30003322.html.

34 'Kazakhstan to Build 5G Infrastructure in Three Largest Cities, Plans to Expand to Other Population Centres', *Astana Times*, 3 June 2019, https://astanatimes.com/2019/06/kazakhstan-to-build-5g-infrastructure-in-three-largest-cities-plans-to-expand-to-other-population-centres/.

35 Huawei's website had a lengthy explanation, later removed, of how it planned to bring 'intelligent surveillance' first to Belgrade and eventually to the entire country. The page is available at https://archive.li/pZ9HO#selection-11355.0-11355.497.

36 Gisela Grieger, 'China, the 16+1, and the EU', European Parliament Briefing, September 2018, https://www.europarl.europa.eu/RegData/etudes/BRIE/2018/625173/EPRS_BRI(2018)625173_EN.pdf. See the table on p. 4.

37 Ivana Karásková et al., 'Empty Shell No More: China's Growing Footprint in Central and Eastern Europe', Association for International Affairs, 2020, pp. 43, 56, https://chinaobservers.eu/new-publication-empty-shell-no-more-chinas-growing-footprint-in-central-and-eastern-europe/. This report was prepared using a regional collaborative research and editorial platform called China Observers in Central and Eastern Europe (CHOICE) and was funded by the US-based National Endowment for Democracy (NED). There is a considerable infrastructure of China-sceptic observers in Central Europe, including ChinfluenCE, which shares personnel with the CHOICE project and is also funded by the NED. Other important nodes include Slovakia's Central European Institute for Asian Studies, Poland's Asia Research Centre, Prague's Sinopsis project and Hungary's Central and Eastern European Centre for Asian Studies. China, meanwhile, has worked to support think tanks sympathetic to it. There is a 16+1 think-tank network managed by the Chinese Academy of Social Sciences and think tanks

have been a feature of the new Silk Road more generally. See Anastas Vangeli, 'Diffusion of Ideas in the Era of the Belt and Road: Insights from China–CEE Think Tank Cooperation', *Asia Europe Journal*, vol. 17, no. 4, December 2019, pp. 421–36, https://link.springer.com/article/10.1007/s10308-019-00564-0.

38 See the country reports in John Seaman, Mikko Huatari and Miguel Otero-Iglesias (eds), 'Chinese Investment in Europe: A Country-level Approach', European Think-tank Network on China (ETNC), December 2017, https://merics.org/en/report/chinese-investment-europe-country-level-approach. The ETNC is a consortium of European think tanks that study China. The report was published by the French Institute of International Relations, Elcano Royal Institute and the Mercator Institute for China Studies.

39 Kate O'Keeffe, Drew Hinshaw and Daniel Michaels, 'U.S. Presses Europe to Uproot Chinese Security-screening Company', *Wall Street Journal*, 28 June 2020, https://www.wsj.com/articles/u-s-presses-europe-to-uproot-chinese-security-screening-company-11593349201.

40 Karásková et al., 'Empty Shell No More: China's Growing Footprint in Central and Eastern Europe', p. 44.

41 'Huawei Announces Plans to Invest Eur100mln by 2018 in Romania, Moves On with Employment Plans', Business Review, 9 July 2013, https://business-review.eu/featured/huawei-announces-plans-to-invest-eur-100mln-by-2018-in-romania-moves-on-with-employment-plans-45994; and Aurel Constantin, 'Huawei Romania: "A Friend in Need Is a Friend Indeed"', Business Review, 3 April 2020, https://business-review.eu/news/huawei-romania-a-friend-in-need-is-a-friend-indeed-209198.

42 Ericsson, 'Ericsson and Magyar Telekom Launch Commercial 5G in Hungary', 9 April 2020, https://www.prnewswire.co.uk/news-releases/ericsson-and-magyar-telekom-launch-commercial-5g-in-hungary-845762905.html; 'Serbia and Nokia Continue Cooperation, Vicic Says', FoNet, 9 December 2019; and Nokia, 'Nokia Announces Private LTE Network in 450MHz for Polish Energy Company', 7 April 2020, https://www.lightreading.com/private-networks/nokia-announces-private-lte-network-in-450mhz-for-polish-energy-company/d/d-id/758739.

43 See Karásková et al.'s introduction to 'Empty Shell No More: China's Growing Footprint in Central and Eastern Europe'; Martin Hála, 'CEFC: Economic Diplomacy with Chinese Characteristics', China Digital Times, 8 February 2018, https://chinadigitaltimes.net/2018/02/martin-hala-cefc-ccp-influence-eastern-europe/; and Erik Brattberg and Philippe le Corre, 'The EU and China in 2020: More Competition Ahead', Carnegie Endowment for International Peace, 19 February 2020, https://carnegieendowment.org/2020/02/19/eu-and-china-in-2020-more-competition-ahead-pub-81096.

44 Tian Dewen and Tian Yuewan, 'Europe Can't Afford to Fully Ban Huawei', *China Daily*, 8 July 2020, https://global.chinadaily.com.cn/a/202007/08/WS5f04ff6fa310834817257da3.html; and Andreea Brinza, 'How Russia

Helped the United States Fight
Huawei in Central and Eastern
Europe', War on the Rocks, 12
Mar 2020, https://warontherocks.
com/2020/03/how-russia-helped-the-
united-states-fight-huawei-in-central-
and-eastern-europe/.

45  Andrius Sytas, 'Lithuania Seeks to
Ban "Untrustworthy" Phones After
Chinese Censorship Concerns',
Reuters, 24 September 2021, https://
www.reuters.com/technology/
lithuania-looks-ban-untrustworthy-
phones-after-chinese-censorship-
concerns-2021-09-24/.

46  Tomoya Onishi, 'Vietnam Carrier
Develops Native 5G Tech to Lock
Out Huawei', Nikkei Asia, 25
January 2020, https://asia.nikkei.
com/Business/Telecommunication/
Vietnam-carrier-develops-native-5G-
tech-to-lock-out-Huawei.

47  David Hutt, 'China Throws Hun
Sen an Economic Lifeline', Asia
Times, 1 May 2019, https://asiatimes.
com/2019/05/china-throws-hun-
sen-an-economic-lifeline/; and
'Rapid Economic Growth Props
Up Cambodia's Strongman', The
Economist, 17 April 2019, https://
www.economist.com/asia/2019/04/17/
rapid-economic-growth-props-up-
cambodias-strongman.

48  May Kunmakura, 'Huawei the First
Authorised Cloud Provider', Phnom
Penh Post, 23 September 2021, https://
www.phnompenhpost.com/business/
huawei-first-authorised-cloud-
provider.

49  Pheakdey Heng, 'Digitising
Cambodia's Economic Future', Khmer
Times, 4 January 2019, https://www.
khmertimeskh.com/565882/digitising-
cambodias-economic-future/.

50  Bhavin Patel, 'Cambodia Edges

Toward Digital Payments', Official
Monetary and Financial Institutions
Forum, 22 June 2020, https://www.
omfif.org/2020/06/cambodia-edges-
towards-digital-payments/.

51  'Huawei Inks Accord with Ministry
for 5G Technology', Asia News
Network, 27 January 2020, https://
asianews.network/huawei-inks-
accord-with-ministry-for-5g-
technology/.

52  Ran Li and Kee-Cheok Cheong,
'Huawei and ZTE in Malaysia: The
Localisation of Chinese Transnational
Enterprises', Journal of Contemporary
Asia, vol. 47, no. 5, July 2017, pp.
758–62.

53  Ibid., pp. 761–2, 766. On the
role of the Malaysian state in
development, see Takashi Torii,
'The Mechanism for State-led
Creation of Malaysia's Middle
Classes', Developing Economies, vol.
41, no. 2, June 2003, pp. 221–42,
https://onlinelibrary.wiley.com/
doi/abs/10.1111/j.1746-1049.2003.
tb00939.x.

54  Zunaira Saieed, 'Kuala Lumpur Set
to Become Smart City Next Year',
Star, 25 April 2019, https://www.
thestar.com.my/business/business-
news/2019/04/25/kuala-lumpur-set-
to-become-smart-city-next-year.

55  Barry Naughton, 'Chinese Industrial
Policy and the Digital Silk Road',
Asia Policy, vol. 15, no. 1, January
2020, pp. 31, 33–4, 36, https://www.
nbr.org/wp-content/uploads/
pdfs/publications/ap15-1_2_
digitalsilkroadrt_naughton_jan2020.
pdf. See also Maximiliano Facundo
Vila Seoane, 'Alibaba Discourse for
the Digital Silk Road: The Electronic
World Trade Platform and "Inclusive
Globalization"', Chinese Journal of

*Communication*, vol. 13, no. 1, 2020, pp. 68–83.

56 Hong Liu and Guanie Lim, 'The Political Economy of a Rising China in Southeast Asia: Malaysia's Response to the Belt and Road Initiative', *Journal of Contemporary China*, vol. 28, no. 116, March 2019, p. 216, https://doi.org/10.1080/10670564 .2018.1511393. On the 2018 shift to a type of anti-Chinese politics, see Elsa Lafaye de Micheaux, 'Malaysia Baru: Reconfiguring the New Malaysian Capitalism's Dependency on China – A Chronicle of the First Post-GE 2018 Economic Reforms', *Contemporary Chinese Political Economy and Strategic Relations*, vol. 5, no. 1, April/May 2019, pp. 77–135.

57 Mary Lennighan, 'Ericsson Bags Malaysia's Only National 5G Network Deal Ahead of Huawei', Telecoms.com, 2 July 2021, https:// telecoms.com/510414/ericsson-bags-malaysias-only-national-5g-network-deal-ahead-of-huawei/.

58 Elliott Zaagman, 'Tencent: How a Global Investment Empire Flies Under the Radar', TechNode, 13 January 2020, https://technode. com/2020/01/13/tencent-how-a-global-investment-empires-flies-under-the-radar/; and Shunsuke Tabeta, 'Beijing Exports "China-style" Internet Across Belt and Road', Nikkei Asia, 21 October 2019, https:// asia.nikkei.com/Spotlight/Belt-and-Road/Beijing-exports-China-style-internet-across-Belt-and-Road.

59 Alex Fang, 'US Says Huawei Tide Is Turning, as Countries Shun China 5G', Nikkei Asia, 26 June 2020, https:// asia.nikkei.com/Spotlight/Huawei-crackdown/US-says-Huawei-tide-is-turning-as-countries-shun-China-5G.

60 Elizabeth Law, 'S'pore MOUs with Shenzhen a Lift for Smart City Initiative', *Straits Times*, 18 June 2020, https://www.straitstimes.com/asia/ east-asia/spore-mous-with-shenzhen-a-lift-for-smart-city-initiative.

61 See the introduction by Ashank K. Kantha and C. Raja Mohan to the symposium volume *China's Digital Silk Road: Implications for India* (Delhi: Institute of Chinese Studies, 2020), pp. 12–14; V. Rajaraman, 'History of Computing in India, 1955–2010', IEEE Computer Society, 2012; and Rafiq Dosani, 'Origins and Growth of the Software Sector in India', Walter H. Shorenstein Asia-Pacific Research Center, Stanford University, 2005, https://aparc.fsi.stanford.edu/ publications/origins_and_growth_of_ the_software_industry_in_india.

62 Biswajit Dhar and Reji K. Joseph, 'India's Information Technology Industry: A Tale of Two Halves', in Kung-Chung Liu and Uday S. Racherla (eds), *Innovation, Economic Development, and Intellectual Property in India and China: Comparing Six Economic Sectors* (Berlin: Springer, 2019), pp. 93–117.

63 Joji Thomas Philip, 'NSC Points to Huawei, ZTE's Links with Chinese Military', *Economic Times*, 15 May 2013, https://economictimes. indiatimes.com/news/politics-and-nation/nsc-points-to-huawei-ztes-links-with-chinese-military/ articleshow/20056800.cms; and 'India Investigates Report of Huawei Hacking State Carrier Network', Reuters, 6 February 2014, https://www.reuters.com/ article/us-india-huawei-hacking-idUSBREA150QK20140206.

64 Apurva Chaudhary, 'Updated:

India's Intelligence Bureau Seeks Ban on WeChat; Report', MediaNama, 17 June 2013; and Shadma Shaikh, 'How WeChat Faded into Silence in India', FactorDaily, 8 October 2018, https://archive.factordaily.com/how-wechat-faded-into-the-silence-in-india/.

65  Chan Jia Hao and Archana Atmakuri, 'When India Meets China's Digital Silk Road', *South Asia Journal*, 4 March 2019. Fiberhome is a fibre-optic and broadband company that is on the US Entity List.

66  'Reliance Jio Ready to Cover 80% India in Second Half of 2016: Mukesh Ambani', *Economic Times*, 22 February 2016, https://economictimes.indiatimes.com/industry/telecom/reliance-jio-ready-to-cover-80-india-in-second-half-of-2016-mukesh-ambani/articleshow/51083911.cms.

67  Thomas K. Thomas, 'From Free Basics to Stake in Reliance Jio, Zuckerberg Gets the Mojo Back into Facebook's India Strategy', *Hindu Business Line*, 22 April 2020, https://www.thehindubusinessline.com/info-tech/from-free-basics-to-stake-in-jio-zuckerberg-gets-the-mojo-back-into-facebooks-india-strategy/article31402579.ece.

68  Ananth Krishnan, 'Following the Money: China Inc.'s Growing Stake in India–China Relations', Brookings India, March 2020, pp. 20–3; and Amit Bhandari, Blaise Fernandes and Aashna Agarwal, 'Chinese Investments in India', Gateway House: Indian Council on Global Relations, February 2020. See also Santosh Pai and Rajesh Gosh, 'Mapping China's Participation in India's Digital Economy', in *China's Digital Silk Road: Implications for India*, pp. 31–44, 45–55.

69  Stephanie Findlay, 'Bharti Airtel and Amazon Team Up for India Cloud Market Push', *Financial Times*, 5 August 2020.

70  Gautam Chikermane, '5G Infrastructure, Huawei's Techno-economic Advantages and India's National Security Concerns: An Analysis', Observer Research Foundation, 10 December 2019; and Sanjeev Miglani and Neha Dasgupta, 'Exclusive: China Warns India of "Reverse Sanctions" if Huawei Is Blocked – Sources', Reuters, 6 August 2019, https://www.reuters.com/article/us-huawei-india-exclusive-idUSKCN1UW1FF.

71  Manish Singh, 'Google Invests $4.5 Billion in India's Reliance Jio Platforms', TechCrunch, 15 July 2020, https://techcrunch.com/2020/07/15/google-invests-4-5-billion-in-indias-reliance-jio-platforms.

72  Manish Singh, 'China Expresses Concern Over Its Absence in India's 5G Trials', TechCrunch, 6 May 2021, https://techcrunch.com/2021/05/05/china-expresses-concern-over-its-absence-in-indias-5g-trials/.

73  Campbell Kwan, 'Quad Countries Announce Slew of Tech Initiatives Including Shared Cyber Standards', ZDNet, 26 September 2021, https://www.zdnet.com/article/quad-countries-announce-slew-of-tech-initiatives-including-shared-cyber-standards/.

74  Nachiket Kelkar, 'India's 5G Networks Will Rely on Indigenous Technology', *Week*, 5 September 2021, https://www.theweek.in/theweek/business/2021/08/26/indias-5g-networks-will-rely-on-indigenous-technology.html.

75  See, for example, Wenyuan Wu,

'How Africa Is Breaking China's Neo-colonial Shackles', Interpreter, 30 October 2019, https://www.lowyinstitute.org/the-interpreter/how-africa-breaking-china-s-neo-colonial-shackles; and Brahma Chellany, 'China's Creditor Imperialism', Project Syndicate, 20 December 2017, https://www.project-syndicate.org/commentary/china-sri-lanka-hambantota-port-debt-by-brahma-chellaney-2017-12.

76  'Zhū Zǐ shuō tànzhōnghé' [Zhu Zi Talks About Carbon Neutrality], WeChat (Weixin), 30 June 2021, https://mp.weixin.qq.com/s/9ae5x9hQtKoIlbQVazPSWA?fbclid=IwAR3yAATNICOtLSZRE0erzqfqhbDSU25opBmzG0XWENMOglPExck7mmEZ94Y.

77  See Jonathan E. Hillman, *The Digital Silk Road: China's Quest to Wire the World and Win the Future* (New York: Harper Business, 2021), chapter 7.

## Conclusion

1  'With Almost Half of World's Population Still Offline, Digital Divide Risks Becoming "New Face of Inequality"', Deputy Secretary-General Warns General Assembly', United Nations, 27 April 2021, https://www.un.org/press/en/2021/dsgsm1579.doc.htm.

2  'Full Text: Keynote Speech by Chinese President Xi Jinping at APEC CEO Dialogues', Xinhua, 19 November 2020, http://www.xinhuanet.com/english/2020-11-19/c_139527192.htm.

3  'Full Text: Xi Jinping's Speech at Opening Ceremony of China–ASEAN Expo', CGTN, 27 November 2020, https://news.cgtn.com/news/2020-11-27/Full-text-Xi-Jinping-s-speech-at-opening-ceremony-of-China-ASEAN-Expo-VKLtNAQRWw/index.html.

4  Josh Ye, 'TSMC Founder Morris Chang Says China's Semiconductor Industry Still Five Years Behind Despite Decades of Subsidies', *South China Morning Post*, 22 April 2021, https://www.scmp.com/tech/big-tech/article/3130628/tsmc-founder-morris-chang-says-chinas-semiconductor-industry-still.

5  Laura Silver, Kat Devlin and Christine Huang, 'Unfavorable Views of China Reach Historic Highs in Many Countries', Pew Research Center Report, 6 October 2020, https://www.pewresearch.org/global/2020/10/06/unfavorable-views-of-china-reach-historic-highs-in-many-countries/.

6  Keith Bradsher, 'China Tightens Grip on Rare Minerals', *New York Times*, 31 August 2009, https://www.nytimes.com/2009/09/01/business/global/01minerals.html.

7  Frank Tang, 'China's Rare Earth Export Plunge Caused by Coronavirus, Not Beijing Agenda, Industry Group Says', *South China Morning Post*, 18 August 2020, https://www.scmp.com/economy/china-economy/article/3097847/chinas-rare-earth-export-plunge-caused-coronavirus-not.

8  'Explainer: US Dependence on China's Rare Earth – Trade War Vulnerability', Reuters, 3 June 2019, https://www.reuters.com/article/us-usa-trade-china-rareearth-

explainer-idUSKCN1T42RP; and White House, 'Factsheet: Securing a Made in America Supply Chain for Critical Minerals', 22 February 2022, https://www.whitehouse. gov/briefing-room/statements-releases/2022/02/22/fact-sheet- securing-a-made-in-america-supply-chain-for-critical-minerals/.

9    Peter Foster, 'Cyber Chief Warns of East–West Split over the Internet', *Financial Times*, 27 August 2020, https://www.ft.com/content/0aacf23f-0f71-4bdf-9ad3-5101ab80b259.

# INDEX

Six *Adelphi* numbers are published each year by Routledge Journals, an imprint of Taylor & Francis, 4 Park Square, Milton Park, Abingdon, Oxfordshire OX14 4RN, UK.

A subscription to the institution print edition, ISSN 1944-5571, includes free access for any number of concurrent users across a local area network to the online edition, ISSN 1944-558X. Taylor & Francis has a flexible approach to subscriptions enabling us to match individual libraries' requirements. This journal is available via a traditional institutional subscription (either print with free online access, or online-only at a discount) or as part of our libraries, subject collections or archives. For more information on our sales packages please visit www.tandfonline.com/page/librarians.

| 2022 Annual *Adelphi* Subscription Rates | | | |
|---|---|---|---|
| Institution | £922 | US$1,705 | €1,364 |
| Individual | £316 | US$541 | €433 |
| Online only | £784 | US$1,449 | €1,159 |

Dollar rates apply to subscribers outside Europe. Euro rates apply to all subscribers in Europe except the UK and the Republic of Ireland where the pound sterling price applies. All subscriptions are payable in advance and all rates include postage. Journals are sent by air to the USA, Canada, Mexico, India, Japan and Australasia. Subscriptions are entered on an annual basis, i.e. January to December. Payment may be made by sterling cheque, dollar cheque, international money order, National Giro, or credit card (Amex, Visa, Mastercard).

For a complete and up-to-date guide to Taylor & Francis journals and books publishing programmes, and details of advertising in our journals, visit our website: **http://www.tandfonline.com.**

Ordering information:
**USA/Canada:** Taylor & Francis Inc., Journals Department, 530 Walnut Street, Suite 850, Philadelphia, PA 19106, USA. **UK/Europe/Rest of World:** Routledge Journals, T&F Customer Services, T&F Informa UK Ltd., Sheepen Place, Colchester, Essex, CO3 3LP, UK.

Advertising enquiries to:
**USA/Canada**: The Advertising Manager, Taylor & Francis Inc., 530 Walnut Street, Suite 850, Philadelphia, PA 19106, USA. Tel: +1 (800) 354 1420. Fax: +1 (215) 207 0050. **UK/Europe/Rest of World**: The Advertising Manager, Routledge Journals, Taylor & Francis, 4 Park Square, Milton Park, Abingdon, Oxfordshire OX14 4RN, UK. Tel: +44 (0) 20 7017 6000. Fax: +44 (0) 20 7017 6336.

# THE ADELPHI SERIES

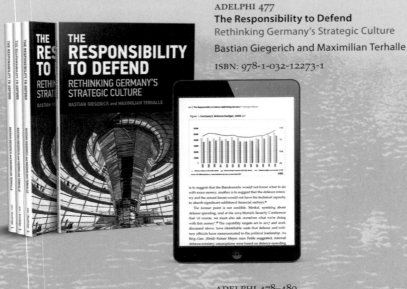

ADELPHI 477

**The Responsibility to Defend**

Rethinking Germany's Strategic Culture

Bastian Giegerich and Maximilian Terhalle

ISBN: 978-1-032-12273-1

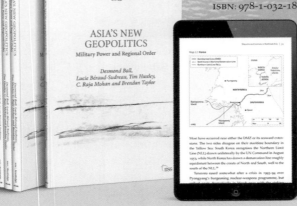

ADELPHI 478–480

**Asia's New Geopolitics**

Military Power and Regional Order

Desmond Ball, Lucie Béraud-Sudreau,
Tim Huxley, C. Raja Mohan, Brendan Taylor

ISBN: 978-1-032-18736-5

## IISS THE INTERNATIONAL INSTITUTE FOR STRATEGIC STUDIES

www.iiss.org/publications/adelphi

ADELPHI 481–483
**Japan's Effectiveness
as a Geo-economic Actor**
Navigating Great-power Competition

Yuka Koshino and Robert Ward

ISBN: 978-1-032-32139-4

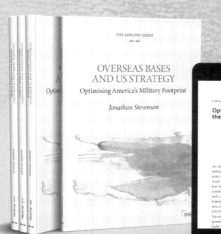

ADELPHI 484–486
**Overseas Bases and US Strategy**
Optimising America's Military Footprint

Jonathan Stevenson

ISBN: 978-1-032-39609-5